Peace for the Troubled Heart

PEACE
for the
TROUBLED HEART

Reformed Spirituality

HERMAN HOEKSEMA

Edited by DAVID J. ENGELSMA

REFORMED FREE PUBLISHING ASSOCIATION

Jenison, Michigan

Scripture cited is taken from the King James (Authorized) Version

Reformed Free Publishing Association
1894 Georgetown Center Drive
Jenison MI 49428-7137

www.rfpa.org
mail@rfpa.org

ISBN 978-1-936054-05-3
LCCN 2010939729

Back cover and interior design by Gary Gore Book Design

Contents

Preface   ix

Part I. Pilgrimage

Chapter 1
The Pilgrim's Confession   3

Chapter 2
The Pilgrim's Goal   11

Chapter 3
Desiring the Heavenly Fatherland   18

Chapter 4
Sojourning Safely   26

Chapter 5
Compassionate Remembrance   32

Chapter 6
Rejoicing in Heaviness   38

Chapter 7
Rest for the Weary   46

Chapter 8
We Fly Away   53

Part II. Suffering

Chapter 9
Nothing Strange   63

Chapter 10
The Fellowship of His Sufferings   71

Chapter 11
The Suffering of This Present Time   79

Chapter 12
Suffering in the Flesh   87

Chapter 13
Angry with His People   95

Chapter 14
How Long, Lord?   103

Chapter 15
Two Viewpoints of the Same Reality   111

Chapter 16
Looking at Things Not Seen   119

Chapter 17
Not Troubled   127

Chapter 18
The More Excellent House of Mourning   135

Chapter 19
The Joy of Many Temptations   143

Chapter 20
Glorying in Tribulation   151

Chapter 21
Zion, A Secure Refuge   159

Chapter 22
A Safe Refuge   167

Chapter 23
Saving Mercies   174

Part III. Struggle

Chapter 24
Internal Warfare   185

Chapter 25
Life through Death   193

Chapter 26
Walking in Darkness   201

Chapter 27
Patient in Tribulation   209

Chapter 28
A Threefold Requirement   217

Chapter 29
Strength through Weakness   225

Chapter 30
Holding Fast Our Profession   233

Chapter 31
Striving for the Faith of the Gospel   241

Chapter 32
Labor for the Rest   248

Chapter 33
God for Us   256

Chapter 34
Who Shall Separate?   264

Chapter 35
Fear Not, Little Flock!   272

Chapter 36
Fear Not!   279

Chapter 37
The Battle Is the Lord's   287

Preface

HERMAN HOEKSEMA'S exegetical and dogmatical writings are well-known. The same cannot be said of his devotional writings. By the publication of this book of Hoeksema's meditations, long buried in past volumes of the Reformed periodical, the *Standard Bearer*, we give especially Christian readers access to his devotional writings.

Beginning with the first issue of the magazine in October, 1924 and continuing until September 1, 1947, Hoeksema wrote the meditation in every issue of the *Standard Bearer*. The very first article in the first issue of the magazine was Hoeksema's meditation on Psalm 145:9a, 20b, "Jehovah's Goodness." In the span of almost twenty-three years, Hoeksema produced more than four hundred meditations.

These meditations are deliberately and distinctively devotional. In language that is often poetical, they breathe the rich experience of the believing child of God.

Hoeksema's meditations express and form genuine Reformed spirituality.

Always exegetical (whereas much purported spirituality is rooted in the emotions of the teacher), always biblical (whereas much purported spirituality is fanciful), and always doctrinal (whereas much purported spirituality is mystical), the meditations of Herman Hoeksema are instructive as well as moving (whereas much purported spirituality merely titillates the feelings for a fleeting moment).

From the approximately four hundred meditations, I have selected the thirty-seven that make up the content of this book. The overarching theme is the struggle and suffering in this life of every believer as a pilgrim on the earth. I have distinguished these meditations as three categories and divided the book into three corresponding parts: pilgrimage, suffering, and struggle. Of course, there is some overlapping of thought. A pilgrim must suffer, and suffering demands struggle.

As an expression of *Reformed* spirituality, these meditations implicitly renounce both the error of supposing that the Christian experience is all exuberant joy and exhilarating power, as well as the error of dreaming that the Christian life is (or ought to be) earthly conquest by those who are at home in this world.

As an expression of *Reformed* spirituality, these meditations address the members of the church not as unbelieving doubters, but as believers who struggle with doubts and fears.

As an expression of *Reformed* spirituality, these meditations do not obsessively concentrate on the struggles within the believer. They do justice as well to his and the church's struggles against a hostile world of ungodly men and women.

As an expression of *Reformed* spirituality, these meditations are not content to leave the believer plagued with doubts and fears. Hoeksema's meditations are gospel, every one: "Believer, you *need* not doubt or fear! You *must* not doubt or fear! You *may* not doubt or fear! you *will* not doubt or fear!"

The title of the book is taken from the especially profound meditation in part two on John 14:1: "Not Troubled."

A number of these meditations were originally written in Dutch. Marvin Kamps has ably translated them into English, retaining the devotional character of the language.

It is our intention to publish more volumes of Hoeksema's meditations on other themes and of a somewhat different, though consistently devotional nature.

DAVID J. ENGELSMA

PART I

Pilgrimage

1

The Pilgrim's Confession

"These all died in faith, not having received the promises, but having seen them afar off, and were persuaded of them, and embraced them, and confessed
that they were strangers and pilgrims on the earth."
—Hebrews 11:13

The pilgrim's confession!

We confess that we are strangers and pilgrims on the earth.

It is a confession—if it is not merely lip service—that expresses
what lives in our hearts and, relative to all things earthly, rules our
entire life on the earth.

Only two confessions are possible: One is either a stranger and
a pilgrim or one is a citizen on the earth and seeks and finds one's
home here below.

If you choose the latter, that is, if you seek your permanent
home on the earth and you do not acknowledge or seek another
home for yourself, your whole world view—your thinking, willing,
desiring, and striving—is limited by the horizon of this present
time. Then you seek the things below that lie under the law of
time. Then you strive to possess as many earthly things as possible. Then you chase after the full enjoyment of earthly pleasures.
You view earthly things not as a means to achieve a purpose, as a
way to an end, but as the goal of all your striving and labor, of all
your drudgery and struggling. Then you are without God in the
world and also without hope. For then, from the vantage point of
the present, you will look toward the future and constantly seek

better things, peace-giving realities for your soul, since present realities can never give you peace and satisfaction. But your hope is a continually disappointing expectation, a mirage that you chase in the vanity of your earthly life until death and eternal darkness put an end forever to your vain expectations.

Then your motto is: Let us eat and drink, for tomorrow we die.

Then you will attempt to keep what you have so that you may be identified with the rich and with the possessors of this world. If you belong to the poor and indigent of the earth, you will strive to steal from those possessors of the world whatever you can. You do not understand any explanation of, and you can have no peace with, the suffering of this present time. You do not practice submission in the midst of painful realities, nor do you have any patience with adversity. You have no comfort in circumstances of grief and sorrow, but are held captive by the fear of death all your life long.

Then you become more and more convinced: Vanity of vanities, all is vanity!

How radically different is the world view, the assessment of life and attitude toward life, of him who confesses that he is a stranger and a pilgrim in the earth!

His horizon reaches out far beyond the horizon of time to the distant reaches of eternal life. There, in the eternal, in the heavenly, in the consummation of all things, is his home, his destination, the goal of all his striving and the fulfillment of all his expectations. He seeks the things that are above. Upon them he sets his heart. His treasure is in heaven. He sees and evaluates all things in the light of that eternal hope. He specifically seeks not the things below, the things that are on the earth. Temporal things are in themselves not his goal, but are the means to achieve his goal, as well as the means to fulfill his life's purpose—God's purpose here on the earth. Then he struggles to climb to the top of Zion. Then he hopes with a living hope that never disappoints. It is a hope that stretches far beyond the temporal into the eternal, that reaches far beyond the range of the earthly unto the heavenly, that is victorious over the world, and that defeats even death itself.

He is then thankful in prosperity and patient in adversity.

He has an explanation for the suffering of this present time, for he knows that all things must work for his good and must serve to the attainment of his eternal dwelling place.

He has comfort even in death.

He sings through his tears.

He confesses that he is a stranger and a foreigner in the earth.

Then he can die in faith.

Looking to the promise.

Glorious confession!

Strangers and pilgrims.

Those who are described in the text confessed that truth about themselves.

In this manner they died. They died in the faith, that is, according to faith. This means that they died as those die who did not in this life receive the promises and viewed the fulfillment of the promise from afar, but who believingly embraced and confessed that they were strangers and pilgrims in the earth.

They were not yet home.

Such is the underlying thought of both strangers and pilgrims. Being a stranger has essentially the same meaning as being a pilgrim. There is, however, a difference of emphasis. Being a pilgrim implies that you are not a citizen in the country where you temporarily reside. In this foreign land you have no rights of citizenship; a language different than your own is spoken there; you are not at home or comfortable there; your family and friends do not live there; the common customs are foreign to you. The country is not your fatherland. Being a stranger emphasizes that you dwell only temporarily in that land, that you reside in an unfamiliar house, find shelter, and are cared for regarding the needs of the body and soul. But with respect to both descriptions the fundamental idea is that of not yet being home. You do not have your residence here. Your home is elsewhere and you seek it elsewhere. You reside here only temporarily and you intend to be here only temporarily. You do not put down any roots. You do not seek to establish any continuing relationships. You are a traveler and must travel farther.

Stranger and pilgrim *on the earth.*

Note well, the meaning of this confession is not that you are a stranger *in the world,* although that is true. In the midst of the world that lies in evil, the world from a spiritual and ethical perspective, you are undoubtedly a foreigner. You are indeed in the world, but not of the world. With the world you have no fellowship. However, this is not the meaning here. You are never a guest in the world. You do not form any temporal friendships with the world as it lies in sin. Besides, what the world offers and proposes to you cannot be of benefit to you. Its pleasure is not your pleasure. Its striving is not your striving. You do not drape yourself with its banner. Darkness has no fellowship with the light. Rather, the meaning is that these all confessed that they were strangers and pilgrims on the earth. This includes the whole of earthly life, all earthly things, relationships, and experiences— money and possessions, name and position, husband and wife, parent and child, brother and sister, friend and acquaintance, servant and master, pleasure and happiness, sickness and suffering, prosperity and adversity.

Amid all those earthly things you behave as a stranger and a foreigner.

You live as a stranger, you appreciatively and thankfully enjoy whatever you may temporally receive from the hand of the Lord.

Yet you do this as a pilgrim.

No matter how hospitable your temporal residence may be, and no matter how long you may with pleasure dwell in that hospitable house, you never make it your home.

You never give your heart to it.

Your temporal shelter and your temporal accommodations must serve the purpose of continuing your journey.
You must travel farther.

———————

The pilgrim's confession.
The content of this confession is that while on the earth and in the midst of all earthly things, we are strangers and pilgrims. From what rich source does that confession draw its strength? Certainly not from our natural existence.

Truly, apart from the consideration of the sin that lives in us, by which we are always inclined to seek our salvation in the things of this world and to seek our happiness far from God, we are of the earth earthy. We have by nature an earthly body and an earthly soul. We are adapted to the earth. We have earthly senses, and we appropriate earthly realities. We are dependent upon the earth and have earthly needs and earthly desires. Our longings are directed to the earthly. Precisely because of this, though our confession is that we are strangers and pilgrims on the earth, we can nevertheless feel at home on the earth in various circumstances and at certain times. Just as a traveler in a foreign country sometimes can live comfortably for a few days in a friendly and hospitable home and does not feel the need to press onward on his journey, so too the pilgrim-Christian can become attached to his foreign residence during times of earthly prosperity and temporal pleasures, when he experiences that life is good, so that he would not forsake it except for necessity.

Apart from any consideration of sin, we are of the earth earthy. We wish not to be unclothed, but clothed upon.

Consequently, the confession that we are strangers and pilgrims on the earth could never arise from our earthly nature.

But according to our spiritual existence we are actually pilgrims on the earth.

God makes his people pilgrims.

In his eternal counsel before the foundation of the world, he appointed them as foreigners, for he chose them and foreordained them in order that they should be made like unto the image of his Son, so that the Son would be the firstborn among many brethren. He chose them unto eternal, heavenly glory and unto citizenship in the heavenly Jerusalem. He also causes them to be foreigners temporally on the earth, for he gives to them the new, eternal life through the resurrection of Jesus Christ from the dead, and he calls them out of darkness into his marvelous light.

The new life is resurrection life!

It is differentiated from the life of the world not only because it is free from the law of sin and death, and thus free to express itself according to the law of the Spirit of life, but also because it is from above.

It is the life of heaven.

By virtue of having received the new life that is from above, they have actually become citizens of the Jerusalem that will presently descend from heaven as God's blessing.

Their conversation is in heaven.

There is their real, eternal home.

And out of the principle of the new life springs forth the confession that they are strangers and pilgrims on the earth. For here is not their continuing city.

They seek the city that comes down out of heaven.

———————

A confession of hope!

These all *confessed* that they were strangers and pilgrims on the earth.

They not only *were* that, but they also *revealed* it. They lived in the consciousness that they were strangers on the earth. They gave witness of that fact and expressed it before each other, before others, and before the whole world.

"These all" were the saints named earlier in this chapter—Abraham, Isaac and Jacob. They were those who confessed their pilgrimage. They told others about it. This fact is obvious from what follows: "For those who declare such things reveal clearly that they seek a country." This truth the aged Jacob literally confessed. When the king of Egypt asked him how old he was, he answered: "The days of the years of my pilgrimage are an hundred and thirty years: few and evil have the days of the years of my life been, and have not attained unto the days of the years of the life of my fathers in the days of their pilgrimage." Such is always the confession of God's people in the world.

They confessed it as well by their walk of faith.

They showed clearly that they were pilgrims who sought a fatherland, for being obedient to the calling of God through faith, they forsook country and home and family circle in order to live in tents as pilgrims in a foreign land. And they remained steadfast. Truly, had they thought about their former fatherland, they would have had opportunity to return.

But now they desire a better, a heavenly, country.

God's people are always called to make this confession, not merely with the mouth—while by their walk they seek the things below—but also in actuality. Confession and walk go together. Not as if it is the calling today of believers literally to dwell in tents. Not as if they may not be citizens of an earthly country. Not as if they must go out of the world or hole up alone in the cell of a monastery. Such is precisely not their calling. Such would make their confession impossible. Their specific calling is to seek the better fatherland by means of all earthly things, to regard everything they have as means—upon which they never set their hearts and which they do not seek for their own sake—to seek the things above.

They always seek first the kingdom of God and its righteousness.

With their eyes focused on the eternal inheritance.

For they saw the promises, believed them, and embraced them as their own. Therefore, they could confess that they were strangers and pilgrims on the earth. Those promises are the eternal promises of God in Christ. They are ultimately the one promise that God the Lord proclaimed throughout all the ages of time from the first paradise unto the Christ. The final fulfillment of that one promise yet today lies in the future—the promise that will be fulfilled when Jesus Christ returns from heaven. That promise we expect, in order that we may enter into the life of the new Jerusalem in its full revelation (though we possess it now only in principle), when the new Jerusalem will descend out of heaven from God, when sorrow and death will be no more, when God will wipe away all tears from our eyes, when our God will make all things new, and when his tabernacle will be eternally with men in the new heaven and the new earth.

That promise they saw from afar.

But we see it before our very eyes.

For we see Jesus! We have seen his day. Fundamentally the promise is fulfilled already now.

We have come to the heavenly Jerusalem.

Its final revelation lies immediately before us.

The hope of the pilgrim!

2

The Pilgrim's Goal

"For here have we no continuing city, but we seek one
to come."

—Hebrews 13:14

Christian, press on!

At the end of your way, there is a city—the city that has foundations, prepared for you from before the foundation of the world by your God.

It is your goal.

Until it is reached and you have entered through its pearly gates, you may not, you cannot, you must not tarry. Onward you must go; ever onward you must press, never once tarrying or abiding, never fearfully or hesitantly clinging to the things you might meet on your pilgrim's journey.

Does not the pilgrim dwell in a tent?

He has no city.

In a city one abides, digs foundations, builds firmly to erect a lasting and permanent dwelling place, a continuing home. There are the ties that bind, the treasures one loves, the joys one seeks. There is one's life. In a tent, however, one tarries but for a night, to rest and recuperate, in order to pull up the stakes at daybreak and press forward and travel onward until the final goal is reached.

The Christian's life is not like that of the continuing citizen, but like that of the passing stranger, pitching his tent by the wayside to tarry but for a night. Onward, ever onward points the way, now rugged and steep, now for awhile on the level and even, but mostly narrow and rough. At sundry stations you may stop long enough to put up your Ebenezers and pray over them, gratefully acknowledging the Lord Jehovah's help in the past and hopefully imploring his care and guidance and protection all the rest of the way. Sometimes the way may lead you through the midst of a city, fair and beautiful, stealing the love of your heart, tempting you to abide and to bid farewell to the pilgrim's life.

But you cannot stay, and you must not tarry.

No city here has foundations.

No dwelling place here is continuing.

The goal lies yonder, at the very end of your earthly way, when time is no more and the heavenly light of eternity's morn beckons you.

The light of the heavenly Jerusalem.

Thither you must press.

On, Christian, on!

———————

Oh, Zion eternal!

Glorious city of God!

How thou art the chief joy of all who have their garments washed in the blood of the Lamb and who love the light!

Surely, I know that I know but little of the glory and beauty and heavenly joy and eternal pleasures of that city. But even the little I know of the final goal is abundant comfort in the narrow way.

I know that of its heavenly beauty I can but stammer in earthly language, and of its glorious reality I can but conceive in earthly images. But even the partial and earthly image of that eternal city so sets my heart aglow with joy and hope and so fills it with earnest expectation and yearning that for the glory of it, I am gladly willing to sacrifice every earthly joy and pass outside of the gate of every earthly city.

For I do know that it is the city of God.

God is the chief joy of the heavenly Jerusalem. His presence fills the city. His blessed covenant friendship perfected is the very essence of all its bliss and rejoicing. Unlike the earthly Jerusalem, built of wood and stone, it has no temple. If you entered the gates of Jerusalem that once was, and if you would inquire as to the dwelling place of the Most High, and you would be pointed to a building made with hands. If, approaching the temple and entering through its outer gate, you would repeat your query, bystanders would direct your gaze to the sanctuary proper, at the same time warning you that you could not enter there to see the face of God. It was all so imperfect, earthly, and prophetic of things to come. But when you enter the heavenly city through its pearly gates, you need not inquire, for there is no temple there. God himself and the Lamb are the temple of that city, and its preeminent joy and glory is that there the tabernacle of God is with men; he will dwell with them, and they shall be his people, and God himself shall be with them and be their God.

He fills the city. I know that it is the city of all the perfected saints, the bride, the Lamb's wife. They walk there in garments white, for they had them washed in the blood of their redeemer, the mighty Lamb of God. There shall be no sin, no corruption, no stain of defilement and pollution left on the robes of its elect inhabitants. Wreaths of victory they wear on their heads, for the battle is ended and won through him who loved them even unto death. I know that there shall be no enemy there to harass and attack and inspire with fear, for the fearful and unbelieving, abominable and murderers, whoremongers, all sorcerers and idolaters and liars, and dogs shall not enter in any wise into that city, but shall have their part with the old serpent in the lake that burns with fire and brimstone, which is the second death.

I know that there shall be no shadow of death there, no pain or sorrow, no trouble and affliction, no fear or distress, for God shall himself dry the tear-stained faces of his weary pilgrim-children and fill their hearts with everlasting joy.

I know that there shall be neither hunger nor thirst, for the inhabitants shall drink of the fountain of eternal life and eat of the fruit of the tree of life and be abundantly satisfied with the goodness of their God.

His face they shall see
In his light they shall walk.
His name shall be in their foreheads.

They shall have put off all imperfection and all that is of the earth earthy, they shall know as they are known, and forever and ever they shall behold the beauty of the Lord their God.

There shall be no night there.

All the weary night shall be past, changed into eternal day.

There shall be perfect peace.

Glorious city of God!

Chief joy of all God's children!

———————

Press forward, Christian, you must!

For here we have no continuing city.

Not only because here there is nothing that abides, although this is also true. Nothing is permanent in this world. There is no city here that can boast of lasting fame, for the world is a child of time, and chance and change are ever busy. We are like the grass that flourishes in the morning and withers before the sun goes down. We are like the delicate flower of the field that blooms but for a moment and soon dies and is past, even so that its place knows it no more. The life of generation after generation is like a passing show, a pageant, always coming, always moving, always disappearing behind the veil of death. As we are, so are all things. Nothing is stable; all things move. A stream is life, and all things drift along with it. For the world passes away and the lust thereof, and there is in all the world nothing to which our soul can cling.

In this sense it is true for all men: we have no continuing city here. All things loudly preach: Prepare your house, for you will die.

The man of the world, the inhabitant of proud Babylon, may dig deeply, lay his foundations firmly, and raise his dwelling place in the midst of this world proud and beautiful. He may close his eyes to the reality of fleeting things and say to his soul, "My house shall stand for aye."

But he is a fool.

Yet a little while and the world shall be no more. Every home, every city, and every proud structure built upon the foundation of this world shall perish with the world.

For the Christian this is not all.

He has no continuing city here in the sense that wherever he looks and in whichever direction he may turn his seeking gaze, nowhere in the world does he find a place to satisfy his soul and to build his permanent home. He is a pilgrim not only because all things pass away, but also because of the state and condition of his own heart and soul.

He is a stranger here, for he was born from above.

By nature he is from below and an inhabitant of this world, seeking the things below. But he has received new life through the resurrection of the Lord Jesus. His new life is from above, not from below. His new life is the life of the city that has foundations, whose builder and artificer is God. His new life stands antithetically against the old, for the old was of darkness, while the new is of the light; the old was of his father the devil, while the new is of God through Christ; the old loved what was evil, while the new loves that which is good and pleasing to God; the old life was of the earth earthy, while the new life is of the Lord from heaven.

He has become a citizen of the new city, and he walks here with the life of that city in his breast. Therefore he can find no continuing city here, no place where he would care to build and to abide forever.

He longs and hopes and yearns and presses forward, until through the gate he will enter into the city.

Christian, here you have no continuing city.

Press forward you must.

————

Seek that city!

Seek it you must, but not as one who gropes in darkness and knows not the way, neither is certain whether he will ever enter.

The way is certain.

You need not doubt as to the direction. It always starts outside the gate.

There is erected outside of the gate and on a little hill a cross, an accursed tree. On the tree there is the Man of Sorrows. The world would not have him. Jerusalem loved him not. As a thing abominable and a reproach, he was cast out to suffer without the camp. Nor will the world ever let him in again. The sign of the cross remains the symbol of his relation to the world and of the attitude of Jerusalem, whose spiritual name is Sodom and Gomorrah. But on that accursed tree this Man of Sorrows shed his lifeblood, that you might have properly washed garments to enter the city of eternal light and joy.

Over that hill, by that cross, and outside the gate leads the way.

One cannot miss it.

Go out of the gate, therefore.

Have your garments washed in his blood.

And bear his reproach. This you cannot escape on the way to the eternal city. Washed by him, you are one with him, and being one with him you will share his reproach. For the servant is not greater than his master. If they have hated him, they will also hate you. The way, then, is unmistakably certain.

But seek the city. Know that it is more precious than all the pleasures and treasures of the world. Set your heart on it. Long for it. Hope for it. Strive for it. Fight for it. Suffer for it. Bear the cross and the reproach of him who suffered outside of the gate for it. Press on and on until you enter through its gates and have the victory forever.

It is coming.

It is not yet. Its glory is not yet revealed, for we are saved in hope, and hope that is seen is not hope.

But it is certain in its coming. God prepared it for you in his eternal and immutable counsel. It cannot fail. The end of the pilgrim's journey that starts outside the gate, and on which you are called to bear the reproach of the sufferer of Golgotha, is the beautiful city of God.

It is about to come.

Yet a little patience and a little suffering, yet a little struggle and a little battle, and the end of your journey will be reached.

A very light affliction, quickly passing and then eternal joy.

Seek that city!

Press on!

3

Desiring the Heavenly Fatherland

"But now they desire a better country, that is, an
heavenly: wherefore God is not ashamed to be called
their God: for he hath prepared for them a city."
—Hebrews 11:16

The heavenly fatherland!

The eyes of the saints of all ages have been focused upon it.

It is the object of their desires. That they seek. To that desiring, to that seeking of the heavenly fatherland every other desire and striving is subordinate and subservient.

For that they hope. In that hope they are blessed, for it is a hope that never vanishes away and that never puts to shame.

The world too always looks forward. It also focuses its attention on the future. The world is driven toward the future, for we are children of time. In time we journey, live, and strive within the limits of the development of earthly things. Temporal and earthly things lie under God's curse. The suffering of this present time is bound unavoidably and inseparably to time. Death lurks in every moment of our earthly existence. The fear of death dogs our footsteps and permeates everything we do. Present reality never gives peace. The present always manifests vanity. When the future moment for which we hope becomes the present moment, it is always disappointing. We are always seeking for something better than the present. Relentlessly swept along on the rushing stream of time, we always reach out toward the future.

Vanity of vanities!

A hope that always disappoints, because something better than the present cannot be found in earthly and temporal realities.

The longings and pursuits of a world that is far from God and that always wants something better meet with disappointment upon disappointment and have the same ultimate end—the despair of death in everlasting horror.

But the saints are desirous of a better, that is, a heavenly fatherland.

They always confess that they are strangers and pilgrims on the earth. The object of their desires is not below. The distant gaze of their hope is not obscured by the horizon of things temporal. They die as the world does, but in faith and with the confession that they in hope cling steadfastly to the promise that they have seen from afar.

And those who say such things demonstrate clearly that they are seeking a fatherland.

At the same time, they demonstrate that the fatherland that they seek does not lie behind them.

Of the fatherland from whence they have gone out they do not think.

They are desirous of a better fatherland—better than everything, better than the world, better than anything the earthly and temporal can offer.

The heavenly fatherland!

Let it be said with emphasis: Fatherland!

Not just any country is a fatherland.

Even though someone in a certain country may have many treasures and possessions, even though he is an owner of much real estate in a certain country, that does not make that country his fatherland. Yet a country can be our fatherland even though we do not own the least part of it. It is more than idle fantasy when we sing, "The precious ground where once my cradle lay."

No one feels this more poignantly than an emigrant who, when he is a young adult, forsakes his fatherland to establish residence in a strange land. After living a few years in a strange land, he becomes really a stranger on the earth. The old fatherland still draws him, but he would not feel at home there any more, and the new country of choice will never become his fatherland.

A fatherland has the love of our hearts. It is the country where we have our residence in the fullest sense, the place where we feel entirely at home. We live among our own people there. The ties and bands of life are found there. All the relationships of life are found there. Our mother tongue is spoken there. Our citizenship is there. In our fatherland we have been born and bred. There we have a permanent place. We are pilgrims and strangers everywhere else, even though we are laden with temporal things and earthly prosperity. The fatherland is entirely entwined in our life, and the whole of our life is joined to the fatherland. Wherever we are in the world, our hearts draw us toward the fatherland.

So it is with our heavenly fatherland as well.

Certainly, the heavenly fatherland is a country—a real country—in a much greater sense than all the countries of the world. The earthly Canaan was an image of that country. The saints of the old dispensation were promised the land of Canaan. Abraham was called out of his father's house and family relationships in order to journey to a country that the Lord would show him, the land of promise that Jehovah would give to him. He believed and embraced the promise, forsook his fatherland, and journeyed to the land of promise. Yet he was a pilgrim and a stranger there as well. He lived with Isaac and Jacob in tents and confessed that he was a pilgrim on the earth. Even though he never inherited the land into which Jehovah led him, he saw the promise from afar and died in faith. The promise caused him to see in the earthly Canaan an image of the fatherland that had been promised him, but yet it was not the fulfillment of the promise. Always and ever he desired and sought a better, that is, a heavenly fatherland. That better fatherland was not merely an abstract concept, but a real country—the new heavens and the new earth, the coming world, the incorruptible and undefiled inheritance.

It is emphatically a fatherland.

In that fatherland are all the relationships of the saints, who are strangers and pilgrims here. In that fatherland is the highest realization of God's covenant of friendship: God's house of many mansions, the most intimate fellowship with the Almighty, the experience of his favor, the knowing even as we are known, the seeing of one another face-to-face, the heavenly revelation of the charms and sweetness found at God's right hand. There God's love is eternally complete and finds its echo in our complete love of him. There we will serve him perfectly with a service of love that never disappoints, as co-workers with God as his covenantal friends. There is our citizenship, and there our joint citizenship with all the saints is perfected. There we will have fellowship in perfect light with all those who in faith reverence his name. There everyone speaks the same language. There everyone performs the same service. There all live and walk in Christ Jesus in perfect light. There everyone bears the image of the heavenly. There is no death, no sin and no failure, no sorrow and no complaint, no struggle and no distress, and no fear. There is the rest of the perfect service of God.

Everything is on the exalted plane of the heavenly.

Everything in the freedom of the eternal.

The heavenly fatherland!

Better, infinitely better, than any fatherland on the earth.

So much better, even as life is better than death, as light is better than darkness, as heaven is lifted up above the earth, and as the eternal is more excellent than time.

The saints earnestly long for the fatherland.

They are overcome with homesickness for the better, heavenly fatherland. Being desirous of the better fatherland, they are strangers and pilgrims here. Just as someone who is far from home and family and who lives alone in a strange country can be overwhelmed with homesickness, so the saints yearn for the better fatherland. They are ever mindful of that land in the country of their pilgrimage. The thought of the fatherland remains with them in all that they do. The longing for the fatherland rules their life: all their actions, their behavior and activities, their speaking and hearing, their struggles and battles, their sadness and joy. They, indeed, live here as citizens of the heavenly fatherland.

They are, indeed, pilgrims and sojourners upon the whole earth.

They seek the fatherland.

They struggle to the heights of Zion.

For they have the promises.

They see the promise from afar. They believe it, embrace it, and place all their trust in it.

They have the new life, the principle of citizenship in the heavenly fatherland in their soul.

They are regenerated unto a living hope through the resurrection of Jesus Christ from the dead.

The attraction of that life is toward that which is above, to the eternal, to the heavenly.

The better fatherland!

A longing that never makes ashamed!

The world's expectations will perish, but the hope of the saints will never be put to shame.

For God has prepared for them a city.

There is no essential difference between the fatherland and the city as pictures of the eternal, incorruptible inheritance that God has prepared for those who love him. This is plain from the text itself: They are desirous of a better, that is, a heavenly fatherland, and God has prepared for them a city. It is also clear from verse ten: "For he looked for a city which hath foundations, whose builder and maker is God." A city is not merely a group of houses, but a fellowship of citizens who live together under their own governance.

There is a difference only of viewpoint in these expressions.

The city is a picture of the permanent in contrast to the tent as a picture of the temporal and transitory. The city has foundations, the tent does not. In a city one builds one's house, one establishes a residence with the intention of remaining there. In the earthly land of promise, Abraham, Isaac, and Jacob dwelt in tents. Thereby they confessed that they had not reached their final destination and that they lived in a land that to them was foreign, even when they were in the land of promise. They did this because they hoped for the city that has foundations, whose builder and maker is God.

The city is a picture of the eternal, final, perpetual rest.

God has prepared such a city, such a place of eternal rest, such a place of permanent residence in the heavenly fatherland!

The city has been prepared for God's people, whom he knew from before the foundation of the world, whom he foreordained to be conformed unto the image of his Son. That city was built with a view to them, in regard to their needs, according to their longings, in harmony with their glorious life that they now already in principle possess, and which they will soon receive in heavenly perfection. They have been formed for the city, and the city has been formed for them. They belong to the city, and the city belongs to them. There they find the everlasting fulfillment of all their desires. There will be their eternal blessedness.

The city has been prepared.

It is finished.

It awaits only its revelation in the day of the glory of Christ.

It was prepared when Abraham, Isaac, and Jacob lived in tents in the land of promise as pilgrims in a strange land, for God had prepared that city in his eternal counsel before the foundation of the world. In his counsel is everything that will occur in time and that has been so arranged in wisdom by the divine architect and master builder that it must serve to the realization of that eternal city that has foundations.

In principle it has also been prepared in Christ.

It was realized when he came in the likeness of sinful flesh—the Son, Immanuel, God with us. It was realized when he shed his lifeblood unto death on the accursed tree at Golgotha for our sins, making perfect sacrifice unto God, satisfying God's justice, and meriting for his own the forgiveness of sins, eternal righteousness, salvation, and glory. It was realized when he arose in glory as the firstfruits of them who slept and ascended into glory at the right hand of the Father as the Lord of lords and King of kings.

Then that city was prepared for us.

For we have not come unto the mount that might be touched and that burned with fire, nor unto blackness and darkness and tempest. But we are come unto Mount Zion, unto the city of the living God, the heavenly Jerusalem, and to an innumerable company of angels, to the general assembly and church of the firstborn, which are written in heaven, and to God, the judge of all, and to the spirits of just men made perfect and to Jesus, the mediator of the new covenant.

Jerusalem that is above.

The mother of us all.

The city is not yet revealed, but it has been prepared, in order to be revealed at the end of time.

Therefore, God is not ashamed to be their God.

They, the pilgrims and strangers on the earth, call him their God.

And God the Lord, who has prepared a city for them, is not ashamed to be called their God by those who confess that they seek a city that has foundations and that they are longing for a better, that is, a heavenly fatherland.

If it were not true that he prepared the city, would he not be ashamed to be called the God of that people in the world?

For in the world they experience tribulation for his name's sake. They were mocked, disgraced, persecuted, and hunted down.

Throughout all the centuries, they experienced more misery than all mankind. They were killed all the day long. They were pilgrims on the earth, poor and despised. They wandered in deserts and in mountains, in the holes and caves of the earth. They wandered about in sheepskins and goatskins, endured mockings and scourgings, bands and imprisonments. They were pulled asunder, hewn in pieces, stoned, and put to death by the sword. The world was not worthy of them. And in the midst of it all, they had to listen to the world's mockery, "Where is your God upon whom you depend and in whose word you trust?"

But he is not ashamed to be called their God.

For he has prepared for them a city!

4

Sojourning Safely

"He suffered no man to do them wrong."
—Psalm 105:14

Sojourners in the world are the people of God. Pilgrims and strangers in the earth God makes them. According to a figure of which the Bible is fond, God's children dwell in tents. An abiding dwelling place, a permanent home, they neither possess nor desire here below. As they cast their eyes about them on the things on earth, they unite in singing with the poet of Psalm 39:

> *I am a stranger here,*
> *Dependent on thy grace,*
> *A pilgrim as my fathers were,*
> *With no abiding place.*

Then, lifting up their heads and with the light of a new city reflecting in their longing eyes, they travel onward, repeating after the poet of Psalm 17:

> *When I in righteousness at last*
> *Thy glorious face shall see,*
> *When all the weary night is past,*
> *And I awake with thee*
> *To view the glories that abide,*
> *Then, then, I shall be satisfied.*

The reason for their sojourner-attitude and pilgrim-spirit is that they are citizens of another, that is, a heavenly country. They are born from above, and they have been begotten again unto a lively hope through the resurrection of Jesus from the dead. Of the life of the risen Lord they partake. Their new life is neither of this world nor a revival of a life in days of yore, in paradise lost. It is the life of a new city, of the heavenly Jerusalem, of the eternal kingdom, still to be revealed in the full splendor of its beauty. It is a life not from below but from above, not earthly but heavenly. It is not mournfully glancing back upon a lost estate, but hopefully looking forward to an eternal inheritance. It is decidedly other-worldly. They become citizens of another country not by any external process of naturalization, but by the inner process of spiritual renewal. Thus they are strangers and sojourners on the earth, pilgrims with their faces set toward the city that has foundations whose builder and maker is God.

Of these strangers on the earth, the psalmist affirms that in their earthly pilgrimage they always are well-protected and safely guarded. For God "suffered no man to do them wrong." As it was in days of hoary antiquity and of the patriarchs, thus it is with these pilgrims throughout the epochs of history, and thus it will be until the last of them will appear in Zion before God.

Sojourners they are, traveling safely.

How wonderful is this safety of God's children in the world!

There is no strength in their number. They are but few—yea, very few indeed—at any given moment in history. How few were the sojourners that traveled with the father of believers when he was called to leave his father's house and kin and become a stranger in the earth. How small was the number of those who as tent-dwellers sojourned with Isaac and Jacob in the land of promise as in a strange country. How small a band they were when they bent their necks under the cruel yoke of Egypt's bondage. How insignificant proportionally appeared their number when they inhabited the land flowing with milk and honey in the midst of the mightiest nations of the earth. Even when finally the gates of Jerusalem are thrown open to all the nations of the earth and many tribes turn their faces toward Zion to learn the will of Jehovah, how comparatively small is their number, especially when counted according to the election of grace.

Surely, counted by themselves, apart from any comparison with the world, they are a great throng. When for these pilgrims all the weary night is past and time shall be no more, they will constitute a multitude, the symbol of whose number is in the firmament's countless stars and in the uncountable sand on the seashore. Innumerable will be their host when the last one of them shall have buried the pilgrim's staff in the valley of death, and bearing the palm branch of victory and wearing the glorious crown of life and the spotless white robe of righteousness, will sing with all the redeemed of God eternal hallelujahs before the throne of God and the Lamb. Then they shall be a multitude that no man can number.

But now, in the days of their sojourn and pilgrimage, their number is quickly expressed. For they are few—very few indeed.

What hinders the enemy to come upon these few strangers and to swallow them up alive?

Considering the smallness of their number, the safety of their sojourn is a marvel.

———————

How perilous is the road they are called to travel, for they are in the world, yet not of the world. The road of their pilgrimage leads directly through the world, and the world hates them. Under the leadership of and in alliance with the prince of darkness, that world is filled with enmity and raves with furious hatred against these pilgrims traveling to the heavenly Jerusalem. For the life of their risen Lord they strive to live, and their conversation and walk are not according to the fashion of this world. The world's song they do not sing; the world's dance they do not dance; the world's wealth they do not treasure; in the world's pleasure they have no pleasure; in the world's glory they do not glory. They decline to worship the world's god. Of the city that has foundations they sing, in the Lord they rejoice, and in him they glory. Anointed of the Lord they are, a holy nation of royal priests, and they show forth the praises of him who has called them from darkness into his marvelous light. The world they condemn.

Small wonder that the world hates them and is enraged against them with the same fury that made them nail the Lord of glory to the accursed tree. A united power of darkness are the world and its prince. They lurk in secret places, they conspire in the dark, and they marshal all their strength to harm these few wayfarers and strangers in order to blot out their existence in the earth and to prevent them from entering into the promised inheritance.

How defenseless seems the position of these sojourners on the earth!

Yet, in spite of their small number, their perilous path, and their hateful enemies, and the fact that the power and authority and wealth of this world are not on their side, how perfect is their safety as they journey onward to the city of their hope!

Why?

God suffered no man to do them wrong.

He was Abraham's shield, Isaac's protector, Jacob's guide, and Israel's deliverer. He is the refuge and high tower of all his people throughout their earthly sojourn, and he never fails nor forsakes them.

This is quite sufficient, for he is God Almighty.

He ordained all things with a view to the salvation of these sojourning strangers; he made all things with a view to their glorification; he moves and directs all things with a view to the realization of their eternal inheritance. Without him no creature moves. Without him no hateful heart registers another beat; without him no malicious mind contrives a single plan; without him no reviling tongue utters another syllable. No murderous sword strikes a blow, no human power condemns, no human army moves, no devil stirs in the darkness of the abyss, but by his will. No lion roars, no serpent sneaks, no pestilence stalks, no fire burns, no water drowns, no death lurks, but when he allows. If he does not suffer, nothing in all the wide creation stirs.

Still more: when they do move, beat, contrive, speak, strike, sneak, lurk, they do so to serve his purpose. He it is—the Almighty—who suffers no man to do these sojourners wrong.

How safe they are!

Peace, be still!

How can he allow any creature to harm his people?

They are as dear to him as the life of his Son. To touch them is to touch the apple of his eye, for God is not only the Almighty, but also the God who loved these sojourners from before the foundation of the world. He knew them in eternal love. Knowing them, he chose them. Choosing them, he ordained that they should be made like unto the image of his Son, that he might have many children and his Son might have many brethren. And ordaining them, he revealed to them the greatness of his love by sacrificing his most beloved for their ransom. Having shed the blood of his Son in their stead, he redeemed them to his praise by the power of his grace!

His love is in them. His name is in them. His glory is connected inseparably with their salvation. The price of the precious blood of his Son he paid for them.

How could he?

No more than he can deny himself can he surrender the glory of his own name, make void the power of his own Son's blood, alter his counsel or change himself, or allow any man, devil, or any other creature to harm his beloved, his anointed prophets, sojourning in the world.

A mother may forget her sucking babe.

But the Almighty never forsakes his people. He suffers no man to do them harm.

My soul shall not be greatly moved!

Does not this firm confidence and comforting assurance appear idle and without sufficient ground in the light of actual history?

Superficially considered, it would seem so.

How these sojourners suffered in the world! How large a measure of the suffering of this present time was meted out to them! How they were reviled, how they suffered reproach and were made a sorry spectacle in the world! How they were persecuted, chased over the earth, subjected to poverty and misery, shut up in dungeons and holes of horror! How they were tortured without mercy, cruelly sawn asunder or burned at the stake amid the mocking shrieks of the enemy! History depicts these sojourners as a small band of silent sufferers, with marred visages, utter amazement in their looks, well-nigh succumbing, as did their master, under their crosses as they were driven to the place of slaughter, all the while moaning, "For thy sake we are killed all the day long!" The trail these wayfarers leave is a bloody trail.

Yes.

But he suffers no man to do them wrong.

The enemy may devise mischief, may touch us, make us suffer for a time, rave against us in bitter hatred, and kill our bodies.

But God is for us. Therefore all things are for us and work together for our good. Heaven and earth and hell move only at the bidding of our Lord, and therefore at the bidding of the same love that was manifested on Golgotha's hill. As gold is tried by fire, so God's people are tried by sufferings and tribulations inflicted by raving enemies and furious devils. These all are our servants. We are more than conquerors through him who loved us.

Be of good cheer, pilgrim on the way to Zion! Through suffering, the way leads to glory.

Presently the Lord will give you beauty for ashes, oil of joy for mourning, and the garment of praise for the spirit of heaviness.

The crown for the cross!

5

Compassionate Remembrance

"For he knoweth our frame; he remembereth that we
are dust."

—Psalm 103:14

What fervent love and tender compassion glows in this poetic
expression of Father's attitude toward his children in the world!

"Like as a father pitieth his children, so the Lord pitieth them
that fear him. For he knoweth our frame, he remembereth that
we are dust."

The Lord never forgets the weakness and frailty of our frame.
And mindful of our frailty he is always compassionate and deals
with us in delicate tenderness, always careful never to overburden,
always filled with tender mercy and sympathizing with us as we
bear our burdens.

Man in merciless oblivion is sometimes forgetful of the frame
of the dumb animal he employs to carry his burden or to draw his
load. He will pile up a burden far too heavy in comparison with
the strength of his beast and drive it with lashing whip accompanied by angry oaths over rough and well-nigh impassable roads to
his destination.

Or cruel Pharaohs, forgetful of and without compassion for
the weak frame of their toiling slaves, require of them a task well-
nigh impossible to perform.

Or man himself, oblivious of the weakness and frailty of his
own frame, forgetting that he is but dust and tender as the flower
of the field, incessantly toils and labors until he succumbs, weary
and exhausted, a physical and mental wreck.

The Lord does not deal so with those who fear him.

He is not hard and cruel, but tenderhearted and merciful to them. Like as a father pities his children, so the Lord pities those who fear him, for he is their Father and they are his children. With a love, deep and constant and eternal as his own heart, he loved them, adopted them, redeemed them, and transformed them. And with a compassion as profound, fervent, and constant as his love, he remembers their infirmities, is mindful of their weaknesses, acquaints himself with their griefs and sorrows, tenderly considers their sufferings and afflictions, longs for their final deliverance, and hastens to their redemption. Nor is he forgetful of the frailty of their frame. He remembers that they are dust, for he made them. Out of the dust he formed them, and dust they are, he knows. And in all his dealings with them and in every way he leads them, with a view to all the tasks he requires of them and regarding all the burdens he makes them to bear, he constantly remembers that they are dust-children—tender and delicate, limited in strength, easily overburdened, needy and weak, and soon overcome, as the tender grass and the flower of the field.

Dust-children he made them, and he never forgets. Loving them, he is filled with compassion and tender mercy for his children in the dust. And in this mindful tenderheartedness, he treats them delicately, gently, never overburdening their frame.

What fervent compassion!

Bless the Lord, O my soul!

———————

Father remembers in mercy that we are dust!

What blessed knowledge!

Experience would often seem so different and contrary to this blessed assurance from our heavenly Father. Our weak frame, originating in the dust, often seems cruelly overburdened with loads of grief and affliction. Not infrequently it seems to break down accidentally, crushed by a weight it was not calculated to bear. And it would appear as if the Lord forgot either that he formed us of the dust or to be merciful over his children.

Does it never seem so to you?

Does it seem so when burning fever consumes the life of your tender and frail darling and wrecks its delicate frame, as the blasting breath of a hot wind causes the gentle flower to wither and die; or when a dearly beloved mother, whose love and care seems indispensable and whose family cannot spare her, is suddenly snatched from her family by the cruel hand of him who rides the pale horse; or when constant pain and suffering is your lot, continually leading you along the edge of the grave, yet never mercifully guiding you into it, so your daily supplication is "how long, Lord?" Does it seem as if the Lord has forgotten that he made us out of the dust or without mercy burdens us with loads we were never formed to bear? Is he oblivious of the delicate frame of your babe? Does he forget mercy when mother is made to succumb? Is he forgetful of your continual burden of suffering and woe?

Or, again, how often are not the enemies of his children made to triumph over them! How fearfully dark is the night of their suffering when they are killed all the day long and led as sheep to the slaughter! How are they chased over the earth, filled with reproach, cast into holes and dungeons, beaten with many stripes, burned at the stake or sawn asunder, cruelly tortured to death! They are made to pass through fire and through water many times. And the plaintive song often rises from their souls, oppressed with grief and enveloped in darkness:

> I asked in fear and bitterness,
> Will God forsake me in distress?
> Shall I his promise faithless find?
> Has God forgotten to be kind?
> Has he in anger hopelessly
> Removed his love and grace from me?

Yet, like as a father pities his children, so the Lord pities those who fear him. And he knows our frame and remembers that we are dust.

He never forgets.

A load of sickness and pain never breaks the dust-frame of his children because he was forgetful of its frailty and overburdened it. It never breaks accidentally. When it does break it is only because he comes to break it. And when he comes to break that dust-frame, he does so in his mercy and compassion because he knows that thus it is best.

He never makes his children bear a load of grief and pain, of sorrow and distress, of tribulation and persecution, without mercifully remembering that the bearing frame is dust. And when the load becomes too heavy for mere dust-children to carry, yet it must be borne, he adds grace to dust and mercifully makes his strength perfect in weakness.

And, oh, what wonders are accomplished when the strength of his marvelous grace is made to sustain the frailty of human dust! Then the Lord's dust-formed children pass through the fire, and it does not burn them; then floods submerge them, yet they are not drowned; then the night of tribulation can be frightfully dark, yet they rejoice; then suffering day-by-day may be their lot and may wreck their mortal frame, yet they sing,

> *Though I am weak God is most high,*
> *And on his goodness I rely;*
> *Of all his wonders I will tell,*
> *And on his deeds my thoughts shall dwell.*

For he remembers that we are dust. And in eternal love and paternal pity he sustains our frame by the wonderful power of his all-sufficient grace.

Blessed assurance and all-comprehensive comfort to know that for the sake of Christ our savior, this God is our God and merciful Father—always remembering, always compassionate, always dealing tenderly, leading gently, sustaining powerfully—our God in prosperity and adversity, our God in health and sickness, our God in life and death, our God forever and ever.

Bless the Lord, O my soul!

This is not all!

He remembers in mercy and pities his children not only while they are dust, but also because they are dust.

Of dust he formed them. He never forgets.

From the dust he called the first man Adam and made him a living soul. And because Adam and his children were formed from the dust, they are limited by the dust and stoop toward the earth earthy. All God's children in the earth bear the image of the earthy. They have an eye of dust and see only earthy things; they have an earthy ear and hear only earthy sounds; they have an earthy tongue and speak only earthy language; they possess an earthy frame and live in earthy dependence, an earthy life. Formed from the dust, they are limited by the dust, stoop toward the dust, and return to the dust. God's dust-children bear the image of the earthy.

Yet in everlasting lovingkindness he predestined them for heavenly glory. He ordained that they should be conformed according to the image of his Son. In his unfathomable love he willed that they should be children of the dust and bear the image of the earthy only for a time, in order then to bear the image of the heavenly, to possess a heavenly frame, to see heavenly beauties, to be charmed by heavenly music, to speak a heavenly language, and to be clothed with heavenly glory.

Such is the purpose of the love wherewith he loved them.

While they were still dwelling in the dust and bearing the image of the earthy, he began to realize in them the purpose of that everlasting love by instilling into their hearts the first drop of that heavenly child-life, through the Spirit and grace of the risen Lord, the Lord of heaven, the second Adam, the quickening Spirit. In principle they have become children of heaven and they are quickened unto a new hope. Yet they are still dwelling in the dust. The heavenly things they long to see they do not see as yet; the heavenly things they like to hear, they hear only in hope; the heavenly tongue with which they yearn to speak, they do not know as yet; the heavenly glory with which they hope to be clothed is still hidden in a cloak of dust.

As children of heaven, they still dwell in the dust. The full manifestation of that heavenly life is hidden in their dust-frame, and the full expression of that life is hampered by their dust-frame.

But the Lord knows their frame. He remembers that they are dust. He never forgets his purpose. For the mercy of the Lord is from everlasting to everlasting over those who fear him.

In that everlasting mercy he pities his children while they dwell in the dust.

And that unfathomable mercy cannot rest until he delivers his children from their dust-frame—weak, mortal, earthy and corruptible—and makes them partakers of the image of the heavenly—in heavenly frame, in power and honor, immortal, incorruptible, and glorious.

Then they shall no more see as in a glass darkly, but face-to-face. Then they shall know as they are known and no more in part. In his everlasting temple they shall walk with him, talk with him, rejoice with him, reign with him, and see the beauties of the Lord in perfected, covenantal communion.

Everlasting friendship!

6

Rejoicing in Heaviness

"Wherein ye greatly rejoice, though now for a season,
if need be, ye are in heaviness through manifold
temptations: That the trial of your faith, being much
more precious than of gold that perisheth, though it
be tried with fire, might be found unto praise and
honour and glory at the appearing of Jesus Christ."
—1 Peter 1:6, 7

Ye rejoice, though in heaviness!

Putting it very briefly, such seems to be the contents of these verses from the first epistle of the apostle Peter.

Apparently a very strange paradox, indeed. Is it possible that two such contradictory states of mind exist side by side at the same time in the soul of the same individual? Can one be burdened with oppression, yet also leap with joy at the same moment? Can one weep and laugh, grieve and rejoice, groan and sing, all at once?

Yet it is only one of a multitude of similar paradoxical statements frequently applied to the Christian as he advances on his pilgrim-journey through this world. He dies every day, yet he lives and shall never die; he is full of troubles and afflictions, yet he walks in heaven; he is persecuted and made a spectacle, so that all the world triumphs over him, yet he has the victory; he is poor and in want, yet he possesses all things; he is saint and sinner, prince and pauper.

And so he smiles through his tears.

Even as nature does, when it displays on the dark background of departing clouds the bow of God's faithful covenant.

The Christian, as the apostle Peter pictures him, is a pilgrim and sojourner in this world, all the way to glory.

He is an elect stranger.

He is such because he was born again, born from above, born again through the resurrection of Jesus Christ the Lord. He walks with the beginning of a new life in his heart, a life that is not of this world but of the world to come, not of darkness but of the light, not of the earth but of heaven. The operation and power of that new principle of life within his bosom makes him look and strive upward, causes him to be out of harmony with the world around him as it seeks the things below and walks in darkness. He is in the world but not of the world, and the world knows him not.

This sojourner is often in heaviness because of manifold temptations.

For the Lord leads his pilgrim-children through many a dark and dreary night to the city of everlasting light. There is the suffering that characterizes the present time in general. A goodly portion of it the Lord allotted to his own children. Pain and anguish according to the body, or sorrow and grief of soul are often their lot. Waters of a full cup are wrung out to them. And who knows not the heaviness of which the apostle speaks, when every morning the sun rises to find us struggling and moaning in the valley of affliction, and every night spreads its shadows over us, only to hide for a while our grief under its dark cover and to swallow up our groaning in its black stillness? Besides, there is the suffering that is inevitably his lot who walks the path where Jesus trod and who, according to God's gracious election, is placed as a pilgrim of light in the midst of the darkness of this world. For the world does not know these strangers and cannot tolerate them in their midst. Could they but sing and dance and seek the things below with the world, the world would know them and recognize them as their own. But they cannot. And in their pilgrim-life, advancing from strength to strength, until they appear in Zion before God, they condemn the world and the ways of the world. Therefore, the world hates them, even as they hated him, through whose resurrection they are begotten again unto a living hope. Hence they must be in manifold temptations, in trials and tribulations, in the midst of reproaches and persecutions. And often they are led as sheep to the slaughter all the day long.

Thus it was with the church of Peter's day. Thus it frequently is. Thus it always is in principle. Thus it must be until the appearing of Jesus Christ our Lord.

Surely, the Christian and the church may for a time hide the light. The pilgrim may put off his stranger's garb and appear in the many-colored robes of the world. Then the hatred of the world may seem to change into goodwill, and the fire of the trials may apparently be extinguished.

But the faithful pilgrim must suffer. And the more he lets his light shine, the more he will experience that his way is one of manifold trials.

He walks his way in heaviness. Fear, anguish, poverty, and oppression are often his lot.

Yet, although he is in heaviness, he rejoices.

Rejoices greatly!

In heaviness rejoice!

Wonderful paradox! Strange contradiction!

It is expressed still more emphatically by the staunch and very profound James, when he was inspired to write, "My brethren, count it all joy, when ye fall into divers temptations."

Strange, yet how real in the life of the pilgrim-Christian in the midst of this world!

Not, indeed, as if he loves the trials and sufferings for their own sake. He does not deceive himself into believing that sufferings are to be desired in themselves. Neither is he a Stoic, practicing to compel his earthly frame to bear the keenest pain and deepest grief without apparent emotion. On the contrary, when he is oppressed, he is in heaviness, and he reveals it; when he is in pain, he cries and groans; when sorrow overwhelms the soul, he weeps bitter tears. He is afraid in danger; fear creeps into his soul in the darkness of the night; he dreads the coming storm; he trembles when the enemy kindles the fires of persecution.

Deeply and keenly he feels the suffering. According to the flesh, there is no reason for him to rejoice.

He longs to be delivered.

Yet, while he must thus suffer according to the flesh and be in manifold trials and in heaviness of soul, there are for him abundant reasons to rejoice according to the spirit, according to that other, that new, that heavenly life, he received through the grace of his Lord.

For the tribulation is only for a season. The sufferings of the present time do not last forever, and they do not last long. They are for a little while. The pilgrim's journey is short. Soon all the weary night is past. And assured of this flitting and passing character of the suffering of the present, we rejoice on the way in many things we possess now in principle, and will possess in perfection as soon as the brief way is finished. We rejoice in the possession of the new life, begotten through the resurrection of the Lord. We rejoice in a blessed, incorruptible inheritance that is kept in the heavens for us. We rejoice in a sense of safety and security, for however dark the way is and however strong the enemy and fiery the trials are, we know that we are kept by God's power, through faith, for that blessed inheritance, and that there is no reason to fear or be dismayed. And, thus, in heaviness the pilgrim-Christian rejoices in many things, sings in his suffering, and smiles through his tears, always advancing with the hope eternal in his bosom.

Then the heaviness is only "if need be."

It is not more severe than strictly necessary. It does not last when there is no more need of it.

Of this we may be assured. There is a loving Father in heaven; there is in the sanctuary a merciful high priest who loves his brethren and has sympathy with all their afflictions and tribulations, because he was tempted in all things even as they are, except without sin.

Although it may seem to us sometimes that the way is controlled by the enemy, yet the way we travel is our Father's way, and it is constantly under the all-powerful direction of our merciful high priest. And, hence, we may be certain that we are led in manifold trials not because our Father loves to see us suffer. He and the merciful high priest before his throne long to deliver us as soon as possible.

Suffering only for a season, with the firm hope that the most glorious morning will dawn upon us, that an unspeakably rich inheritance is waiting for us, and that it will be revealed to us as soon as the dark night is passed.

And in tribulation, only because it must be.

The paradox may seem very strange, yet it is very real: we greatly rejoice, although in heaviness!

Ye greatly rejoice!

Rejoice in your spiritual and heavenly possessions!

Even though you must be in heaviness for a season, if need be, because of your manifold temptations.

And if the manifold trials are necessary with a view to our everlasting glory and our entering into the possession of the inheritance incorruptible, we will count it all joy that we may fall into them.

For then we begin to understand somewhat the darkness of the way in which the Father leads and from which he will not deliver us until all is finished. Often, it is true, we do not comprehend our Father's ways in detail. His thoughts are higher than our thoughts, and his ways are higher than our ways. Wondrous and often unfathomable are they. We cannot account for every curve in the road; we do not understand the reason for every cloud of evil that lowers upon us; we cannot see the necessity of every billow of affliction and all the fire of trial. But we begin to understand the general reason and necessity for these manifold temptations.

They are for our faith what fire is to the gold in the refiner's pot.

That fire must serve to test, to assay, to purify and refine the gold, to separate from it all the foreign elements, to bring out the riches of its yellow gleam, the beauty of its lustre. So must the fire of manifold temptations serve to reveal the beauty of faith, by putting it to the test, by refining and purifying it unto the appearing of Jesus Christ.

Nothing is more precious than our faith. It is the living bond of fellowship with Christ, the tie that binds us to him, the spiritual power whereby we draw our life, our all, from him. It is in us the root of our whole life, for by faith we live and fight the battle. By faith we are righteous, and through faith we hope and purify ourselves even as he is pure. Faith is the power through which God preserves us and keeps us unto the incorruptible inheritance. By faith we are saved through grace. And it is the gift of God. It is all his work in us. To live by faith is to live not of ourselves, but of Christ through the grace of God who chose us unto glory.

The wonderful power and beauty of that work of God in us must be revealed. In the day of Christ Jesus the Lord, it must appear in all its luster and splendor, unto praise and honor and glory, that the author of it all may receive the praise and honor of all his wonderful work and that we may enter into everlasting glory.

For this purpose faith must be tried.

For even as tested gold is beautiful gold, so faith, refined and tried by the fire of temptations manifold, is beautiful.

Here, and especially when all is bright and smooth according to the flesh, the beauty of that work of God in us, whereby we are ingrafted into and live from Jesus Christ our Lord, is often hidden under sin and imperfection. Many foreign elements are still mixed with the gold of our faith.

Hence it must be tested, refined, purified, and approved.

The manifold trials are the fires that serve this purpose. Through them the genuine is separated from the counterfeit. So often we are inclined to intermix that which is of ourselves, of our own power and wisdom and righteousness, with the work of God and the operation of Christ in us and would have some of self and some of him. We attempt to put our trust partly in self, even while confessing that all our confidence is in him only. We boast of our own work while we are speaking of his; we rely on our own righteousness while professing to lean on his; we divide the glory and praise between his work and our own. And as it is with the individual Christian, so it is with the church of Christ as a whole in the world. The tares grow with the wheat. The work of man often would force itself to the foreground, although the church confesses that it is all grace, the grace of the Lord Jesus. But let the trials come, let the battle rage, let suffering and affliction be our portion, let the enemy rage, the devil and the world persecute and kindle the fires of temptation for the pilgrim-Christian and for the sojourning church, and see if they all do not serve one and the same purpose: to test the true faith, to separate it from all that is of man, to cause the child of God to cast away all that is not of Christ, and henceforth to lean only on him and give all the praise and glory to him.

Let faith be cast into the fire of temptation. There is no danger that it will perish. It stands the test. Storms may rage, and billows may roll. But when all is past, faith still stands. Fires of tribulation may be kindled. But when the fires have burned out and have consumed everything that is not of faith and therefore not of Christ, faith will still prevail.

And through these trials faith will increase its power, and its beauty will be enhanced. Hateful though he may be, the devil must serve to polish Christ's work in us. Dreadful though they be, the trials of this present time must work for our salvation and the praise and honor and glory of the Lord at his appearing.

Therefore, we rejoice, even though for a season, if need be, we must rejoice weeping.

Rejoice because of what we now possess, which no fire of trials can possibly destroy.

Rejoice because of what is coming in the future, when all the weary night is past.

Rejoice, too, because these very trials must serve our salvation
and the glory of the Lord.

And behold, he shall quickly appear!

And his reward is with him!

The inheritance incorruptible.

Everlasting joy!

7

Rest for the Weary

"Come unto me, all ye that labour and are heavy
laden, and I will give you rest."
—Matthew 11:28

Toiling!

Do you know by experience the sad and disheartening implication of that word?

Nay, if you would understand its meaning, do not summon before the eyes of your imagination the picture of the daily laborer in the shops or of the husbandman in his field, who rises early in the morning and returns home in the evening, tired and weary and longing to forget the burdens of the day in restful sleep. For however heavy the work may be that he finds waiting for him every morning, and however fatigued his frame may be when the daily task is finished and he lies down to rest, in the evening of every day he returns home in the consciousness that the task is accomplished and that he may forget the struggles of the day.

Rather, imagine the man who is groaning under burdens too heavy for human strength to bear. Or think of the man who is laboring at a hopeless task. All the strength of body and mind he exerts to exhaustion. To accomplish the work is the ambition of his life. From early morning until late at night he struggles and strives and ponders and plans. Incessantly he labors with all his might. Yet he fails. And after all his attempts he finds in the end that he is farther from the goal than at the beginning. Real toil is to strive with all our strength of body and mind for an end that is never achieved. It is to labor hard and incessantly at a hopeless task that can never be accomplished.

And are you acquainted with the spiritual significance of the word?

It is the spiritual toilers under burdens too heavy for them whom the Lord calls in the text.

It is a toiling that in its deepest root is born from the heart's desire to get right with God, to know that we have peace with the Most High, and that his favor is with us. The heart, then, somehow realizes that God's lovingkindness cannot be enjoyed and that we cannot be the objects of his favor, except on a basis of a righteousness that is valid before him. For he is righteous, we know, and spotlessly holy. The heart feels, too, that this basis of righteousness and justice cannot be established, except the law is fulfilled and all its demands are perfectly satisfied. And we begin at the task to gain the desired peace in the way of accomplishing our own satisfaction of the entire law. But as we labor and toil to fulfill the law of the Lord, we experience that she is a severe mistress. And though we may labor with all our might, anxious to hear from her the sentence that it is enough, repeatedly she flings us back with her terrible words: "Cursed is he that does not abide perfectly in all that is written in me!" And toiling on still, we find that we increase our guilt daily, that the task is a hopeless one, and groaning under heavier burdens than before we commenced the struggle, we are inclined to abandon the attempt and hang the harps in the willows, still longing, yet despairing.

Are you sin-weary?

Do you find the burden of the law too heavy to bear? Have you toiled with it, groaned under it, and been oppressed by it, until you succumbed in grief and despair? Take courage, then.

For the wise and the prudent do not know this weariness. They either care not to be righteous or they boast of a righteousness that is a vain thing before the Lord. And never would they acknowledge that the natural man can only increase his sin daily.

Take courage, for the Lord calls you by name. "Weary toiler, come unto me!"

He will give you rest!

Rest.

Blessed word!

Thrice blessed for the weary and toiling soul!

It is not simply to cease from toil and struggle; it is far more. It is to cease from work in the consciousness—to know that the task is accomplished, the work is done, and the end is achieved and to rejoice in the finished product. It is the glorious feeling of body and soul that we may enter into and enjoy the fruit of a completed work.

Thus it is naturally.

And thus it is spiritually.

Ah, what a task that must be accomplished is pressed down upon our weary soul! What mountains of sin and guilt that must be removed rise up before our consciousness: sin in our actual walk, sin with all the members of our body, sin in our thoughts, sin in our deepest heart, sin in all our planning and desiring, sin in what we did and said and thought and wished, sin in what we did not do and think and say and wish, sin in the present, sin in the past, sin everywhere as far as eye can see.

And then, when we penetrate more deeply into this horrible reality of sin, we find that it is not merely a matter of acting, but a matter of our very being. For out of the heart are the issues of life. And that heart is corrupt, hopelessly corrupt, and from it, as a boiling and bubbling fountain, arise all our actual sins. Before we can hope to remove the mountain of our actual guilt, that heart must be cleansed. The corrupt fountain of iniquity must be changed into a clear stream of love.

And searching more deeply still into this awful mystery of sin, we discover that the deepest source of this foul fountain of iniquity is not even in our individual hearts and lives, but is connected with a rushing stream of sin and guilt that leads us for the source back into paradise of yore. And we find that it will be of no avail to even attempt to cleanse the fountain of foul sin in our own heart, unless we could first cleanse that deepest and original source of it all.

What a task!

How disheartening to know that there is no life, no peace, no comfort and joy for our troubled soul, unless the task is finished, guilt is blotted out, the stain of sin is removed, the heart is cleansed, the foul fountain of iniquity is changed into a stream of living love! And then, to have struggled and toiled until all our strength was exhausted, and to know that we utterly failed, so utterly that the end of all our toil is greater sin and heavier burdens.

And then to learn that there is rest!

To know that the task is accomplished, that the stream of our guilt is washed away, that we may cease from toiling in the blessed knowledge that all is finished, that there is righteousness and sanctification, wisdom and redemption, peace and joy and comfort and eternal life in God's blessed communion.

Comfort, weary toiler, for you.

The task is accomplished.

Accomplished for you.

Rest!

I will give you rest!

He is the rest-giver because he accomplished the task.

He put his shoulders under our burdens, the burdens of our guilt and sin and condemnation. For the Father gave to him a people from before the foundation of the world, a people whose savior he was to be, their head and their redeemer, and whom he was to bring from the horrible slavery of sin and death into the glorious liberty of the children of God. He, therefore, was to take their place, to assume their burdens of guilt and sin, to carry them way

49

down into the dark and deep valley of his agony and death, and to leave them there forever.

And he did so, according to the will of his Father.

He did put his shoulders under their heavy burdens, under which they would have been crushed into death and hell.

And he was strong, for his name is Almighty God.

He was able to bear these burdens even unto the accursed tree of the place of skulls, to enter with them into the dark abyss of death and hell, to toil and labor with them until he had shaken off the load of guilt and the shackles of death. First from Calvary, then soon from Joseph's garden, he might send forth the glad tidings: It is finished!

He accomplished the task.

With him there is rest.

And the rest-giver he is, too, because he causes us, by the irresistible operations of his Spirit and grace, to enter into his rest.

By nature we would not even seek to enter into that rest. Surely, we may seek rest, but we do not desire his rest. We seek and imagine that we possess rest in the accomplishment of our own righteousness, which is abominable to Jehovah. But he never forgets his people, neither leaves them alone. He enters into their hearts and minds by the Spirit of grace. In their hearts he knows how to create unrest and worry. He reveals unto them the greatness of their sin, the abomination of their vain righteousness, their impotency to fulfill the demands of the law, their proneness to all evil, and the corruption of their heart and mind.

With unrest he fills the heart until every last basis of self-confidence is removed, until from the heart the cry is wrung, "O, God, be merciful unto me, a sinner!"

When all the wisdom and prudence, all the righteousness of works, all self-conceit and self-confidence to carry our own burdens and remove them is uprooted, and the heart longs for a righteousness that is not its own but God's, he stands forth in all the beauty of his salvation, in all the glory of his power and says,

"Weary toiler, it is finished. The task you labor to accomplish is completed. The work is done!"

"It was done for you."

"Completely finished by me."

"I will give you rest!"

Come unto me!

Blessed summons, when by the gracious call of his Spirit, he makes it resound in our soul!

And blessed soul that obeys that summons and comes.

It is a coming that is the result of Father's drawing, for no one can come unto him except the Father who sent him draw him. The drawing is first, and the coming is second. The drawing is the cause and the coming is the result. It is the drawing of that love that is always first, and the coming of faith that relies on that love.

It is a coming that begins when we cast away all our own righteousnesses and every basis of confidence in self. For we cannot come unto him with aught of self. Empty and poor and naked, weary and exhausted, as the drowning man who struggles with the tempestuous sea until all his strength is gone, thus we must come to him who is our all.

It is a coming that continues when we see Jesus as we never see him with our natural eye, full of grace and glory and life and rest and peace, the fullness of our wisdom and righteousness and sanctification and complete redemption, and when our soul, hungering and thirsting after righteousness, desires to possess him above all the treasures and pleasures of the world.

It is a coming by which we draw nearer when we hear him address us, as with the natural ear we could never hear, so clearly and distinctly as if he were calling us by name. "Weary toiler, heavily burdened one, cease from toiling at your impossible task. I have finished it. Come unto me and rest!"

It is a coming whereby we know and trust that when he bore the burden of his people's sin, our transgressions and our iniquities were also upon him, so that we believe his promise and trust for life and death with all our soul in that promise: I will give you rest!

And that promise he fulfills.

He fulfills it when he sheds forth the love of God into our hearts, that love in which there is no fear, and when he gives us the faith by which we joyfully shout of redemption: "We, therefore, being justified by faith, have peace with God through our Lord Jesus Christ." He fulfills it when, if we would return to the old burdens and the slavery of sin and death, he draws us back unto himself and assures us: "Your sins are forgiven." He fulfills it when amid the battle and strife of this present life in the midst of the world, he makes us partakers of the peace that passes all understanding.

And he will fulfill it to the last.

For the final rest is not yet.

There still abides a Sabbath for the people of God.

The eternal Sabbath.

And the rest-giver will surely bring that final rest. When all of life is over and all the weary night is past, and the last one of his toiling people shall have been brought into the rest he accomplished, then he shall come again and lead his people into the perfect rest. Then the toiling and groaning creation shall be delivered from the yoke of vanity and corruption and shall partake of the rest of God's children.

God through Christ shall have completed his work.

And into that completed work we shall enter.

God's tabernacle over all!

The rest of eternal joy!

8

We Fly Away

"The days of our years are threescore years and ten;
and if by reason of strength they be fourscore years,
yet is their strength labour and sorrow; for it is soon
cut off, and we fly away."

—Psalm 90:10

We fly away!

Whoever pauses for a moment on the eve of the last day of the year to glance back upon his course of life, now finished, discovers to his amazement that his experience corroborates this testimony of sacred Scripture.

He does so not without amazement, because in the daily course of life he is oblivious to the rush of the stream of time by which we all are relentlessly and swiftly carried away.

Partly the explanation for this is that the wings of time, upon which we are relentlessly carried away, move so quietly. Time is so soundless. We do not notice its violent rush. It is not like the wind, which we certainly do not see, although we hear the sound of the wind and observe and measure the speed of the wind. In a high-speed commuter train we are conscious of its rate of speed, which is indicated by the rapidity with which the mileposts pass by. Yet time glides past unnoticeably, and the reality that we are really flying away with furious speed is not part of our daily awareness.

Partly the explanation for this is that time characterizes our very being. We are children of time, born in time, and our entire existence is conditioned by time. We fly away gladly. There is no opposition, no conflict between the violent rush of time and the searching and striving of our hearts. This is also true of the natural man, even though this reality is so paradoxical. Man, who has no hope outside the parameters of time, and whom the fear of death pursues all his life long, is inwardly propelled, so that he unhesitatingly cooperates with the rush of time in order to arrive at his end. The present moment never satisfies him. The natural man always seeks his peace in the future. He reaches out to the future, to what lies before him, although before him lies nothing but weariness and misery and what awaits him eventually is nothing else but eternal destruction.

Consequently, in the ordinary course of life, we do not notice the dizzying advance of time, which ever races onward. But if on Old Year's Eve we stand still for a moment in our thoughts and look back to the past, we come to the realization that we experience this biblical message as reality.

We fly away.

A whole year is again past, and we can hardly comprehend it.

Time incessantly advanced. It did not speed up because of our impatience, nor did it slacken its pace because of our haste and because we were so busy. And now we have come to the end of the year. It seems as but yesterday when we wished each other a happy new year.

Truly, we flew away.

Much has happened, many things and in many forms. There was rejoicing and complaining, singing and crying, praying and cursing, hoping and despairing, feasting and gathering in the house of sorrow. There was rejoicing over infants who were born into this world, and there was pain because our way led to the grave as we walked behind the bier of a loved one. There was weariness and misery, drudgery in vanity, struggling and battling onward without victory. There was war; and there was an end to war, but without peace.

As we look back now on all of these and on a thousand other experiences and take stock of them all, we come to the conclusion that the declaration of the text is confirmed in our experience: "Yet is their strength labor and sorrow."

"For it is soon cut off."

"And we fly away."

Serious language!

Joyless words, because of profound grief.

Language that views and evaluates our earthly life, which is so very brief and limited, as well as so very fleeting.

An evaluation made from the perspective of the dreadful wilderness in which a whole generation perished, was consumed, and died off, under the oppressive burden of God's wrath.

A generation that could not enter into God's rest because of its unbelief.

A generation that indeed lived in that day in the house appointed to Moses, but which in principle and in reality was the house of the Son of God. The people heard the voice of God's Son, even as his voice came emphatically to them in many different ways—through the miracles in Egypt, in the thunder at Sinai, through Moses' word, in the water that flowed from the rock, and in the bread that rained down from heaven.

They did not pay heed to that voice.

Against that voice Israel rebelled in unbelief. They followed their idols! According to the lust of their flesh, they longed to return to the fleshpots of Egypt.

And God had sworn in his wrath, "They should not enter into my rest."

And now the situation was hopeless: God by his wrath had cast down that generation in the wilderness. There was no escape any more. In the wilderness, existence was characterized by toil without fruit, suffering without deliverance, wasting away without hope, and death without resurrection. Therefore, the man of God could sing,

> *Man in thy anger is consumed,*
> *And unto grief and sorrow doomed.*
> *Before thy clear and searching sight,*
> *Our secret sins are brought to light.*

Beneath thy wrath we pine and die,
Our life expiring like a sigh.

How is our earthly life any different, when viewed as it is in itself apart from the grace of the Lord Jesus Christ? Viewed from this perspective, the tone, should one wish to sing this song, must become very somber and melancholy. From this perspective, as a revelation of the wrath of the great and awful God who sees our secret sins in the holy light of his presence, our existence becomes dark and dreadfully suffocating.

Concerning the days of our years.

Those days of our years upon which the dreadful fury of God is oppressively poured out without reprieve.

Those days are only seventy years, or at the most eighty. This does not mean that the majority of the people live that long. Nor does it mean that seventy or eighty years is the average span of human life on earth. Absolutely not! The extreme measure of human existence is given in the text. If everything is normal, and if nothing out of the ordinary happens, then it is possible that the strongest among men may observe Old Year's Eve seventy or eighty times.

The intent of these words is not to make known the length of our life, nor to cause us to contemplate the brevity of life, but rather to impress on our hearts that we are perishing: man in thy anger is consumed and unto grief and sorrow doomed. Living, we die. Existing, we perish. Seventy or eighty years the strong in their earthly existence can endure the burden of the anger of the Most High God. Then they also are consumed.

Dust thou art, and unto dust thou shalt return!

That word was not God's original creation ordinance. God did not create man to die, but formed him to live. A dwelling place was given to him next to the tree of life in the midst of the garden. He was not created to die, but to be God's friend and to live in eternal blessedness with his creator. To that end he had been formed. Just as the generation that perished in the wilderness, so also did man originally live in God's house, and he heard the voice of his God. No, even more must be said. He was granted the privilege to dwell in God's rest. For God rested on the seventh day from all his work, and man entered into the rest of God's completed work. He might eat of the tree of life not to live seventy or eighty years, but to live unto all eternity.

But man did not obey the voice of his God.

In rebellion man shook his fist against the Most High.

And God banished him from the rest, far from the tree of life. There this word is appropriate: "Dust thou art, and unto dust thou shalt return." That is the word of God's wrath.

Because this word pursues him, penetrating to the marrow of his bones, man must vainly pine away in the fearful wilderness of this accursed world for some seventy or eighty years, subservient to God's purpose, instead of living in God's house with him in eternal blessedness!

Concerning the days of our years.

They are but seventy or eighty years.

Years of pining away under the anger of God.

Somber language!

———————

And yet there is light.

Light in darkness.

Light in which the sadness of the seventy or eighty years is changed to joy.

For God has provided something better for us.

He spoke of another day. He gave his honor to no one else. He did not break his covenant. He made man's rebellion subservient to the realization of a much better covenant, whereof Jesus has become the guarantor. God began another work—the work of deliverance, forgiveness, justification, adoption unto children, resurrection from the dead, and eternal life in the tabernacle of God with man.

And again man entered into rest.

God reconciled the world unto himself through the death of his Son, not imputing their sins unto them. God merited for us eternal righteousness and called life out of death, paradise from the wilderness, and heaven out of hell by the resurrection of Jesus Christ from the dead.

In him is rest.

And because God spoke of another day, this terrifying, melancholy psalm may and does end with the prayer, "O satisfy us early with thy mercy; that we may rejoice and be glad all our days."

Seventy or eighty years.

Yes, but whosoever hears the voice of the Son of God in his new and eternal house does not lament the brevity of this transitory time of earthly existence, but looks longingly to the perfect rest.

Light in the darkness.

The light of life!

———————

We fly away.

It is soon cut off.

This idea indicates the relentlessly fleeting character of our earthly life and existence. Not for a moment do we stand still. We are born into a fleeting, transitory existence. We fly away from the very first moment of our lives, and we do not stop anywhere on our way. Sometimes we would like to tarry for a moment somewhere, but we cannot even for a moment escape or free ourselves from this rush of life that hastens onward. Flying onward, we fly away.

Above all, in these words is implied the idea of the speed with which we move through this life.

Everything is flying away, and we fly with it.

That a year has gone by indicates that our planet has completed its circumnavigation of the sun. The earth traveled almost six hundred million miles, which means that it—and we with it— flew at a speed of about forty thousand miles per hour. So it is with the whole of our life. We are always in a hurry. The child rushes to become a man; the man rushes to bring forth a new generation, and then he hastens onward to his end. The tempo of human life becomes ever faster.

We fly away.

And that fast tempo is in our very blood. We want it that way. We experience it. We cooperate with it.

If we view this very rapid passing of time from the perspective of the dreadful wilderness, from the perspective of God's wrath, of the hopelessness that we have been banned from God's rest, then this somber, dark language of deepening sadness and the dreadful fear of death is appropriate.

There is no hope.

The farther we proceed in our fleeting journey through time, the more oppressive the wrath of God becomes. We fly always from anger unto anger. There is no escape anywhere. We fly, yes indeed, but in the midst of death.

Let us eat and drink, for tomorrow we die.

Vanity of vanities!

But there is light!

There remains a rest for the people of God.

Whosoever believes already partakes of that rest—the rest of the resurrection of the Lord Jesus Christ, the rest of the forgiveness of sin, of the free favor of God, of liberty, and of the rest of God's eternal home. Therefore this somber, sad psalm can jubilantly close with the prayer, "And let the beauty of the LORD our God be upon us!"

Whosoever flies away with that rest in his heart views the rapid tempo of his earthly life in another light.

He flies away, yes, but toward the eternal house of his Father.

To the rest of God's covenant.

Joyful hope!

A somber discourse.

The very best of it is labor and sorrow.

The very best we can expect in this world is what the world boasts about for the blink of an eye, of which the world is so proud, and in which it seeks its pleasure, its wealth and honor, its enjoyment and happiness, its friendships and bands of love—all that is the most excellent, the best of life.

But it is all labor and sorrow.

Dark, somber language! Do you perhaps say that all of this is stated much too strongly? Is our life of seventy or eighty years too darkly tinted by the text? Is there no source of happiness? Is there no pleasure and joy in this otherwise wearisome life?

Go then to the dreadful wilderness. Know that there the whole of life lies under the wrath of God. Indeed, life is soon cut off. Death permeates and operates in all the joy and pleasure of this world. And man, who flies away, knows it all too well. Even more significantly: the most pleasant realities of life in this wilderness of God's wrath work your everlasting destruction. Labor and sorrow!

But view this labor and sorrow from the perspective of the rest, and everything changes.

The very light affliction of this present time works for you an eternal weight of glory.

There is no night there, no sorrow or weeping.

Oh, the loveliness and beauty of the Lord our God!

PART II
Suffering

9

Nothing Strange

"Beloved, think it not strange concerning the fiery
trial which is to try you, as though some strange
thing happened unto you."

—1 Peter 4:12

There is sometimes in nature an hour of breathless, awful expectancy.

When in the late afternoon of a sultry summer day the gentle zephyr even holds its breath and ceases to stir even the sensitive leaf of the poplar and when blue-black clouds thickly pack on the horizon and the distant rumble of thunder announces the approach of a storm, all nature stands in awe, fearful and still, expectantly, until the storm breaks loose, the wild wind howls and lashes the trees, lightning sets the heavens ablaze, stroke upon stroke, and the roaring thunder reverberates through the air, peal upon peal.

So there is betimes, in the history of the church, an hour of oppressive stillness.

When the enemies of the church are seated in high places of authority and power, and latent hatred of God and his Christ and his people begins to manifest itself, when slanderers of the righteous and accusers of the brethren are bestirring themselves to report evil things about the children of light, and there are signs of secret conspiracies and plottings against the church, the people of God stand in fearful anticipation of the things that are at hand, until soon the storm of persecution breaks loose, prison doors are opened unto them, scaffold and stake are erected, and their blood is shed for righteousness' sake.

Such an hour of approaching woe and suffering is dreadful, frequently worse than the actual tribulation itself. Imagination, creating a picture of the impending woe, brings the hour of actual tribulation to our mind in all its horror, and fearful apprehension fills the soul with oppressing grief. Thus the suffering servant of Jehovah is overwhelmed with the awful anticipation of the hour of darkness, and crawling in the dust of Gethsemane's garden, he expresses all the burden of his grief in one significant sentence: "My soul is exceedingly sorrowful even unto death."

Thus it is with the individual child of God and frequently in the history of the church. There are periods when the fiery trial is not yet, but is impending and expected, moments of oppressive stillness before the breaking of the storm of persecution and tribulation.

And such an hour it was for the church when the apostle Peter wrote these words to them: "Beloved, think it not strange concerning the fiery trial which is to try you." In general, though not always in that specific sense in which the church of Peter's day saw the signs of approaching tribulation, such an hour it is always for the people of God in the world. For the enemy is always there. He whose lordship over us is our only comfort is always hated. And the servant is never greater than his Lord. The word of that Lord is always with us: "In the world ye shall have tribulation."

Beloved, think it not strange.

———————

They might deem such fiery trials strange indeed!

For why should they have to suffer and be oppressed so terribly? In fact, why should the children of God have to suffer at all? Did not their Lord bear all their griefs? Did he not fully atone for all the guilt of all their sin and iniquity? Are not their transgressions blotted out in the blood of their redeemer? Do they not walk about clothed with the garments of righteousness? And if their sins are actually forgiven and forgotten, blotted out in boundless grace, is it not strange that they still must suffer and pass through fiery trials?

Still more.

Are they not beloved children of the living God? Surely, he loved them with fathomless love from before the foundation of the world, with a love that is measured only by the sacrifice of his only begotten Son. They are dear to him as the apple of his eye. And his watchful eye is continually over them in love, for the keeper of Israel never slumbers and never sleeps. Besides, he most surely is powerful above all gods. Yea, besides him there is no God. All things, all the raving enemies included, are constantly in his power, and without his will they cannot and do not stir. How then can God tolerate the enemy to rave in furious enmity against his beloved and permit the power of darkness to triumph over them? Is it not strange that our Father in heaven should permit his beloved children, for whom he sacrificed the life of his Son, to pass through these fiery trials and tribulations?

Neither is this all.

They might think this approaching fiery trial strange from a human point of view. For why should men hate them? They are no evildoers. They do not murder or steal, they are no busybodies in other men's matters, they are no dangerous element of a country's population, nor a sore upon society. They do well and walk as children of light. They do the will of their Father in heaven.

How strange, then, that upon these children of the living God, walking as children of light, tribulation should come and they should have to pass through fiery trials!

Yet, beloved, think it not strange.

For there is nothing strange in it.

This suffering for righteousness' sake is not strange from a historical viewpoint, for so they have persecuted the prophets who were before you. Tribulation would be astonishing for the church at any particular period of history, if in the general course of his-

65

tory the righteous prospered and were esteemed, while the wicked suffered and the evildoer met with general condemnation. If the children of God, the men of old who walked with God, the prophets of the Lord, had been men of high esteem, honored by all, while the workers of iniquity they upbraided in their messages from God were locked behind prison doors or led to the scaffold, surely some suffering child of God might think so uncommon a thing as suffering for righteousness' sake to be strange and marvelous. But this is not the case. The church in fiery trial is in good company. Always the righteous suffered. Ever since the blood of righteous Abel was poured out near the gate of first paradise, the righteous suffered for righteousness' sake. They were hated; reviled; dragged before courts civil and ecclesiastical; condemned as evildoers; deprived of property, honor, name, position, liberty, and life; sunk in dungeons and miry holes; chased over the earth; mocked; spit upon; burned at the stake; and cruelly sawn asunder. Thus was done to the captain of our salvation who did not know sin, neither was guilt found in his mouth. On him they fulfilled all their wicked pleasure until he was crushed and broken. Of all the righteous none was righteous as he; of all the despised none was hated as he; of all who passed through fiery trials, none was tried as he. As they did with the prophets who were before him and with the servant of the Lord, of whom all those prophets spoke, so they did with the apostles and with the church. Wherever and whenever there are righteous in the world, there they must endure fiery trials.

Beloved, think it not strange when men falsely accuse you and speak evil of you. Marvel not when they who call themselves your brethren (but are not) plot and conspire against you and cast you out of their synagogues.

Historically, you are in good company. For so they have persecuted the prophets who were before you.

Strange it would be if it were otherwise. Think it strange when all men speak well of you. But when they hate and rave and plot and conspire and commit their works of darkness and unrighteousness against you and cause you to pass through fiery trials—nothing strange!

Nor is the matter strange in principle.

Is it a marvel that darkness and light are mutually exclusive? Do you think it strange that the lie persecutes the truth? Is it so uncommon that Belial hates Christ? Is it at all unusual that he whose proper name is Diabolos slanders God?

Would you deem it strange that all through history the children of the devil hate and rave against the children of God?

Surely, there is nothing strange in it. The church is Christ's body. And him the world hated. For in him is the Father. Christ is the light that should come into the world. Doing in all things the will of the Father, he caused the light to shine. But the world loves the darkness rather than light, and the world keenly resented the clear and bright rays of light emanating from him who is the light, for they condemned the world and exposed the evil of its works. Therefore the world hated him more than it hated all the prophets who were before him. All the bitter gall of their hatred they poured forth upon him to extinguish the light penetrating the darkness, until there was neither name nor place left for him in the world. And still they hate him. Still their fury is not abated. Still they rejoice in his suffering. But he is no longer in the world. To glory he went, and for the suffering he endured he received a name that is above all names, with power in heaven and on earth. Him they cannot touch any more. But he is in the church, and through the church he becomes manifest in the world. Still the light shines in the world, for the risen redeemer dwells in his people, and they are in the world. They do his will in the flesh. Therefore, the world hates them as they hated him, for his name and his light are in them. And the world is in power. The wicked are strong in number, influence, wealth, position, and authority.

Therefore, the people of Christ in the world are partakers of his sufferings. They pass through fiery trials. If they are faithful, the world will surely hate them. And the more they are faithful in walk and conversation, and the more they allow their light—his light—to shine into the darkness, the more they will experience that the servant is not greater than his Lord, and that even as they have hated and do hate him, so they will and do hate them.

Beloved, think it not strange concerning the fiery trial which is to try you.

There is nothing astonishing in it.

Deem it not strange that God should allow his beloved to pass through these fiery trials.

They are trials. There is joy and hope in the words the text uses to indicate the suffering of God's people in the world. Even as gold is tried in the refiner's furnace, so God tries his people.

There is joy in this thought, for it implies that God, not the enemy, is in control of the situation. It often appears to be so different! So frequently it seems that God's people are the helpless victims in the hands of those who hate them. Thus it appeared with the suffering servant on the accursed tree. Thus it would seem to be with the faithful all through history. The enemy would appear to be supreme. But more than mere appearance this is never. Behind and above the hateful world and the power of darkness stands the Lord of his church. He is the great shepherd of his flock, and he employs the devil and all his servants as his dogs. They are mere instruments in his hands and nothing more. If it were not so, the sufferings and tribulations of the church could never be trials. The devil does not intend to try, but to destroy, the people of God. But God's thoughts are higher and his counsel shall stand. The devil's persecutions are God's trials. Ultimately the church is not a victim of the enemy, but even in suffering is the beloved of the Lord.

Think it not strange. By these trials the church is purified. How many are they who in times of peace and prosperity affiliate themselves with the church for various worldly reasons. There are those whose membership in the church is a matter of mere custom or heritage. Others call themselves brethren for business purposes, for a good name and personal honor, or because it is hardly civilized to have no church-connections. These are wolves in sheep's clothing, enemies of the truth, and a dangerous element in the midst of Christ's flock in the world. But by fiery trials this foreign element is eliminated, while always the remnant according to election is preserved. The devil and his subjects are employed to purify the church!

Beloved, think it not strange that the Lord should work thus. For his name is Wonderful.

By these trials the church is strengthened. How the tie of love in the Lord is strengthened in the church by means of these fiery trials! For as sheep huddle together when the wolves are around, so God's people feel themselves united as never before and seek the communion of saints when the enemy threatens. Besides, how faith and trust in him who is Lord alone are confirmed in times of tribulation! How the eye is drawn away from and the heart is weaned from the things that are below, and the mind is fixed steadfastly on the eternal inheritance when around us the enemy raves, and we must pass through fiery trials! What a sweet peace, more precious than all the world, fills the soul in the assurance that we may be partakers of his sufferings! Surely, the powers of darkness are instruments for the confirmation of God's people and the preparation for their inheritance with the Lord.

Beloved, think it not strange. But rather rejoice. For we are more than victors, even our enemies being our servants! After a little while we shall rejoice with exceeding great gladness, for as we have suffered with him, so shall we also be glorified together. Then it shall become manifest that the sufferings of this present time are not worthy to be compared with the glory that shall be revealed in us. Then we will understand that the fiery trials instigated by the devil and his host were means to keep us in the way and to prepare us for eternal joy.

Therefore, beloved, when clouds of evil lower and the thunder of affliction rumbles in the distance, when suffering and tribulation seem at hand and the enemy raves in drunken triumph, be not afraid, neither think it strange, but rather rejoice!

The enemy is your servant.

The bearing of the cross is to fit you for the crown!

10

The Fellowship of His Sufferings

"And the fellowship of his sufferings, being made
conformable unto his death."
—Philippians 3:10

The excellence of the knowledge of Christ Jesus, my Lord!

This excellence always is the almost inexhaustible subject of
the apostle's message, as he now writes, "And the fellowship of his
sufferings, being made conformable to his death."

Speaking from personal experience, he testifies how the knowledge of Jesus Christ his Lord is above all else most precious to him
and is to be desired above everything else that is to be desired on
earth. So incomparably precious is this knowledge that for that
knowledge of Christ, Paul esteems everything else as loss and
dung. Moreover, Paul wants to cause the congregation to see the
excellence of that knowledge and to taste it, so that with him they
would voluntarily despise everything rather than being devoid of
that knowledge.

He wants to gain Christ.

He wants to be found in Christ, not having his own righteousness of the law, but the righteousness of God through faith in
Christ.

Paul wants to know, taste, prove, and experience Christ.

He wants to know the power of his resurrection.

And the fellowship of his sufferings.

He wants to become conformed unto his death.

His sufferings.

But is it possible to long for fellowship with suffering?

Is it not true that we oppose with all our strength any occasion for suffering, that we fear it, attempt to escape it, and fight against it as much as possible?

Oh, to know him in the power of his resurrection; to know that justifying, renewing, quickening, sanctifying, glorifying power that engenders a new and living hope—we readily understand the glory, excellence, and desirability of that. But what is the value of the fellowship of his sufferings? Is the knowledge of that fellowship also an aspect of the excellence of the knowledge of Christ? Is it possible that anyone would regard everything else as loss and dung, preferring the knowledge of the fellowship of Christ's sufferings?

That is how the apostle saw it, and that is how sacred Scripture sees it.

There is even more. There is in this passage a rising to new heights of revelation regarding this concept. The apostle rises ever higher, constantly higher. Ever more deeply the apostle drinks from the fountain of the knowledge of Christ. He brings forth and continually displays ever more excellent and precious riches from the treasure of that knowledge of Christ.

Having gained Christ.

To be found in him.

Having but one desire: to possess his righteousness alone through faith, and at the same time rejecting all the righteousness of the law.

To know him!

To know the power of his resurrection!

Even more, to know the fellowship of his sufferings in which we become conformable to his death. It is the most excellent of the excellences of the knowledge of Christ. It is absolutely the most desirable of the treasures of this knowledge.

His sufferings.

But is it not impossible to have fellowship with that suffering? Is it not impossible to taste that suffering? Did he not suffer alone?

Was it not absolutely necessary that he die alone? Is his suffering not *the* suffering? Did he not descend into the deepest depths of hell, in order in the depths to bear the burden of God's wrath against the sins of those whom the Father had given to him, there to be terrified and filled with inexpressible dread? Did he not descend, in order to experience the living and the most terrifying God as a consuming fire that rages eternally against all unrighteousness, and there in the depths of hell and before the face of that most dreadfully holy God, who filled him with horror, to say, "Lord, my God, I will love thee from the heart; I will love thee here as well; I will love thee even as I now experience thy holy wrath"? Is it not exactly for this reason that his suffering is satisfaction, and as satisfaction, also reconciliation? Was it not *the* offering for sins, which never again may or can be repeated? Is not his suffering unique? Is it not, therefore, the end of all suffering for the brethren, the death of death?

Did he not have to descend to the depths of hell, so that we would never be required to stand there?

How can I then drink from the cup that Christ drank empty? Can I suffer as he suffered? Can I stand next to him in the depths of his sufferings, in order to suffer with him the burden of God's wrath and to drink with him from his cup of suffering?

No, God be thanked! Considered thus, it is not only true that we *cannot* drink from his cup, but it is also true that we never *have to* drink from that cup.

He suffered so that we would not eternally suffer.

He suffered so that unto all eternity, we need not bear the wrath of God.

He died so that we would not die, but would have life.

He suffered alone, absolutely alone.

It is his suffering!

The fellowship of his sufferings.

But how then is there a fellowship with that suffering, if his suffering is necessarily unique, and if we cannot partake in his atoning suffering?

Or does the apostle here perhaps mean something else?

Is he thinking not about a fellowship by which we also endure his sufferings, but about a participation in the suffering and death of the savior through faith, by which we know that at Golgotha Christ shed his blood for us and gave his life for our sins?

Oh, the knowledge of this fellowship of his sufferings is really most glorious. After all, whoever has fellowship with the cross of Christ has felt the power of that cross in his heart. He has learned to know the misery of the fellowship of sin in which he lies bound by nature. He has tasted the ineffable grace by which he was cleansed through the blood of Christ, and thus justified before God and delivered from the bondage of sin and death. He knows the joy of the forgiveness of sins. In the consciousness of this aspect of faith in the suffering of the savior, he may indeed declare with joy, "I count all things as loss and dung, for the excellence of the knowledge of Christ."

But no, that cannot be the meaning of this portion of Scripture, as true as it is in itself.

For then the apostle would have continued to speak not of the fellowship, but of the knowledge of the *power* of Christ's sufferings.

Then he would not have spoken first about the power of the resurrection of Christ, only then to advance to the knowledge of the fellowship of his sufferings.

Moreover, is it not evident that God's word in this passage aims at a different fellowship of suffering than that wherein we have our righteousness through faith, when his word ends with the still more marvelous declaration: "being made conformable unto his death"? Besides, does not Scripture mention a fellowship of his sufferings in which we also suffer with him, for him, because of him, and in his work? Is it not true that only if we suffer with him, will we be glorified with him? Does not the apostle testify that the sufferings of Christ abound in us? Does not the apostle encourage himself by speaking of the remnants of the sufferings of Christ, which the apostle fills up in his own flesh?

There is a cup of agony that Christ had to drink alone.

There is a suffering of Christ for us, into which only he could enter and into which we cannot enter.

But there is also a fellowship of Christ's sufferings. For on the one hand, Christ bore on our behalf the suffering of God's holy wrath. On the other hand, according to the will of God, he bore the suffering of the hatred of this world, so that the world would be condemned. He was the servant of the Lord. He stood in the midst of the world for the cause of the Lord, the cause of the living God. He was the light in the darkness and was never known by the darkness. He glorified the Father in word and deed in the midst of the world that lived from the principle of animosity toward God. He was the truth in the midst of a world of lies. And the world hated him. This world—of depraved necessity—had to hate him because it loved the darkness more than the light and its works were evil. In that deadly hatred the world caused him to suffer. They treated him as a pariah, made no place for him, cast him out, heaped slanders upon him, made him the object of their piercing mockery, spit upon him, lacerated his back with a whip, reckoned him with the transgressors, and nailed him to the accursed tree.

From that perspective there is a fellowship in Christ's sufferings.

There is a suffering of Christ throughout all the ages!

There was a suffering of Christ in the old dispensation. Why had the saints in the old dispensation suffered uniquely? Why had Abel, Enoch, Noah, Moses, and the prophets suffered? Why were they strangers in the earth? Why were they driven to the holes and caves, scattered, exiled, and sawed in pieces, if it were not because the whole world scorned the Christ? For Christ's sake, for the cause of Christ, they suffered in a world filled with enmity toward God. And it was Christ who suffered in these saints.

Also today there is always that suffering of Christ because his people are partakers of his anointing. He is in them. His life is their life; his will is their will; his cause is their cause. He is revealed through them, for they proclaim his word. They confess his name. They keep his commandments. He is indeed exalted, but the world still hates him. He is indeed in glory, but there are still remnants of his sufferings that he fulfills in his people.

He suffers in them because the world hates them just as they hated him.

In them Christ is vilified, slandered, spit upon, and time and again crucified anew.

They suffer for his sake, for his cause.

The fellowship in the sufferings of Christ in the world.

Christ in us, and we with Christ.

Throughout all the ages.

His sufferings!

That I may know him.

And may know the power of his resurrection.

And may know the fellowship of his sufferings.

Does not this idea transcend our understanding? The apostle desired to know the fellowship of Christ's sufferings. He does not speak of a theoretical or theological knowledge, a knowledge that can be obtained by investigation, but he speaks of a self-examining, experiential knowledge.

He longs to taste the fellowship of the sufferings of Christ. He longs to experience them in his own sufferings.

There is in the knowledge of the sufferings of Christ something so excellent, so precious, and so inexpressibly blessed for him, that for the sake of the knowledge of Christ, he has learned to regard everything else as loss and dung. He would not want to be without the knowledge of the sufferings of Christ for anything in the whole world.

What then is that blessing, that inexpressible delight in the knowledge of this fellowship of sufferings?

Does the apostle seek the sufferings in themselves? Is he inspired by a vain spirit, by which (as some think) some of the ancient martyrs were motivated when they sought out dungeon and scaffold, in order to receive sooner a more glorious crown in heaven? Not at all! No, the apostle does not desire the suffering, not in itself. Nor does he have in view a more glorious place in heaven. After all, he does not speak about the excellence of the knowledge of that suffering, but he speaks about the blessedness of the knowledge of the *fellowship* of Christ's sufferings. Not the suffering is glorious, but the fellowship. He desires not to taste merely the sufferings, but in the sufferings to taste that his suffering is the suffering of Christ—to taste that he belongs to the same fellowship of sufferings as the sufferings of all the saints who went before him. All of it was the sufferings of Christ, so that in death they were made conformable to the death of Christ. That is inexpressibly blessed.

Rejoice and be glad!

Blessed are you when men slander and persecute you and speak all manner of evil against you falsely for my name's sake. Then you stand in the fellowship of the suffering that fell centrally upon the Christ. They in like manner persecuted the prophets who were before you. Likewise, they persecuted Christ. In the same manner they have spilled the blood of the apostles and of the faithful witnesses.

Then you are blessed, but not because of the suffering itself.

On the contrary, that suffering is real suffering.

Consequently, from the depths of that suffering you cry out and make known your needs to God in heaven.

But you know yourself to be blessed in the knowledge of the fellowship of the sufferings of Christ and in being made conformable to his death. Blessed you are in the knowledge that persecution is not because of you, but because of Christ, who is in you. Blessed in the experience that the world hates you, because it is the world and you are born of God, because they are evil and their works are evil, and because you testify against them and their works. You know yourself to be blessed because it is inexpressibly sweet to experience receiving grace in order to will to suffer for righteousness' sake, for God's sake in his cause. It is blessed to choose for suffering in righteousness rather than to enjoy the friendship and joy of the world in unrighteousness.

Blessed are you.

Blessed because, in the knowledge of that fellowship of suffering, you enjoy the testimony in the midst of suffering that you are more than conquerors.

You have that testimony before the world that persecutes you, for they are condemned in and through your suffering. They know that they are not the victors, but that you are through death.

You have that testimony in your own heart. You know that the Christ, who is in you, sits on the right hand of God. He has the victory over the world.

Rejoice and be glad!

For great is your reward in heaven eternally!

11

The Suffering of This Present Time

> "If so be that we suffer with him, that we may be also
> glorified together. For I reckon that the sufferings of
> this present time are not worthy to be compared
> with the glory which shall be revealed in us."
>
> —Romans 8:17, 18

If so be that we suffer.

Occasionally the even flow of the language and argumentation of Romans 8, which is like a mighty stream, increasing in force as it rushes on, carrying us irresistibly forward on its current to the ocean of God's eternal and unchangeable love in Christ Jesus, seems interrupted, checked.

If so be…

The same warning note was sounded before in the chapter: "But ye are not in the flesh, but in the Spirit, if so be…"

It seems as if this note of doubt is in conflict with the basic conception of the whole, as if the words introduce a discordant note into this grand song of assurance, of positive hope, and of certainty of victory. There is no condemnation for those who are in Christ Jesus. The law of the Spirit of life has made me free from the law of sin and death. God condemned sin in the flesh, in order that the righteousness of the law might be fulfilled in those who walk not after the flesh but after the Spirit. Although the body is still dead because of sin, the Spirit is life because of righteousness, and the Spirit of him who raised Jesus from the dead shall also quicken our mortal bodies by his Spirit that dwells in us.

Blessing upon blessing, glory upon glory.

We shall live, for we are led by the Spirit of God, and they who are so led are children of God, and children of God shall never die. Heirs they are of God and joint heirs with Christ, and with him we shall be glorified forever.

If so be…

This apparently discordant note cannot be missed in this song of salvation and victory, as long as it is sung in the church on earth.

Assurance is a matter of the individual.

Let every one examine himself, for if any man has not the Spirit of Christ, he is none of his.

And if any man should refuse to suffer with him, let him not take this song of victory and glorification upon his lips, for he will not be glorified with him.

Here you must choose: If so be…

To suffer with Christ.

Awful way, yet blessed privilege!

The word of God speaks here of the suffering of this present time.

Suffering indeed characterizes this present time and is inseparably connected with it, so that no man passes through the present time without becoming subject to this suffering.

This is true of all men.

This present time is the time of sin and death, of wrath and the curse of God. The wrath of God is revealed from heaven upon all unrighteousness and ungodliness of men and causes them to suffer. What pain and agony, what sorrow and grief, what torments of death are endured in soul and body by all—men and women, old and young—from the moment they join the unhappy throng of Adam's children, doomed to death, until the moment they sink into the sleep of death! Who can adequately describe the agonies of sickrooms and deathbeds in homes, in hospitals, and in asylums; of the sufferings of the dying, writhing with pain, gasping for breath, desperately struggling to maintain their hold on life; of bleeding hearts, silently grieving in hopeless bereavement that cannot be healed and will not be comforted? The shadow of death darkens the way of all who travel through this present time; the fear of death pursues them all their life; the despair of death blasts their every hope; death is actually in every moment of this present time.

Suffering is universal; it is the lot of all.

How can one successfully refuse to share in the suffering of this present time? Where, then, is a way of escape? And how, then, can the apostle present this suffering as if it were a matter of our free choice whether or not we take our share, bear our crosses, and travel the way of suffering and death? How can he say, "If so be"?

It is not of this universal world agony that he is speaking, for he speaks of suffering with Christ.

To suffer with him implies that we share in the very special and unique agony that he endured. It means that we partake of his suffering and suffer even as he did.

To be sure, not as if we can share in or add to the agonies of soul and body he endured when he became obedient unto the death of the cross; when he bore the wrath of God instead of and in behalf of his own; when God was in him reconciling the world unto himself, not imputing their trespasses unto them, causing all their iniquities to be loaded upon his head; when he tasted death as only the Son of God was able to taste it in human flesh; and when he fully atoned for all their sins. That suffering is forever unique. It must remain forever alone. We cannot share it with him. Neither is it necessary that this suffering of the Lord should be repeated in us or perfected by us. It is finished. It alone will forever be the ground upon which we shall be glorified with him.

Yet, to suffer with him signifies somehow to suffer as he did.

He suffered in the world.

The world hated him because it is from below, and he is from above; it is in darkness, and he is the light; it loves darkness rather than light, and he came to radiate the light; it is of its father the devil, and he is sent by the Father to do his will; it has its delight in the lust of the flesh and the pride of life, while his meat was to do the will of the Father. In short, he came from God to speak of God and to represent his cause in the midst of a world that is motivated by enmity against the Most High. Therefore the world hated him, despised him, persecuted him, left him no room, performed all their will upon him, contradicted him, treated him with contempt, led him captive like an evildoer, spit upon him, buffeted and scourged him, preferred a murderer above him, and nailed him to the accursed tree.

He suffered of evil men for righteousness' sake.

To suffer with him is to suffer in fellowship with him. The wicked world still hates Christ. If Christ is in us and through his Spirit dwells in us, he must become manifest in our walk in the midst of the world, in our confession of his name, and in all our life and conversation. The word of Christ will be fulfilled in us, that even as they hated him, so they will hate us for his name's sake. The suffering of Christ, which he suffered personally from the world while he was in the world, must be filled. Its measure was filled by the saints of the old dispensation who died in faith, not having received the promises; it was filled centrally by Christ himself in the fullness of time; and it must be filled by the saints of the new dispensation.

The suffering of Christ in and through his church in the world.

It is a suffering like unto his suffering.

If we suffer with him, we suffer not as evildoers, but for well-doing and for righteousness' sake. Also now that suffering assumes the form of reproach and shame. It involves the loss of name and position in the world, of honor of men, of possessions and liberty, yea, of our very lives.

The saints of Rome were acquainted with the suffering of this present time.

They were placed before the choice of denying Christ and bending the knee before the gods of Rome and before Rome's Caesar, or of losing all. They chose rather to suffer with Christ. They endured the forfeiture of their possessions; they were deprived of their liberty and put into holes and dungeons; they were subjected to cruel tortures, were beheaded, burned as torches in Nero's garden, and thrown before the wild beasts for the entertainment of the world that hated them.

And we?

The world has not changed. Still the word of the Lord is true: they have hated me, they will also hate you.

Are you willing to endure all rather than to deny him?

We shall be glorified together with him, if so be ...

———————

Unavoidable suffering!

Unavoidable this suffering with Christ is as the only way to glory with him.

Another way there is not.

Such is evidently the implication of the conditional limitation: if so be ...

We are children and heirs of God, joint heirs with Christ, to be sure. Our inheritance is the incorruptible and undefilable glory that never fades away. Joy unspeakable is awaiting us in the day of the revelation of Jesus Christ. But remember: if so be that we suffer with him, in order that we may also be glorified together.

To be sure, this implies irrevocably that we will never be glorified with him, and that all this glorious confession of being children of God and his heirs and joint heirs with Christ is cancelled, if we are not found willing to suffer with him.

There is but one way—and do not imagine another—to the glory with Christ: the way of suffering with him.

This does not mean that our suffering with him may or can ever constitute the ground of our glorification, for our hope is in Christ. All other ground is sinking sand indeed. Not your or my works, not our piety or religion, not our confession of the name of Christ, not our suffering can make us worthy of that glory. Though you would give all your goods to the poor and though you would give your body to be burned, it would avail you literally nothing with respect to your part in the glory that shall be revealed in the children of God. Only the death of the Son of God can merit such glory for those who are lost in sin and dead through trespasses. His perfect obedience is wholly sufficient. We shall be glorified together with him, as belonging to him, as being one plant with him through the grace of God, both in his death and in his resurrection.

Still more must be said.

Quite contrary to the notion that our suffering with Christ has meritorious value with a view to the glory we shall inherit, the truth is that our suffering is a gift of God's grace to us. It is only because of the grace of Christ that we may suffer with him; it is solely through the power of his grace that we are able and willing to suffer; and it is a glorious privilege of grace that we suffer with our Lord.

Notice that we suffer with him in order that we may be glorified together.

God's purpose is attained. His purpose it is to lead us through the suffering with Christ to the unspeakable joy of glory.

Yet the limitation remains: if so be . . .

The way of suffering is unavoidable as a way to glory. In another sense you may avoid it, for this suffering is your voluntary choice. There is a way out—the way of friendship with the world that crucified your Lord. You may avoid the way of suffering with Christ; you may save your name, your honor among men, your possessions and your position in the world; you may save your life.

But only in the way of denying the Lord who bought you.

Only by becoming a friend of the world.

If you are a friend of the world, you will be accounted an enemy of God.

If you deny him, persist in denying him, and thus avoid the suffering of this present time, you are none of his; the Spirit of Christ does not dwell in you; you are no child of God, no heir of his, no joint heir with Christ, and never shall you be glorified with him!

If so be…

———————————

Be not dismayed!

Hesitate not to choose the way of suffering with Christ, for the suffering of this present time is not worthy to be compared with the glory that shall be revealed in us.

You may reckon, and your reckoning may comfort you in all your tribulation.

The word of God gives us the example of such reckoning and reckons for us. The glory and the suffering are compared and carefully weighed in the balance.

On the one hand, the glory that shall be revealed in us is evaluated. It is a glory that is prepared, for God prepared it from before the foundation of the world for those who love him. It was made ready in Christ, in his resurrection and in his exaltation at the right hand of God. It is about to be revealed. It is still hidden in all our sin, imperfectness, and suffering, because we still bear the image of the earthly. But it will be revealed in the day of Christ, not merely as a glory around us, but in us, for it is God's eternal purpose that we will be made like unto the image of his Son.

On the other hand, the weight of suffering is estimated—all the agony of Christ and his saints in the world, all the pain suffered, all the bloodshed, all the cries raised to heaven. Terrible, indeed, when considered by itself.

Yet of no account, when compared with the glory that shall be revealed in us.

So unspeakably great is the glory to come!

The suffering is temporal. It is but for a little while. The glory is eternal. The suffering is very limited. The glory is measured by the capacity of our heavenly natures, made like unto the resurrected Lord. The suffering involves only the loss of perishable things within the scope of our perishable existence. The glory consists of incorruptible treasures.

Not to be compared!
Fear, not, little flock!
More than victors are we!

12

Suffering in the Flesh

"Forasmuch then as Christ hath suffered for us in the
flesh, arm yourselves likewise with the same mind: for
he that hath suffered in the flesh hath ceased from sin."
—1 Peter 4:1

Have you, dear brother and sister in Christ, suffered in the
flesh?

Then you have ceased from sin!

Not, you understand, if you merely are acquainted with the
general suffering that is the lot of all mankind because of the with-
ering breath of a holy and righteous God passing over a sinful
world. There is nothing special in that. All the world is writhing
in agony and pain of body and mind and spirit. And the whole
creation groans and travails together. No one escaped the touch of
stalking pestilence or the cruelly impartial sword of him who rides
on the pale horse and whose victims are swallowed up by Hades.
All are acquainted through experience with the heartrending cries
of souls that part forever as far as this present time is concerned,
torn asunder by the hand of death that knows no mercy. Mere suffering in the flesh is no proof that you have ceased from sin.

But are you also acquainted with that other suffering that
comes upon you because while you are still living in the flesh, you
have become a stranger to the life of the flesh? Then you have in
that very suffering a proof that you have ceased from sin. And you
have reason to rejoice in your suffering. For you suffer for righteousness' sake. And such suffering is thrice blessed.

What a stranger the church of today has become to this very

thought, and still more so to the actual experience of suffering in the flesh because to that flesh we have become enemies! The church of today feels itself so at home in the world, and the world assumes such a friendly, almost fraternal attitude to the people of God, that it sounds ridiculously pessimistic to even mention the possibility of suffering for righteousness' sake. The line of demarcation is lost from sight. There is such a gradual shading of darkness into light; there seems established such a lovely truce, if not a permanent peace between Christ and Belial. The common yoke on the necks of those who know the Lord and those who know him not has been made so soft and easy that it must appear too gloomy a conception that the church in the flesh must suffer. The church even appears victorious in the world. Room is made for her; homage is paid to her; the goodwill of the church is appreciated and prized very highly in the world, and by no means without success does the church claim the whole world for Christ! Even as on the mount of temptation Satan showed his willingness to surrender all his world kingdoms to the servant of Jehovah, so the world of today lays all her mighty kingdoms at the feet of the church, and the devil seems ready to surrender his bloody scepter into the hands of the lion of Judah's tribe. Small wonder that many feel and some openly express that the world is not so malevolent and hateful against the children of God. Suffering in the flesh seems to be a thing of the past.

My fellow pilgrim to the city that has foundations, have you perhaps erred from the main road to Zion? If you experience the world as so lovely and Belial as such a peacemaker, and if suffering in the flesh is foreign to your life, then stop a moment and seriously consider the question: Have you lost the way? God's word surely is with you no more. It speaks—read it where you will—of elect strangers, people in the world but not of the world, marching onward, striving and longing for the things that are above and accompanied by the word of their redeemer: "In the world ye shall have tribulation."

You say that you have not suffered in the flesh?

Then either you have never ceased from sin, or you have returned to sin.

Have you not lost the way?

Christ was in the flesh.

How rich in meaning is that simple sentence!

It expresses that he became like unto his brethren in all things, sin excepted. He was man, fully man, partaking of the flesh and blood of the children, living the full life of the human body, being familiar through actual experience with its needs, desires, weaknesses, pains, hunger and thirst, limitations and weariness, and labor and toil. He entered into and lived the full life of the human soul; he thought in human mind, willed with human will, longed with human heart, spoke with human tongue; he was intimately acquainted with human ambitions, aspirations, joys, and sorrows—he acted in all the wide domain of human activity.

Neither is this all.

Jesus entered into all the human relationships involved in living in the flesh. He was a baby among other babies, a boy in the midst of contemporary boys, a young man in relation to other young men, a Hebrew of the Hebrews, a man among men. He lived as a son in relation to his parents, as a brother in the midst of his brothers, as a pupil of his teachers, and as a citizen of Nazareth. He was subject to Jewish law and to the jurisdiction of the Sanhedrin. He stood under the dominion of Herod, Pilate, and Caesar, and he was within the wide reach of the terrible Roman sword. Because of his entering into the flesh, he stood in all the manifold relationships connected with life in the flesh.

Into that flesh he entered. Before the world was, he was, but not in the flesh. In the bosom of the Father, coessential with him and the Holy Spirit, he lived in infinite, divine glory, the life of the perfect covenantal friendship of God triune. He did not partake of the nature and life of the angels, but he entered into the nature and lived the life of his brethren, so that he might deliver them from the power of him who had the dominion of death and bring them into the eternal light of the liberty of the children of God.

Into the flesh, into all the life of human nature and earthly relationships, Christ entered for us.

That God might have many children and himself, many brethren.

In the flesh Christ suffered.

Others lived in the same flesh with him. Brothers and sisters, children with him of the same mother, shared with him the same humble home, ate with him at the same table, slept with him under the same roof, were subject with him to the same parents, grew up with him and lived in daily contact with him. Citizens, inhabitants of the same town, were his fellowmen, his neighbors; they met him daily, walking the same streets with him, and they dealt with him, conversed with him, and knew him as the son of Joseph the carpenter. Priests and elders, Sadducees and Pharisees, were of his flesh and blood, Hebrews of the Hebrews, members with him of the commonwealth of Israel, speaking the same language, worshiping in the same temple, meeting in the same synagogue, searching the same Scriptures, possessing the same covenants, addressing the same multitude, and pretending to be children of the same God. In the same flesh lived kings and governors, men royally appareled, decked with purple and gold and living in ease and splendor, wielding with authority the terrible sword that is divinely instituted for the punishment of evildoers. Judges and soldiers, kings and emperors, businessmen and wise men and leaders of the people, as well as publicans and sinners, lived with him in the same flesh and were active in thought and speech and deed in the same spheres and relationships into which he also had entered. Contact with these others, living in the same flesh was unavoidable.

Shoulder-to-shoulder and elbow-to-elbow, Christ lived with Pharisees and Sadducees, with priests and elders and scribes, with emperors and kings and governors and judges, with soldiers and merchantmen, and with publicans and sinners, in the same flesh.

Thus in this inevitable contact with others in the flesh, Christ suffered. These others inflicted his suffering upon him. They chased him into Egypt by the cruel sword of merciless and madly ambitious Herod. They jeered at him in his hometown, as he opened unto them the Scriptures concerning himself, and led him to the precipice to cast him down into certain death. They opposed his speech and made attempt after attempt to catch him in his discourse. They forsook him in Capernaum, hated him, called him an evildoer in alliance with Beelzebub, the prince of the devils. They captured him, accused him as the vilest criminal, condemned him, maltreated him, spit their contempt upon him, scourged him, pressed thorns on his brow, nailed him to the accursed tree, cast him out of the flesh.

Living in the flesh, Christ suffered.

Why this suffering?

Briefly, because in the flesh he did the will of his Father, and he did so in opposition to those who in the same flesh did the will of their father the devil.

Christ had no sin, neither was guile found in his mouth. Personally he was God's Son. The common guilt of all, imputed to all who are born of women, did not touch him. Prepared in Mary's womb through the power of the Holy Ghost, his human nature was without the stain of sin. He was positively holy. He never committed a sinful deed. On the contrary, it was his meat to do the Father's will. His mind was completely subject to the will of him who is a light and in whom there is no darkness. Never a thought arose in his mind, except it was of the Father; never a desire originated in his heart, except it had God for its object; never a word passed from his lips, except to glorify the Holy One; never a deed by him was witnessed, except it was in most perfect obedience to the Almighty. Challengingly he could look in the faces of his contemporaries, hostile though they were, and without fear of indictment of contradiction ask the question, Which of you can convict me of sin? Because of this positive holiness and righteousness and perfect love of the Father, he who was the servant of Jehovah preeminently, and the friend of God uniquely, took issue with all sin and ungodliness. He served the one master and rejected the other persistently.

But for this he suffered.

For there were others in the same flesh. Others with whom the man Christ came into inevitable contact. Others who loved darkness rather than light, who wished to do and actually did perform the will of their father the devil. These aspired after earthly things, things of the world, things of the flesh, things of darkness, and things of hell. They hated the Father of our Lord Jesus Christ and loved him who is a murderer from the beginning. An earthly name and earthly fame, earthly bread and earthly power, earthly glory and earthly riches, and earthly empires and power, they sought and after them they strove. They were and lived as children of darkness.

Thus the contact between Christ in the flesh and these others in the flesh became conflict, battle, and struggle everywhere. In speech and in deed, the servant of Jehovah, doing the will of his Father in the flesh, condemned these children of darkness and exposed their deeds as evil.

Because of this antithesis, the flesh could not tolerate this servant of Jehovah. They made him suffer in the flesh.

Suffer, until they had cast him out of the flesh.

Fellow pilgrim, arm yourself with the same thought.

If you suffer in the flesh, it is because you have ceased from sin.

Formerly you obeyed with the world the lust of the flesh. You reveled in sin. You walked in darkness. You performed the will of your father the devil. There was complete harmony between sin and you, between the devil and your heart. Therefore, the world knew you and loved you as its own. With others in the flesh you rejoiced and danced and worshiped the world's god. The things below constituted your treasure and claimed all the love of your heart. And suffering in the flesh you knew not, because the flesh was your proper abode.

But the risen Lord suffered for you, and by his suffering overcame for you him who has the power of death. He cleansed you in his precious blood. He cut the shackles of sin that held you. He entered with his own life into yours, turned your love of the devil into enmity, and your hatred of God into love. With that life of the risen Lord in your inmost heart, you confess that you are dead to the world and the world is dead to you, that it is become your meat to do the will of the Father, and that you seek the things above, not the things on the earth.

You have become of God's party.

But you are still living in the flesh. If only with your heavenly life you were immediately and completely delivered—delivered from your sinful heart and the temptations of the old man of sin, delivered from the intimate contact with the world and the children of darkness living with you in the same flesh—there would be no strife, battle, and suffering. But this is not the will of your Father in heaven. You must fulfill the rest of your days in the flesh doing the will of your Father and Christ's Father.

Hence your suffering, if you have ceased from sin. Suffering within, because of the working of sin in your members, causing you to cry out, "O wretched man that I am! Who shall deliver me from the body of this death?" And suffering from without, for with you in the same home, church, society, school, shop, office, city, country, and world, live those in the same flesh who intend to do the will of their father, the devil, and who will not tolerate any other will but his.

Arm yourselves with the same mind.

There is joy in the very thought of this suffering, painful though it may be to the flesh. For though it may be grievous to be despised of men, derided and mocked, presented as an evildoer, cast out of the church or out of society, the fact is that you carry within your heart the sure conviction that it is because you have ceased from sin. If you were of the world, the world would love its own, but now you are not of the world. Therefore, the world hates you as they have hated him whose life is become yours.

Sweet peace! Free from sin. Soon free in judgment. Confidence with regard to the day when he who judges righteously will judge both you and those who have persecuted you!

Be of good cheer!

Christ has overcome the world!

13

Angry with His People

"And they forsook the LORD and served Baal and
Ashtaroth. And the anger of the LORD was hot
against Israel … Whithersoever they went out, the
hand of the LORD was against them for evil."

—Judges 2:13–15

In the crucible of God's anger, God's people are purified.
With the wicked it is not so.
For he is angry with the wicked every day. And they flee from
his burning wrath, always descending on the steeply declining way
of sin, hastening to destruction, until they sink into the pool that
burns with fire and sulfur, where their smoke goes up forever and
ever.

But against his people God's anger burns until they are
cleansed from their iniquity.

As they often foolishly would pursue the way of sin, turning
their faces away from him, the living God, toward hell and destruction, he hems them in from every side; his hand turns against
them for evil whithersoever they go, leaving open to them only the
narrow way of righteousness and life, so that toward it they might
turn to life and liberty!

Often God tries the righteous as silver is tried by fire.
His hot anger against them is the anger of love.
Of holy love, sanctifying!

———————————

The anger of the Lord was hot!
It always is hot against all sin and iniquity.

95

For he is unchangeably holy, loving himself with a holy self-love as the sole good and the overflowing fount of all good, constantly, eternally; willing, too, that all shall love him and acknowledge that he is good.

In that unchangeably holy self-love, the anger of the Most High is as constant as his holiness; it always burns; it always is hot against the workers of iniquity; it constantly consumes all that is corrupt and blazes against those who refuse to glorify him. The anger of the Lord is not a sudden ebullition of ill temper that vanishes as quickly as it bursts forth, but is a constantly burning fire kindled from within the unfathomable depths of his eternally adorable being.

It burns against all iniquity. And when the people of God stand in the place of unrighteousness and walk in the way of perverseness, the anger of the Lord burns against them.

Thus it was with the people of Israel of old.

They forsook the Lord and followed after Baal and Ashtaroth. God's covenantal people they were. Jehovah had given them his revelation and his law, and they knew him; they were to be holy unto the Lord, separated from the nations; and he blessed them with the blessings of his covenant in the land in which he had planted them. Him, their God, they forsook. They deliberately dismissed him from their minds and from their hearts and from their lives. They refused to keep his precepts as they were delivered unto them by his servant Moses. They forsook his service, forsook his sanctuary, forsook the blood of atonement!

And they served Baalim and Ashtaroth.

Baal is Bel, that is, lord. The sun god he was supposed to be, and as such the lord of heaven and the source of all blessings. Not only in Babylonia was he worshiped, but also by the Canaanites and the surrounding nations. Many Baalim there were. Each locality had its own Baal. When times were normal, he received from his worshipers incense and burnt offerings. But when his wrath was thought to be manifested in times of calamity and distress, his servants would appease him by human sacrifices, especially by the sacrifice of children. Ashtaroth represented the female counterpart of the masculine Baal. Like Baalim, there were many Ashtaroth, and their worship usually was connected with immoral rites.

These gods Israel served. For them they forsook Jehovah.

Not, indeed, because of misunderstanding. Knowledge is no virtue and sin is no intellectual mistake.

But these gods were carnal gods, and their worship was a carnal worship; serving them, the people could follow after the lust of the flesh.

Always the lust of the flesh prefers the idols of our imagination to the service of the living God.

Thus Israel forsook their Holy One to follow after the abominations of the heathen. Thus always the church forsakes the living God, in order to put her trust in the vanities of men that indeed are impotent to save, but allow full sway to the lust of the flesh, the lust of the eyes, and the pride of life.

Yet, how was it possible?

How can God's people forsake him? Are they not his workmanship, the fruit of his grace? Is there, then, a falling away of the saints? God forbid! He never forsakes the work of his hands.

First, not all the seed of Abraham is spiritual seed; not all are children of the promise. The carnal element is always present, is often strong, and is always striving for predominance, both in the old and in the new dispensations. It is not all Israel that is of Israel. And wistfully this carnal element constantly has its eyes directed to Baalim and Ashtaroth, to the world and its lust; it cannot rest until it sees the church prostrate before the vanities of the heathen. Its doctrine is always false; its way is always corrupt; its intentions are always wicked.

Second, the spiritual seed is far from perfect. Easily they are lulled to sleep. They fail to watch and pray. They cease from fighting the battle. They do not remove the evil men from their midst. And before they know it, the carnal element predominates, has its representatives in the sanctuary, among the prophets, in the pulpit, and in high places. They who should be rooted out from among the people of God become leaders among them.

And they lead the people of God astray.

Gradually, with subtlety, very wickedly these leaders teach the people to forsake the living God.

And they lead the people to the shrines of Baalim and Ashtaroth, where God's anger burns hotly against his people.

Against Israel is his anger hot.

It cannot escape our attention that there is something very distinctive in this burning wrath of Jehovah against the people of his love. For why should Israel immediately become the object of his oppressing anger as soon as they forsake him and turn to Baalim and Ashtaroth? Why should they feel God's afflicting hand upon them the moment they bow themselves before the abominations of the heathen?

Did not also the surrounding nations serve Baalim and Ashtaroth? Did they not also commit the same wickedness and lewdness as did Israel? Did they not constantly live in rebellion against the living God? Why, then, should the anger of the Lord burn so hotly against Israel and not against these nations? And why should these nations be caused to rejoice, when the hand of the Lord delivers his people into their power, so that they are victorious over the people of God? Behold, these are the ungodly! Pride compasses them about as a chain; violence covers them as a garment. Corrupt they are, and loftily they speak of oppression. Baalim and Ashtaroth they serve every day, and God is not in all their thoughts. Yet they prosper and are victorious over the people of God and rejoice in their victory. And when God's people turn to these same abominations for a moment and bow themselves before the vanities that the heathen serve daily, the anger of the Lord burns hotly against his people, and the hand of Jehovah is against them for evil whithersoever they turn!

Is God angry only with his people when they sin?

Does the fire of his holy wrath consume them alone when they forsake him to serve Baalim and Ashtaroth?

Is he not also filled with wrath against the wickedness of heathen nations?

Oh he is! He is angry with the wicked every day. His face is against them for evil, although his hand does not seem to be. His curse is in the house of the wicked, prosperous though it may appear to be. Even when he causes them to be victorious over his people and when he delivers them into the hands of the wicked, he does so in his constant wrath and anger over them. Instruments they may have to be in the hand of the Lord to chastise his people. Yet they are instruments of wrath, and in serving their purpose they become more than ever vessels of wrath fitted unto destruction, and they realize themselves as such. Not to execute the will of God, neither acknowledging that they are the instruments in Jehovah's hand, do they chastise his people, but with devilish joy they oppress them and would destroy them, rejoicing in the opportunity to afflict them. And in their temporary success they work out their final damnation, heaping up treasures of wrath.

There is an anger of eternal wrath that burns against the workers of iniquity to their destruction, even in the way of prosperity.

A phenomenon that in this world often gives rise to the anxious query: Do not the wicked prosper?

Yes, they do! But remember, it is a dreadful thing to prosper in the way of iniquity. For behind that prosperity, in the way of perverseness and iniquity, there is a divine anger that purposes to lead to eternal damnation!

And do not the righteous suffer? Does not God's anger burn against his people?

Yes! But remember, there is an anger of eternal love that burns against you—not to consume but to heal, not to destroy but to save, not to burn you but your sin, to burn it away and to purge you from it—until you stand without spot and blemish before him who is holy and righteous and dwell in his house forever!

A blessed thing it is to be afflicted in the way of iniquity, for the motive of that affliction is the holy anger of eternal love that leads you to eternal glory.

Against Israel God's anger burned hotly, for he loved his people with an eternal love, unchangeable and sovereign. But he loved them for his name's sake. He loved them as he loves himself. He loved them as he conceived of them before the foundation of the world, as he engraved them in the palms of his hands—holy, righteous, spotless, glorious, precious in his sight.

Hence when they forsake him and turn to Baalim and Ashtaroth, his anger burns against them hotly.

The anger of his holy love!

Salutary was this anger of the Lord!

In purpose and in actual effect salutary for God's people.

Salutary just because whithersoever they went out, the hand of the Lord their God was against them for evil.

They would go out for victory, and everywhere they would meet with defeat. In this defeat they met with the hand of Jehovah that was always against them, that hemmed them in on every side, so that there was no outlet to success and victory.

He gave them into the hands of their enemies who spoiled them. On the surface it would not seem so. Not immediately would they perceive and acknowledge that it was the hand of the Lord that was against them for evil. It was the nations around them who afflicted them, not the Lord whom they had forsaken. Yet it was of Jehovah. By the hand of the Lord was Israel strong, so that one could chase a thousand. By the hand of the Lord were the nations made powerful and victorious over Israel. He it was who surrendered them into the hands of the spoilers.

And his people were sore distressed.

For the nations rejoiced in their power over them.

The nations hated them and bereaved them of all their substance; they oppressed them and killed them all the day long. They caused them to be in bondage, to suffer hunger and thirst, to be in constant fear of their lives, to become a reproach and a byword among the nations.

Yet always it was the hand of the Lord that was against his people for evil. They sought a way of escape from that encompassing evil hand and found none. Gladly would they have pierced the rock wall that enclosed them and on every side and blocked their way to prosperity. If they had been able, they would have removed the hand of the Lord, not knowing that it was Jehovah's, and would have escaped, with Baalim and Ashtaroth, fleeing from Jehovah and running to destruction. They turned hither and thither, always with their vanities, always in the way of iniquity and perverseness. For they were foolish children. And always they would find the way of escape cut off by that evil hand. Whithersoever they went they found humiliation and shame, oppression and defeat. They were hedged about with Baalim and Ashtaroth, with adversity.

Until they understood.

And dropped the lie that was in their right hand.

And forsook Baalim and Ashtaroth to return to the rock of their salvation.

Then the evil hand would be removed. Then the way would be open, the way of victory and freedom, the way to prosperity and glory. For then it was the way of righteousness, the way of the Lord. And in that way they could be saved and taste that the Lord is good.

The hand of the Lord had saved them from the vanities of the heathen!

Purged they were by the anger of Jehovah.

The saving anger of his holy love!

In the crucible of God's anger his people are saved.

Yet, only because they are his people, chosen in Christ from before the foundation of the world.

If it were not for Christ, Israel could never be cast into the furnace of God's anger and emerge purged and glorified. In that furnace—all the history of Israel witnesses it—they must perish, were it not for the mighty Immanuel, the lion of Judah's tribe!

But he is their head forever.

And in the fullness of time he comes and takes upon himself the iniquity of them all. And freely, willingly, as the obedient servant, he steps into the crucible of God's anger, that the fire of God's wrath may burn against him and may burn the sin of his brethren away forever and ever. He descends into the depth of the death of the cross.

But he emerges, for he is risen!

And we are justified.

Purged from sin forever.

Zion is redeemed through justice from sin forever!

14

How Long, Lord?

"How many are the days of thy servant? when wilt
thou execute judgment on them that persecute me?"
—Psalm 119:84

How long, Lord?

How many are the days of thy servant?

It is not inspired by vain curiosity that I ask the question.

I know, and it suffices me to know that the extent of the number of my days is threescore years and ten, or if I belong to those endowed with a special measure of strength, fourscore years. Beyond this I crave for no more definite information. It is well that thou hidest from me the immediate as well as the more distant future and the condition of the way I will be called to travel.

For I am persuaded that thy way, Lord, is wisdom and goodness.

Neither is the question intended as a hopeless complaint that life is all too brief.

Let them complain of the brevity of this earthly life whose portion is below, whose god is their belly, and whose glory is in their shame. They have all their hope in the things of this world. Beyond the horizon of the things of this present time, even the vision of their hope perishes. In the world they prosper. With the world they seek to be satisfied. To the world they cling with all their might. This world they dread to leave. For them the way through this world is all too brief. They may complain that time hastens on and that the end approaches too fast, but I will not.

How many are the days of thy servant, Lord?

This is a question of longing—of the holy impatience that characterizes the attitude of all the saints in the world, of the church, the bride of Christ—a looking for the end; a waiting for the adoption, to wit, the redemption of the body, for their final and public justification and the manifestation of the righteousness of their God; a waiting with patience with respect to the way they must travel and the battle they must fight, the reproach they must bear, and the killing they must endure all the day long; yet a waiting with a holy impatience with regard to the glory that shall be revealed to them. This is the expression of that holy impatience.

Do not the saints always utter this question of yearning? My soul thirsts for God, for the living God. When shall I come and appear before God? How long, Lord? Wilt thou hide thyself forever? Lord, how long will the wicked triumph? How long will they utter and speak hard things? How long will all the workers of iniquity boast themselves? How long, O Lord, holy and true, dost thou not judge and avenge our blood on those who dwell on the earth? Do not the Spirit and the bride always say, "Come"? Do not the saints have the promise, even though the time seems long, that God will quickly avenge the elect who cry unto him day and night?

How long, then, O Lord?

How many are the days of thy servant?

For the end of my days I long.

Not for the end as such do I look with earnest expectation, for that end is death, the dissolution of the earthly house of this my tabernacle, the end of all my earthly life and earthly existence and earthly relationships. I do not desire to be unclothed, but clothed upon.

But the end brings victory, life, and glory!

The end of my days on the earth, although it is the end of much in this earthly house that is dear to me, is also the liberation from all that is a cause of grief to the inward man. It is the end of the body of this death, the end of the law of sin in my members that takes me captive, so that I do not what I would and often find myself doing that which I hate. It is the end of all my connection with the world that is crucified to me and I to it—the word with its glitter and vainglory, its temptations and persecutions, its boast of victory, and its prospering in iniquity. It is the end of my being exposed to the temptations of the devil and his host, the end of death and of the suffering of this present time, the end of the battle, and the end of all apparent defeat.

How many, then, are the days of thy servant, the days of battle and of the suffering of this present time?

I long for the end of them, for that end marks the beginning of everything that for which my soul longs.

Beyond that end, I know and am persuaded, lies the glory of the eternal inheritance. There I expect perfection, freedom, life, victory, and glory. There I know that I will be in God's tabernacle and see him face-to-face, as here I cannot see him. There I will respond with my whole being—body and soul, mind and will, heart and all my desires; eye and ear, mouth, hand, foot, and all my members—eternally, perfectly, in a heavenly fashion and on a heavenly plane, to that perfect vision of God. There I shall know even as I am known.

Beyond that end is the perfect being and fellowship with Christ and with his saints.

There is the incorruptible and undefilable inheritance that fades not away.

There I expect the new heavens and the new earth in which righteousness shall dwell.

How long, O Lord?

———————

How many are my days, the days of thy servant, O Lord?

The question is not inspired by wicked unbelief and lack of confidence, not by grumbling dissatisfaction or murmuring impatience.

Such indeed may sometimes be the motive for asking this question.

It always is the motive when wicked hypocrites, who outwardly travel with the people of God but whose heart is in the world, exclaim, "How long?" Thus it was with the ungodly multitude that was with the church in the desert in the old dispensation. Ah, they loved Egypt with its treasures and pleasures, its fleshpots and delicacies. Had it not been for the brick kilns and hard labor, for the oppression and persecution they endured as Hebrews, never would they have cared to move to the land of promise. When their oppression became hard and insufferable, they were willing—though with bleeding hearts and a carnal attachment to the pleasures of the world of Egypt—to forsake the house of bondage and to seek the land flowing with milk and honey.

In Egypt they groaned with the true children of God, "How long, Lord? How many are our days in the land of oppression?"

Had the land flowing with milk and honey been entered immediately after Israel's crossing of the Red Sea; had their exodus meant only the exchange of one carnal object of their desires for another; had there only been no desert without food or drink, no waste howling wilderness in which all the streams were dry and in which they would be called upon to seek the Lord and to live in daily confidence in him; had there only been no Sinai, no law, no covenant, no long and weary way of battle and suffering; had there only been no mighty enemies to fight in the land of promise...

But now?

They wanted Canaan without God.

They longed for the fleshpots of Egypt or for the land flowing with milk and honey, but not for God's covenant.

They became dissatisfied with the way of the Lord in the awful desert, and in rebellious and wicked unbelief they asked repeatedly, "How long? How many are our days in this desert in which we must perish? How long must we suffer and die? How long must we eat this sickening manna that our soul loathes? Oh, were we still in Egypt with its abundance, its fleshpots and cucumbers, its onions and garlic!"

Such is the desire of the wicked, a desire that sometimes arises from the old nature of the child of God, and which, therefore, must be distinguished from the question of holy impatience: How many are the days of thy servant, O Lord? At times he beholds how the wicked prosper in the world, while his punishment is there every morning. His feet will well-nigh slip at the sight, and he will be inclined to ask, Is there knowledge in the Most High? How long? Or a child of God who has been wandering far into the world and has drunken deeply of the cup of the world's pleasures is chastised and put down on a bed of sickness and agony that will become his deathbed. On that sickbed he may reach the stage when he will long to be delivered from his agony and prefers death to his present suffering. If only he might recover, for he still would prefer to live. Not the longing for heavenly perfection, but the unwillingness to travel the way of suffering thither inspires the question, How long, O Lord? How many are these days of my suffering?

Still it is the question of unholy impatience, rather easily distinguishable from the motive that inspires the poet, for it is inspired by dissatisfaction with the way of the Lord. The way is one of suffering, of self-denial, of cross-bearing, and we do not want to travel it to the end. It is the expression of a desire to have our way turned into one of earthly prosperity, not of a longing to see the glory of God and to enter into the heavenly perfection. It is a lack of confidence in the Most High, who causes all things to work together for good to those who love him, and hence, a lack of submission to his will and way. It is disobedience, rebellion, murmuring against the Lord, refusal to bear the cross.

A very unholy impatience, indeed!

Not so the question of the psalmist.

The saint who asks this question is in a position to call himself "thy servant."

He is Jehovah's servant and is conscious of it. He occupies a position in the midst of the world that enables him to express without shame before the face of the Lord that he is his servant. Surely that presupposes that he is a regenerated child of God, called out of darkness into the Lord's marvelous light, and that he is a partaker of the salvation the Lord prepares for those who love him. But it means much more. It expresses that he conceives of his whole life in the light of Jehovah's covenant as a divine appointment that he must fulfill, and which he keeps gladly. He stands at his post by divine appointment. He is called to represent Jehovah's cause. He is of the party of the living God.

Thy servant Lord, am I. Willingly I abide at my post. I am ready to serve and to fight the good fight, yea, to suffer in the cause of thy covenant in the midst of the world. I do not ask thee to change the way.

But, O Lord, I hope in thy word. My soul fainteth for thy salvation; my eyes fail with longing for the glory that is awaiting thy servant, O Lord!

Here is the battle; there is the victory.

Here is sin and imperfection; there is the beauty of holiness.

Here is death; there is life.

How many are my days?

Lord, how long?

For thy great name's sake, Lord, how long? When will I see the theodicy, the justification of my God?

When wilt thou execute judgment upon those who persecute me? When wilt thou avenge the blood of thy servant upon those who hate thee?

For as thy servant I suffer.

A stranger I am in the earth, for thou hast begotten me again unto a lively hope. Because of thy work of grace within my heart and because of the gracious calling wherewith thou hast called me, I am separated from the world. I love thy precepts and would keep them with my whole heart. I confess thy name before men. I keep myself from the unfruitful works of darkness. The world loves iniquity and hates thy word, and for thy name's sake they hate me without a cause. They have dug pits for me, they persecute me wrongfully, they almost consume me. I am become like a bottle in the smoke, like an empty wine skin hung up in tent or house, exposed to smoke and dirt and heat, parched and wrinkled, covered with soot.

Despised by the world.

And, Lord, I would not have it so. For I am thy servant, the representative of thy name, thy covenant, thy cause, thy friendship in the world.

How long, O Lord?

The more the world triumphs over me as I stand at my post where thou hast stationed me, and the more I suffer for thy name's sake, the more I long for the end of these days of defeat and shame and for the day of my perfect justification, when all the world will have to acknowledge that my cause is the cause of the Son of God and that the cause of Christ is thy cause.

And thy cause must have the victory, for thy name must have all the glory forever.

And the glory of thy name is involved in the suffering and shame and defeat of me, thy servant.

When wilt thou manifest thy glory?

When wilt thou execute judgment upon those who persecute me?

How many are the days of thy servant?

How long, O Lord?

———————

Hark, the answer!

It is implied in the question, for the question concerns the days of thy servant.

This implies that these days are definitely numbered. Numbered they are by divine determination in God's everlasting counsel. Numbered are the days of the whole church in the world. Numbered are the days of each saint in connection with the days of the wicked and of the whole world of this present time.

They must be fulfilled to the very last.

For the days of his servants in the world are determined with perfect wisdom and infinite grace—so determined that all these days, with all they contain, with all the suffering and reproach they bring, with all the battle that must be fought in them, with all their prayers and groanings, with all the iniquity of the world, must work together for the salvation of the saints, for the perfecting of the saints, and for the final condemnation of the wicked world.

And hear the final answer: Behold, I come quickly!

Come, then, Lord!

15

Two Viewpoints of the Same Reality

"All these things are against me."

—Genesis 42:36

"If God be for us, who can be against us?"

—Romans 8:31

All these things are against me?

What a depth of misery opens up before us at this heartrending outcry!

Yawning darknesses of despair appear ready to swallow us up, when we utter this passionate plaint of helplessness.

Things are against us. They conspire to destroy us. They have united their forces to extinguish the very light of our life, to take the last drop of sweetness out of our already bitter cup, to leave us in dark despair. And we are alone, helpless, defenseless, without power to ward off the last threatening blow. Alone, for—note the personal element in the outcry—all these things are against *me*.

Outburst of lone grief, of dark despair!

Yet how often, also in the life of God's children in the world, do circumstances fully appear to justify such plaintive exclamations.

They appeared to justify the old patriarch Jacob.

Had not the days of his life been few and evil?

Did it not seem, at the moment when this passionate outburst of grief was pressed from his heart, as if lately all things conspired to deprive him of children? Did he not stand helpless and defenseless over against these things?

Years ago it was, indeed, but still fresh in his memory, that he had sent his most beloved child away from home to inquire after the wellbeing of his brethren. And Jacob had never seen anything of him again, except the blood-soaked garment the brethren brought to their father as a silent witness that a wild beast had devoured him and that Joseph had without doubt been rent in pieces. The sad departure of the first son of his beloved Rachel had left him comfortless, and when his other children approached him with their vain consolations, he had plainted, "I will go down into the grave unto my son mourning." Time had never completely healed that heart wound.

Now it was cruelly torn open anew.

Famine had ravaged the promised land in which Jacob still dwelt as a sojourner and stranger. The corn had been consumed. Jacob and his family had also heard the news that was rumored abroad that there was corn in Egypt. Long had Jacob hesitated to send his sons to that far country, but the hunger pressed, and he finally let them go. "Look no longer upon one another, for there is corn in Egypt; go and buy from thence, that we may live and not die." Thus had he spoken. Benjamin—Rachel's second son, the only one who could somewhat reconcile Jacob to Joseph's death— Jacob had kept at home, "lest peradventure mischief might befall him." The brethren had gone. When they returned to their anxious father much later than might reasonably be expected, one son was missing, and the rest told a sad story of the strange treatment they had experienced in Egypt and of the harsh words the ruler of that country had spoken to them. They explained why their brother was missing and mentioned to their father the condition upon which he might be fetched home again: they had to return and take Benjamin with them!

No wonder, then, that the old patriarch broke out in sad complaints and wails, "All these things are against me!"

Joseph is not. The old wound is cruelly torn open and again he beholds his bloodstained coat of many colors. Simeon is not, disappeared in a way similar to that of Joseph's removal from the family. And Benjamin must now go? Benjamin, upon whom all his father's love had been concentrated since the death of Joseph?

Did not things seem against him? Did they not appear to conspire to tear his children from his heart, cruelly, mysteriously, one by one?

And did he not stand helpless, defenseless over against these things?

Oh, he might emphatically declare that he would never permit Benjamin to leave home. Did he not know at the same time that things would compel him to let him go with the brethren? Was it not the proposed condition for Simeon's release? Would not the hunger in the land force him to send the brethren to Egypt once more? And had not that strange ruler of the land, where corn could be had, sworn that he would not see their faces again unless they brought Benjamin with them?

All these things are against me!

How apparently justifiable seems the outburst of grief!

And how equally justifiable appears a similar vociferation in the life of God's children!

Men, cruel men, devils, times, circumstances, the very place where they live, their name and position—all things often seem against them. They have a family and they cannot support it. They look for work and it is in vain. Or they have an honorable position, but men conspire to thrust them out. They have a few pennies, but they are consumed. They have a home, but they cannot keep it and must deliver it up. And they see no outcome.

And they consider these *things*. They reason with them. They look at them from every side. They count their possessions, their opportunities, their prospects. They figure and turn things over and over in their mind, until they grow weary with thinking and sleep will not close their eyes at night.

But no matter how they care and worry and meditate on these things, dark despair yawns on every side.

All these things are against me.

Yet, brethren, this loud wail of despair, if heard from the lips of God's children, is only the expression of a viewpoint, a wrong viewpoint, the viewpoint of unbelief.

For listen! However dark the way may appear, is this not true, unchangeably true, true forever and ever: God is for us?

And if God be for us, who can be against us?

All these things are against me.

What things?

Would it not be well, worried brethren, weary with thinking and planning and contriving and calculating, careworn because of your anxiety about all the things that are against you, to enumerate them, one by one, to let them have their full weight of misery, and then to take a look also at the things that do not seem against us?

The anxiety of unbelief, however apparently justified by circumstances, is apt to concentrate all our attention upon the things that seem evil, make us unmindful of many things that are still cause for rejoicing, and tempt us to become guilty of gross exaggeration of the things that seem against us.

We count the evils ten times, a hundred times, the blessings but once!

The sorrows and miseries crowd in upon our soul, the darkness envelops our heart, the thought of all our misfortunes (for such we are prone to call them in that state of mind, even though we know that the very word is coined by the ungodly) solely occupy our mind, until we see nothing but evils about us and the darkness of despair ahead. We become unmindful of the good things of God, of the thousands of reasons to rejoice, of the abundance of blessings, of reasons to be comforted and to rejoice for what he still lavishes upon us.

Such was surely the case with Jacob when he cried out, "All these things are against me."

What things?

As Jacob beholds them now, at this moment of faltering faith and deep despair, they are to be enumerated as follows: "Me have ye bereaved of children; Joseph is not; Simeon is not; and ye will take Benjamin away."

But how greatly exaggerated is the evil of *these things* in the words of the complaining patriarch! How dark he draws the picture of his present circumstances! How utterly forgetful he appears to be of all the goodness of the Lord over him. How he must ignore hundreds of blessings to make these statements!

Notice the sweeping statement: "Me ye have bereaved of my children." But did not the Lord give him far more than he ever gave to Abraham or Isaac his fathers, to see the realization of his covenant in twelve sons and one daughter? And while he spoke of being bereaved of children, was he not surrounded by eleven of them? Was not the statement, then, marked by gross exaggeration? Did he not exceed far beyond the bounds of truth in making it, and was he not oblivious of God's goodness over him? Besides, was it, from Jacob's viewpoint and as far as he knew, not an injustice to the brethren when he accused them of being guilty in the matter? True, they actually were guilty of Joseph's disappearance, but of this the old father was not cognizant. As far as he knew, a wild beast had devoured him. And in the matter of Simeon's absence, they surely were innocent. Again, Jacob's viewpoint of unbelief causes him to mention the case of Joseph in one breath with that of Simeon and Benjamin: "Joseph is not, and Simeon is not, and you will take Benjamin away." But also this was not a statement of reality. Simeon was not dead, but he lived in Egypt. And the brethren had plainly explained that he would be released and would return home with them, if only they might take Benjamin to that strange ruler in proof that they were honest men. Neither was it true that the brethren would take Benjamin away in the sense implied in the statement of the grieving father.

How greatly unjust and guilty of exaggeration, how unmindful of all the blessings Jehovah had bestowed on him is the patriarch as he thus wails and bemoans his condition!

Yet is not the experience of Jacob a common one?

Is it not always characteristic of unbelief, of a faltering faith, that we enhance the evil things until we see nothing except them and are unmindful, forgetful, and unthankful with respect to the blessings the Lord showers down upon us? Is it not true, when the Lord takes away from us one that is dear to our heart, that often we are apt to concentrate all our mind and heart upon the deceased and forget the living loved ones? Do we not often extend our cares and worries far beyond the present day, so that when we are thrust out of our position, when times of abundance are passed and a period of scarcity, of want, of lack of labor and money arrives, we become forgetful that the Lord cares for his people every day and that each day we receive our daily bread?

O we of little faith!

Is God dead?

Or did he turn against his people?

If he is the ever living God, and if he is unchangeably for us, why concentrate all our attention with careworn hearts and minds upon the things that seem evil and become forgetful of all his benefits?

Why not search for all the tokens of his lovingkindnesses that are always more than we can count?

If God be for us, who can be against us?

All these things are against me.

How untrue, how directly against reality was this statement of the patriarch!

That it was so untrue and that he nevertheless uttered it was because at that moment he lost sight of his God.

This is evident already when he spoke of *things* being against him.

In the darkness of unbelief we can see things and nothing but things and forget that the Most High holds the reins and controls and rules with absolute sovereignty over all things. These *things* appear to have power against us; they seem to plot and conspire;

they appear to be implacable and merciless; they cooperate for our destruction. And we feel helpless and defenseless over against these *things*. And in this darkness of unbelief, it is not surprising that fear of them takes hold of our hearts and that we cry out with the patriarch, "All these things are against me!"

Reality is that things are nothing.

The truth is that above all things stands the living God and that men and devils and powers and principalities, and heights and depths, and life and death, and things present and things to come, are in his almighty hand and can do nothing against his will, but always must accomplish what he wills them to do.

The fact is that this almighty God is for his people. He is for them from eternity and his lovingkindness over them moved him to arrange all his divine counsel in such a way that all things must work together for good to those who love God. He is for them in time, and he governs all things according to his counsel, so that they may be conducive to the eternal salvation of the elect. He manifested that he is for them in unfathomable love, for he gave his only begotten Son into the depth of shame and reproach and of the suffering of death and hell that they might live. What shall we then say to these things? What shall we say if things seem to conspire, if men rave against us, if the powers of darkness unite to destroy us, if very death and hell rise up against us? What shall we say to them? Shall we be afraid and complain that all these things are actually against us? Nay, but we shall say that God is for us, and if God be for us, nothing can be against us!

We shall say, He that spared not his own Son, but delivered him up for us all, how shall he not with him also freely give us all things?"

We are more than conquerors through him who loved us.

Nothing can separate us from his love.

For he is God.

He is the almighty, against whom no living or dead things can prevail, whose will they must surely accomplish. He is the all-wise God, who never makes errors, whose counsel is perfect, who will surely realize the purpose unto which he made and governs all things. He is the unchangeably faithful one, whose lovingkindness is from everlasting to everlasting upon those who fear him, who will never fail nor forsake us, who is for us forever.

If he is for us, all things must be for us!

They were not against Jacob, but for him, although he could not see this. Had he had control of things, he would have made an end to the famine in Canaan, kept the brethren home, left Simeon in Egypt for fear that Benjamin might be taken away, and all things would have been against him.

Now Joseph was living, Simeon was living, Benjamin must go, and all must serve the purpose to unite them again and save a great people alive.

No different is it with us, although the way is contrary to our plans.

Only climb through enveloping darkness to the heights of faith.

And say, "God is for us! All is well!"

16

Looking at Things Not Seen

"For our light affliction, which is but for a moment,
worketh for us a far more exceeding and eternal
weight of glory; While we look not at the things
which are seen, but at the things which are not seen:
for the things which are seen are temporal; but the
things which are not seen are eternal."
—2 Corinthians 4:17, 18

We look at the things not seen.

How blessed are they who direct their lives in accordance with
the true wisdom of this seeming paradox!

Blessed now, in the midst of things present and seen: in joy
and in sorrow, in sickness and in health, in prosperity and in adversity, in life and in death—when the soul leaps in exultation and
when the heart is overwhelmed with grief.

Having regard for the things that are not seen, they appreciate
and evaluate all things seen in the light of things as yet invisible
and hidden from view, and they know that the things tangible and
perceptible, the things of their present experience, are temporal
and will soon fade and be no more, to give place to the higher, eternal reality of things that are not seen. Having their eyes fixed
steadfastly on the things that are not seen, they feel confident that
things present are but a means to realize for them the things future—that things temporal are the way, while things eternal are
the end.

Thus they will neither set their hearts on things temporal
when they appear pleasant and joyous and beautiful, nor be over-

come in the struggle and sit down by the wayside in desperation when billows of affliction and waves of grief roll over the soul. They will in all things be more than conquerors.

A thing of beauty, appearing as an integral part in the world of our present experience, is no joy forever.

Our affliction is but for a moment.

Leaning against the railing of our ship, I stood gazing on a late summer evening at a sunset over the Atlantic, my soul enraptured by its marvelous beauty. On a deep background of transparent blue, deeper because the heaven's canopy served as a mirror to reflect somewhat the depths of the ocean's mysteries below, the Lord of heaven and earth painted a work of color—so rich and variegated, yet so harmonious in its form and polychromatic beauty that I stood riveted on the spot, lost in wonderment. As slightly toward the northwest the sun was about to go down in a halo of blazing fire, in the southwestern part of the firmament's dome, a huge fan of featherlike clouds stretched itself through the heavens, rising from a common center on a line of richly dark purple that was drawn near the horizon and parallel to it, reaching out and expanding to points almost directly overhead. From the deep purple at its base and center, the colors gradually and softly shaded into a blazing scarlet, a bright red, then into a beautiful orange that produced a deepening effect upon the dark blue background of the sky. The entire picture seemed to be alive, the colors shifting and leaping upward like flames of fire, then as swiftly gliding downward again and contracting toward the fan's center. The heavens were ablaze with the glory of God, and the firmament poured forth abundant speech.

Then as I would fain have prolonged the scene to fill my soul a little longer with its all-surpassing beauty, the picture quickly faded, the colors lost their brightness, until with the setting sun the whole disappeared from view and the darkness of night spread over the ocean.

A part of this sunset was evidence of all the things that are seen and that are temporal: a vivid testimony of the transitoriness of all the beauty and pleasure and joy of things temporal. To regard the visible things, to gaze at them only, to set our heart upon them as if they were to be evaluated in themselves and were lasting treasures, is foolish and hopeless.

It is no different with regard to the afflictions in the midst of the world of visible things.

He who looks at them without having regard to the things that are not seen will be overcome by present troubles. So were sometimes the saints of old, and it pressed from their hearts the cry that all things were against them. Similar was the experience of the inspired psalmist when he regarded the things seen as things in themselves, and when he almost was inclined to let the murmuring judgment of rebellion that there is no knowledge in the Most High escape from his lips. He regarded the things that are seen, both of the godly and the ungodly, and he set his heart on them. He looked, and behold, the ungodly knew no pains and no bands until their death. They wallowed in pleasure and lived luxuriously; prosperity was their portion all the days of their life. He looked again and found that he was oppressed with grief, although he washed his hands in innocency. His punishment awaited him every morning anew. He could not understand the problem that was presented to his mind by the aspect of things that are seen. It was too painful for him. Bitter dissatisfaction filled his troubled soul until he ceased to look at visible things and regarded their end in the light of the sanctuary of God. Then he was satisfied, for he understood that the things he had seen and had regarded with envy and grief of soul were temporal—both the prosperity of the wicked and the affliction of the godly.

Blessed are they whose confession this is, and who direct their lives accordingly, day-by-day, while we look at the things that are not seen, not at the things that are seen.

———

"Our light affliction, which is but for a moment."

These words express the apostle's evaluation of all the sufferings and troubles of the present time.

Does he not speak too lightly? Is his judgment of the world's pain and death not far too superficial to be regarded seriously?

Is his light appraisal of all the tribulation men endure in the world of things that are seen to be explained from lack of experience on his part? Was he perhaps a man not acquainted with grief? Did the storms of life always pass over him? Was his way perhaps always smooth? Having no personal acquaintance with the sufferings of this present time, and lightly regarding the agonies of others round about him, did he perhaps speak foolishly, when he characterized present grief as our light affliction which is but for a moment?

Did he not know how the world is writhing in the throes of death? Had he never heard how the whole creation groans and travails together until now? Had he never seen how man is frequently born to suffer, to die day-by-day, not for a moment, but for weeks and months and years, for a lifetime—and not lightly, but in unbearable agony?

Yes, he knew. He did not speak foolishly when he said that our present affliction is light and for a moment.

He knew suffering by personal experience. He was acquainted with the sufferings of this present time, with pains of the body and sorrows of heart, with griefs and troubles. And he knew of still another suffering, which the world of things that are seen inflicted upon him just because he had regard to the things that are not seen. He was troubled on every side, persecuted and cast down, always bearing about in the body the dying of the Lord Jesus, always delivered unto death for Jesus' sake. His outward man was perishing, and his inward man was afflicted by his outward man. Sin afflicted him until he cried out, "Who shall deliver me from the body of this death?" The world afflicted him because it is in darkness, while he, according to the inward man, desired to walk in the light. He was persecuted, reproached, scourged, cast out, stoned, imprisoned, condemned to death, oppressed on every side in the world of things that are seen. Knowing all this and having before his mind the things of this present time in all the power of their oppression and tribulation, he nevertheless speaks as he does and characterizes all the sufferings of the present as a light affliction, which is but for a moment. Again, knowing not only his own sufferings, but being mindful also of the tribulation of all the saints, of the church of Jesus Christ in the world of visible things, he includes their affliction and comforts them with the confident assurance that it is only light and evanescent, like streaks of morning cloud dissipated by the rising sun.

But, pray tell, why? Whence this light appraisal of the affliction of this present time?

Surely not because the apostle considers these sufferings lightly and of no account when weighed all by themselves. Then indeed the weight of affliction is heavy enough; then the dark night of suffering seems long and terrible.

Rather, the reason is that he looked not at things that are seen, but at the things that are not seen. The world of visible things—the world of our earthly experience, the things of perception, the things we can see and hear and taste and smell and handle—are the things through which we suffer. They constitute the world in which we are afflicted. But this is not the only reality. There is a world of things not seen as yet, but which is nonetheless real. It is the world of heavenly, spiritual, eternal things. It exists, but it is not yet seen. It exists, but it cannot yet be perceived by the earthly eye. It has existence, because the God of his people conceived of that world before this world of visible things was. It already is, for it was realized through the sufferings and death, the resurrection and exaltation of the Lord Jesus Christ, who is exalted at the right hand of God. Although we cannot see it, yet we look for it by faith in him who is the captain of our salvation and the finisher of our faith. Though that world of heavenly things is hidden from our present earthly view, yet we look at it with the eye of hope through him who loved us even unto death.

We know it is there, and we regard it. Steadily we gaze upon it with the eye of our spirit. And with our eye fixed on that world of invisible things, we appraise our present suffering.

Both present affliction and future glory we put in the balance and weigh. Then there is no comparison.

The things not seen constitute an exceeding weight of glory, and they are eternal.

The affliction of the present, in the world of things that are seen, is light.

It is but for a moment!

———————

Our light affliction—the means to the end.

Only by considering his suffering in the light of the invisible things, not the visible things, can a man be blessed and reconciled with the brief way of his light affliction.

Truly, the mere comparison of present affliction and future glory is comforting for the afflicted soul in the midst of the things that are seen. The mere remembrance of the things that are not seen as the object of our blessed hope is sufficient to make us rejoice in the midst of suffering and to cause us to sing songs in the night.

But the mere comparison does not satisfy. It does not reconcile us even with our light affliction, because it does not reveal the reason. It does not show us the necessity of our present suffering. Why, after all, the suffering? Granted that it is only light and quickly passing and flitting away, when viewed in the light of the exceeding weight of eternal glory that awaits us in the world of unseen things. The fact remains that while we endure it, the burden of it is heavy and the pain of it severe. Were it not far better, then, to obtain the exceeding weight of glory in a different way and to be free from suffering in this world of visible things?

Yes, but our light affliction *works* a far more exceeding weight of glory. There is a causal relation between the affliction and the glory, between our experience in the world of visible things and our glory in the world invisible.

The light affliction is a means; the glory is the end. Our present suffering is the way, and there is none other. The future glory is the destination whither the way is leading. The affliction yields fruit, and the fruit is the far more exceeding weight of glory. The former is necessary to the latter. Without the means we would not gain the end. Unless we travel the way, difficult and rough though it may frequently be, we cannot reach the destination.

Then all is well and we are reconciled with the way.

We may not always understand the exact relation or be able to discern the connection between our light affliction and the glory God has in store for his people. In fact, more often than not we cannot. We grasp a few great and general truths. Did not God himself choose the deep and awful way of sin and grace, with all its misery and death, yea, with the suffering and death of his only begotten Son in its very center, to realize the far more exceeding weight of the glory he has prepared for those whom he loved with an eternal and predestinating love? Was the way of the cross and all its agony of soul and body not necessary for the Lord, in order that he might attain to his glorious mediator's crown? Can we not see that suffering sanctifies, that affliction purifies us as gold is proved by fire? Yea, do we not understand that the outward man must perish day by day and must ultimately perish in death, in order that the inward man may be renewed and finally glorified?

Yea, the earthly house of this tabernacle must be dissolved, and we must be unclothed that we may be clothed upon.

Yet aside from these general truths, we do not fathom the mind of the Most High.

The details of his ways with us we do not understand. Why one must travel in this way, and another in that way, remains a mystery.

Neither do we care to know.

For we walk by faith, not by sight.

One step at a time is enough.

Having regard not to the things that are seen, but to the things that are not seen, and being assured by our God who leads us that our light affliction works a far more exceeding weight of glory, we are confident that all things work together for good to those who love God, to them whom he has called according to his purpose.

Then we are reconciled with the way, although it is rough and steep and the night is dark.

And cheerfully we travel onward, enduring the way for the goal in view.

Eternal glory, exceedingly great!

17

Not Troubled

"Let not your heart be troubled: ye believe in God,
believe also in me."

—John 14:1

The heart can become profoundly troubled.

Just as the deep sea, having been swept up by a howling storm, becomes restless, so that her usually calm surface heaves and groans, her waves, as high as houses, rolling and foaming, rising and dropping precipitously, finding no rest, so too the profoundly deep heart of man under the influences of the raging storms of life can be extremely agitated. The heart becomes so troubled that it can find no rest.

Man's heart is the center of his life from a spiritual perspective.

Out of the heart are the issues of life.

Our thoughts and desires, inclinations and interests, understandings and conceptions, and wants and aspirations all have their source and spiritual root in the heart. As the heart is, so are its issues: our wants, our thoughts and desires, our inclinations, and our ideals and purposes. As the heart is, so is our life. The heart is who we really are.

The expression "to be troubled in heart," therefore, penetrates so deeply and describes something so very dreadful.

It is not a minor disturbance occasioned by life's superficial realities.

There are people who are very easily troubled.

By nature these are superficial persons who have never really been touched to the depths of their existence, whose hearts know no troubling, but who by the slightest, mildest opposition, or by the most insignificant twinge of pain and suffering, react with a show of strong emotions, cast themselves down in dust and ashes, pour forth a flood of tears, hang the harp in the willows, and leave the impression with others that their psychological resilience and strength is broken in many different ways. Just as shallow waters become suddenly tempestuous, so too are these persons easily troubled. Yet do not take them seriously. Their distress is not the troubling of the heart, but only a superficial mental, emotional distress. Their superficial emotions are distressed, but not the depths of life.

The troubling of the heart penetrates to the depths of one's being, affecting even the desire to live.

It is not caused by the appearance of little clouds the size of a man's hand on the horizon of our lives, but by the powerful storms of life that furiously rage over our heads, until there appears to be no possibility of deliverance by the hand of God or men. To be troubled of heart is something quite different from being merely sad of heart. The heart can be filled with pain and overwhelmed by sorrow without being troubled in the sense in which Jesus means it in the text. The disciples, to whom he first directed this comforting word, may indeed have been troubled. There are moments in the lives of God's children in which it would be foolishness for one to urge them, "Let not your heart be saddened." No, when the heart is troubled, we are crushed. We are broken and unable to function. We see neither any escape, nor any reason for or any wisdom in the way that we have to walk. We do not understand what God is doing. The way of God appears to be unjust. The mind has worn itself out trying to understand the way of God, but it was all fruitless. The mind stops thinking. The will finds no rest. There is no calm submission, no unity of our thought and will with that of the Almighty. The heart is troubled, full of unrest and turmoil. The scale of our lives never balances.

The heart is troubled.

So it was for the disciples when Jesus spoke these words.

Their hearts were troubled. They did not understand what was happening. They were not one with the way the savior chose to walk. Wherever they looked for understanding, the darkness of a deep abyss engulfed them.

Yet their hearts would be troubled even more. Deeper and still less understandable would be the way for them in the future that lay immediately before them.

And there were reasons.

It was not a minor, superficial distress that disturbed the feelings of these eleven men. No, furious storms were raging in that hour. There was darkness—such dreadful darkness that their souls were robbed of all understanding. No, they did not yet understand fully what was about to happen. They did not understand the character of the way, where it would go, or the depths through which it would lead. But everything indicated clearly that in the very near future they would lose the most precious possession they had; the Master would be taken from them. He had spoken to them about it repeatedly, but they did not understand him because they never wanted it to happen. In that very night they had seen the threatening signs of that inevitability. They saw it in the marvelous foot washing and the message that the savior gave through it; they saw it in the unmasking and expulsion of the betrayer who left in the depths of the night. They saw it in the institution of the Lord's supper, the signs of which pointed to shed blood and a broken body.

Now they were on the path. Where were they going?

What would happen in this night?

They did not understand. All they knew was that their hearts were troubled, and would be even more troubled.

Soon the troubling would completely dominate them when they would see the Master delivered into the hands of sinners and they would see him suffer, scorned and trodden down underfoot, despised and spit upon. They would be troubled when presently they would see their Lord swallowed up in the terrifying death of the cross. Surely, their hearts were troubled. And they had reasons. Violent storms of life were raging. Apparently their faith was becoming vain. The object of their hope was being taken away from them and the longing of their souls denied!

Such was the experience of the disciples.

So too, although perhaps in a less serious measure, it is for God's children today.

The way becomes sometimes very difficult for them. When only sadness upon sadness is one's lot and only sufferings smother one's soul without relief, it appears as if God destroys his own work, does not achieve his own purpose, does not fulfill his promise, denies his own faithfulness, rejects us, and allows his own cause to endure defeat.

Then our hearts are shaken to the very depths of their hidden recesses. Then peace disappears from our hearts, unrest rules, and torment of soul oppresses us.

Then the soul in all its powers is consumed with contemplation. And it is all fruitless.

Our hearts can become troubled.

———————

Let not your heart be troubled.

Wonderful word of power! So much more powerful and with much more significance, because he who speaks has the right to speak.

If the subject is the storms of life that trouble our hearts, he may indeed speak to us.

It is far too easy for those who have not known the storms of life by experience to give words of encouragement to one who is almost drowning in the pool of life's misery. It is far too easy for one who radiates health to encourage the sick in the way of submission and patience regarding the cross they must bear. It is far too easy for the wealthy to preach to the poor to be at peace with their lot. It is far too easy for those who know no misery and are not familiar with the agony of life, to sing,

In the deepest pain
Our hearts remain
At peace in the Lord!

As easily as such a word of comfort falls from the lips of one who has not known any grief, to that extent it is both superficial and comfortless. The wretched soul feels that the speaker does not understand what he says when he offers admonition and encouragement: "Let not your heart be troubled."

His word has no significance.

It lacks depth.

It does not grip one's heart.

Yet how different is this word of the savior! Was there ever one who had experienced misery as he did? Was there ever a way so deep, a path so dark, a suffering so extreme, that his path was not deeper, his way much darker, his suffering inexpressibly more horrible? Is he not the only one, who exactly for that reason can be our merciful high priest, who can have compassion upon us in our weaknesses because he was tempted in all points even as we are, yet without sin? No matter to what depths our path may take us in the future, most definitely the footprints of the Lord lead us onward!

No, still more.

Let not your heart be troubled. He spoke from a heart of love to his disciples to encourage them. But in what hour and in what circumstances did he attempt to comfort his disciples? Was it not the approaching final hour of which he had often spoken, the hour in which the powers of darkness would be let loose to crush him and apparently to triumph over him? Surely, in just a few hours his enemies would violently assault him and would spew forth the venom and of their hatred and malice in order to kill him. In just a few moments all the unrighteousness of all the brethren would be laid upon him, and the Christ would carry it. In a very short time the curse, rightly belonging to his people, would be his to carry. And he knew it. He knew the way before him. He knew the heavy, suffocating pressures that would press down upon his heart, and he knew what pains and agony would torment his body and soul. It was in that hour of thick darkness that his most fearful suffering was already beginning to fill him with dread, that hour in which he himself had need of comfort. In that hour he spoke lovingly to his disciples: "Let not your heart be troubled."

Wonderful message!

It was so very amazing, because not only did he himself know the misery of suffering as no one else, and not only because in that fearful hour he entered his deepest sufferings, but especially because he spoke with the certainty, the calm and joyful confidence, of final victory!

When he said, "Let not your heart be troubled," this was no empty, vain word, no hollow, insincere utterance, no mere groundless comfort. But it was his intent and purpose to assure his disciples and to cause them to live in the joy of faith in which he himself lived, so that there could be no reason whatsoever for them to be troubled in heart.

Surely he saw before him the deep way of his own suffering. Yet if he had seen only that suffering, his heart would also have been troubled, and it would have been no marvel that the hearts of his disciples would also have been troubled.

He saw, however, much more.

The author and finisher of our faith saw past the depths of sufferings and knew that all was well.

There was no reason to despair, no reason to hang the harp in the willows, even when God's way appears to be so dark.

Let not your heart be troubled.

———————

Be not troubled!

Be at peace—the peace that surpasses all understanding—when in the midst of raging storms and threatening hurricanes, in deep ways of suffering and in the darkest night.

But how? When, after having long pondered it, we cannot understand the way of the Lord and can see the way of the Most High only as being unjust, how will we obtain that peace of heart?

Ye believe in God. Believe also in me.

That is the way.

The way of peace.

In both parts of this statement, you must read an admonition: Believe in God and believe in me. You must not understand this statement as if in the first part Jesus mentions a fact and only in the second part expresses an admonition, so that he intends to say, "Ye believe in God already, now believe in me as well." No, in both instances you have admonition, encouragement, and inspiration: "Beloved, believe in God and believe in me." This twofold admonition is not to be understood as if believing in Jesus and believing in God are two different acts of our spirit, as if these two could ever be separated. Nor is the admonition to be understood in such a way that its two aspects are of equal importance. No, the savior's intent is "Believe in God through me. Believe in God as he has revealed himself in me and through me to you. Believe in the God of your complete salvation."

Believe in God and believe in me.

Let your faith—as it cleaves to God through me, as it knows and trusts in God through me—be a real working faith. Let that faith control your mind, rule your will, and take captive your whole life.

Then your heart will not be troubled, no matter how dark the way may be.

Then the peace that surpasses all understanding will keep your hearts and minds, no matter how dark the night of your suffering may be.

Indeed, God in Christ, the God who so wondrously loved you from before the foundation of the world, has granted to you the highest good, has reserved for you the most glorious salvation, and has foreordained that you should be conformed to the image of his Son and live with him eternally. He is the one who foreordained all things in such a way that they must work together to attain the glorious goal of your eternal blessedness in his tabernacle. Everything, literally everything—all things in heaven and on the earth, living and inert creatures, friend and foe, angel and devil, and all their activity and deeds—he has designated, arranged, and given such a place to them in his eternal counsel that they all must cooperate toward your salvation.

That is why everything is so very certain.

That is why everything, literally everything, is so wise and good. Therefore, there is no enemy that can do you harm, no adversity that can hurt you, no sickness and no death that does not serve your good. There are no storm clouds threatening, no hurricanes raging, no waves rising so high, no nights so dark, and no ranting enemies so hateful that they will ever be able to do anything other than work together for the good of those who love God.

Believe in God, believe also in me.

Believe in the God of your complete salvation.

Know him. Trust in him. Do not look first at the storms of life, at the enemies who would destroy you, but look first to God who has loved you with an eternal, unchangeable love revealed to you in Christ Jesus.

Then your heart will not be troubled. Then you know and feel in the depths of your soul that all is well.

Inexpressible peace!

18

The More Excellent House of Mourning

"It is better to go to the house of mourning, than to
go to the house of feasting: for that is the end of all
men; and the living will lay it to his heart."
—Ecclesiastes 7:2

"Blessed are ye that weep now: for ye shall laugh.
Woe unto you that laugh now! for ye shall mourn
and weep."

—Luke 6:21, 25

A whole year has flown by again.

It was a circular course: we made no headway.

Oh, certainly, Old Year's Eve marks an end. A part of our life's
journey is past. We came closer to the end, the end of our earthly
existence, the end of all things.

But a *telos*, a goal, we have not reached.

What has been is now and will be again. There is nothing new
under the sun.

True, God goes forward, for he never stands still in history. He
never retraces his footsteps, but always progresses from the Alpha
to the Omega. He builds his house, he maintains his covenant,
and he realizes his everlasting kingdom. Christ comes quickly. Yet
he does not come in the way of gradual development, of world im-
provement and cultural advancement, in the way of steadily drawing nearer to perfection and rising to heavenly realities. But he
comes quickly in the way of the miraculous, in the way of catas-
trophe, regeneration, world incineration, the resurrection, and the
renewing of all things.

He came that way once before.

Not as the ripe and most noble fruit of Israel and of our race, but as the impossible one, when Israel was almost extinguished, when our race appeared to be hopelessly lost, having been debauched by its culture. He came from above, from heaven, refusing every display of human culture. He came in a manger.

The wonder of the incarnation.

Therefore, he advanced toward his end. Not the illustrious end of a world power and world magnificence, not in order to cause the glorious earthly throne of David to be manifest again in majestic brilliance, and not to rule over the kingdoms of this world. But he advanced toward the cross, the bitter death that he had to taste as God's judgment, the death of the wrath of God, the bearing of the whole curse, including hell. Therefore, the cross is the end, the proclamation that David's earthly greatness and power is forever finished. The cross is the proclamation of the end of the body of sin, the end of a world that is rebellious before God, and the end of all things.

But he arose!

No, he did not arise in the way of evolution from the dead. Ah, there is no development from darkness toward the light, from the prison of sin toward the liberty and glory of the children of God, from death to life, from hell to heaven. There is only a deep, gaping chasm between them. Nonetheless, he arose by means of the death-destroying wonder.

And he ascended into the highest heavens, in order to sit on the right hand of God.

Yet he neither improved the world, nor pointed out a way that this world could be improved.

He came onto this world's stage. On it he fulfilled the will of his Father and returned whence he came. The stage remains unchanged. We lie here in the midst of death; we toil and struggle; we suffer and die.

Therefore, the new year that lies before us brings nothing new. Earth does not draw nearer to heaven, and the culture does not bring any fruits into the new Jerusalem.

Since that stage has not been changed at the end of your and my way, and at the end of the way of every man, there is always a house of mourning, a house of sorrow; since the stage has not been changed, and this earth is not gradually changed into the world to come; since the body of this death cannot of itself develop into the resurrection body; since your treasure cannot and may not be here on the stage of this world; since you are always dying here, and the end of your way is a house of mourning—you do not want to go to the house of feasting to celebrate by self-indulgent reveling, for in reality your life is lived in the chambers of death.

Weep! Let him who goes to revel in the house of feasting mourn, for he shall grieve and weep.

It is better to enter the house of mourning, for there is the end of all men.

Blessed are you who weep, for you shall laugh.

Although there is no evolutionary escape from our impending death, and although even you who hope in Christ will discover the house of mourning at the end of your way, there is for you the hope that rejoices.

For he comes again!

He will make all things new—new forever!

The house of morning will give way to the house of eternal rejoicing.

Blessed are they who mourn.

They will be comforted!

———————

Better it is to enter the house of mourning.

Better than to enter the house of feasting.

No, do not say that the preacher is too morbid, that he suffers from melancholy, that he is a gloomy person, a pessimist who sees everything in this world with dark-colored glasses and who, therefore, can find nothing good in our earthly life. Do not characterize the preacher as a malcontent who does not have an eye for the blessings of common grace. Do not characterize him as one who discovers the end of a thing to be better than its beginning, sadness to be better than joy, the house of mourning better than the banquet hall, and death better than life.

Do not say that. Do not say it on Old Year's Eve either. No, especially on Old Year's Eve, do not say it.

Can you not see that the vicious circle, the vanity of vanities of the repetition of earthly things, the stage of this world, is not changed into a direct line upward, into an "excelsior" that has its *terminus ad quem*, its final end and highpoint in heaven and in the everlasting perfection thereof? Do you not see that all things groan and sigh continually under the smothering oppression of vanity? Do you not see that nothing has been changed here on the stage of the earthly, nothing has been changed by the incarnation, by the cross, by the resurrection of Christ, and by his ascension into the eternal, blessed mansion of his Father? Do you not understand that although the angels did indeed sing "Peace on earth" in adoration of the infant in the manger, that peace has never come onto the stage of this world, nor ever will? But that peace waits—and of necessity must wait—for the destruction of this stage and for the realization of the new earth and the new heaven in which righteousness dwells?

Do you not hear the booming of the cannons, the rat-a-tat-tat of the machine guns, the roar of the bombers high in the sky? Do you not see the people running to bomb shelters like rats to their holes? Do you not hear the groans of the wounded, the death rattle of the dying, the weeping and anguish of the sorrowful in the homes of many thousands of people? Do you not hear the weeping of the world, even on Old Year's Eve? Will you then either forget all about the weeping of the world, or despite being burdened by it, go to the house of feasting and there attempt to drown out the moaning of fellow human beings and the lamentations of the world with the boisterous songs of drunkards, and to forget the pains of this world with the joy and happiness found in wine?

Should we spend the annual celebration of the end of the year in the house of feasting, now that we have gone through another cycle of the year?

But what will you do then with the body of this death? Or do you not experience every day—you, who are of Christ Jesus and in him and who confesses that through marvelous grace you have become a new creature—that the old has passed away and all things have become new? Do you not experience that all this is true insofar as you have a small beginning of the new obedience? Do you experience through the body of this death that you are pressed on all sides exactly because you possess that new principle of obedience in your heart, with the result that every day you cry out, "O wretched man that I am! Who shall deliver me from the body of this death?" Will you then go into the house of feasting with this cry of anguish in your soul, in order to silence it by means of the vain joy found in the tents of wickedness?

Will you spend Old Year's Eve in the house of feasting?

But are you not aware that by nature and insofar as you belong to the stage of this world, you lie in the midst of death, in the midst of temporal death as well, and that at the end of your way stands a house of mourning, to which your life directly and unavoidably leads? Do you not understand that the whole of your way is symbolized not by the house of feasting, but by the house of mourning, and that it is better, more fitting, wiser, and much more in harmony with reality for you to enter the house of sorrow?

But do you say that this is not the last word?

You know well the weight of the body of this death, but you are also a new creature. You indeed groan about not doing what you would, but you have as well a delight in the law of God. You utter a cry of distress: "Who shall deliver me?" But you know the answer as well: "I thank God through Jesus Christ our Lord!" You lie in the midst of death, but you have life eternal.

Yes, thanks be to God!

Therefore you are blessed in hope, and you rejoice by faith in the Lord.

But you do not enter with that joy into the house of feasting.

You cannot find here on the stage of this world an appropriate banquet hall to celebrate the blessedness that is from above.

The joy of heaven causes you to sing in the house of mourning:

Within his house, the house of prayer,
My soul shall bless the Lord
And praises to his holy name
Let all his saints accord.

You learn this song—you, who have grace to be able to learn it—not in the house of feasting, but in the house of mourning.

For blessed are you. Yes, blessed are you who weep, for you shall laugh.

Blessed are they who mourn—who through faith mourn—and who therefore mourn triumphantly.

They will be comforted!

Enter, then, into the house of mourning.

For there you will find the wise.

The heart of the foolish is in the house of feasting.

Admittedly, you do not have to associate the house of feasting with drunkenness and gluttony, music and song and dance and boisterousness in the most offensive sense. Some have so interpreted the statement of the preacher, because they did not know how else to explain it. The house of feasting is then the place of ungodliness and unfettered recklessness that gives free rein to the lusts of the flesh. But that is not the contrast. Consider only the fellowship of "decent" people of the world at a worldly feast. People eat and drink, they laugh and joke, they are joyful and sing, though they do not know why.

People are joyful when the new year makes its entrance.

People are joyful when the old year takes its leave of them.

At the beginning of the year they sought out the house of feasting, because they thought that it would bring something new, something better. And now the end of the year has arrived. Once again they seek the house of feasting, in order to forget that it is an end.

Obviously the world of unbelievers does not want an end. The fool is afraid of the end. And in the house of feasting the end is not acknowledged. Therefore, in that house is found the fool's heart. For although his way is nothing but vanity, he flatters himself in his foolish pride by saying in his heart, "My house will stand forever." He wants to believe that. Although everything on the stage of this present time loudly proclaims the opposite, still he attempts to convince himself that his house will exist forever. On Old Year's Eve and on New Year's morning he seeks the house of feasting, for there the end is not acknowledged.

But the heart of the wise is in the house of mourning. For in that house is the end of every man.

That house of mourning is indeed the house of sorrow, the chapel of the mortician. There people are given to sorrow. There people weep the loss of a loved one who has entered his own house of mourning at the end of his way.

To that house turn the wise who have the fear of God in their hearts, who have been born from above, who have been regenerated unto a living hope by the resurrection of Jesus Christ from the dead—but who still live their lives on this stage of time, who still lie in the midst of death, who also wrestle against the body of this death, who still groan, being burdened, who still must be unclothed that they may be clothed upon, who still must go through death in order to enter into life. The children of God, therefore, do indeed rejoice with an inexpressibly glorious joy, but they still grieve because of their sin and death. Only they purposely enter into the house of mourning. What would the fool do there? Certainly, he has to go there sometimes. But then he despairs and flees from the house of mourning as fast as possible, in order immediately to deceive his heart with vanity in the house of feasting.

Yet the wise man goes into the house of mourning.

Oh, no, he does not go to comfort all the grieving there. How can he comfort others, when he himself is in the house of mourning? But he goes there because it is the final end of all men.

That truth he lays away in his heart. He sees the end in the light of an eternally new beginning. He sees the end of death, of sin, of the world, of his grieving and weeping, of vanity and of the earthly. He sees everything in the light of eternal life, of perfection, of heavenly blessedness, of the freedom and of the glory of the children of God.

Blessed are you, who now weep.

Your weeping will become an eternal laughing.

In heavenly joy!

19

The Joy of Many Temptations

"My brethren, count it all joy when ye fall into divers
temptations; Knowing this, that the trying of your
faith worketh patience. But let patience have her perfect work, that ye may be perfect and entire, wanting
nothing."

—James 1:2–4

A wonderful message!

If you fall into temptations, all kinds of temptations, then consider the temptations that surround you and that are crafted for
your demise as a cause of great joy. Do not find anything else in
them, but esteem them entirely and completely as joy, as the original language states it. Temptations are only and exclusively a cause
for your happiness.

Whoever understands even in a limited measure, and has
learned by personal experience what is really involved in falling
into temptation does not immediately concur that this is a wonderful message. It is a message that we do not easily accept and
apply to our actual practice in life. It is a message that the most
sanctified can practice only after long and trying experiences.

Oh, it is possible to read this text superficially and to say that
it is such a beautiful and comforting message for God's child, as
long as we ourselves do not actually bear suffering. It is not difficult for a superficial person to quote this text to him whose way
offers nothing but pain and sorrow. A superficial person can so
easily bring this word as long as his own way is strewn with roses.
We frequently see that one who is aglow with health, while at the

bedside of a man or woman who writhes in pain or is overcome with grief, offers comfort by singing,

> *In the greatest affliction*
> *Our hearts remain*
> *Trusting in the Lord.*

But let severe affliction, trouble and distress, fear and pain, and divers temptations come upon you. Let Satan receive permission from the Almighty to touch everything you have, so that as Job you are suddenly cast down into the dust on the rubble heaps of your possessions and find yourself amid ten coffins in which the bodies of your children will soon be buried. Let Satan also receive permission to rack your body with pain. Let the world be offended at your faithful confession and its offense demonstrated by denying you a place in its midst, so that your name and position, your freedom, and even your living must be abandoned for Christ's name sake. Then try to sing it!

Note that the text does not admonish you to be silent in the midst of temptations.

The world can do that sometimes, at least outwardly.

The Stoic made it his philosophy of life to steel himself against all adversity, pain, distress, and sorrow, so that he could smother every complaint of his lips in the face of terrible pain and could endure the deepest suffering without even the slightest observable wince. Even today you meet people who are able to be silent under a heavy burden of suffering, to carry their burden of suffering, and to harden themselves in adversity. Also God's child can sometimes be silent in the midst of oppression, while fearing the Lord and believing that all things have been appointed him by his Father in heaven. He is not rebellious, but is submissive to the will of the majestic, sovereign God. Blessed is he who has learned by grace to be silent amid the greatest afflictions and to trust in the Lord his God.

But the admonition of James aims much higher.

Account it a great joy—as nothing but joy—when you fall into many kinds of temptations.

Glory in tribulation!

Powerful message!

———————

Many temptations!

The term translated in the text as "temptations" could be translated just as well as "trials."

Although there is a great difference in meaning between these words, there is also a very close connection between them.

The same circumstances, experiences, sufferings, and adversities are frequently both trials and temptations.

Yet the two terms view the same experience of life from two entirely different viewpoints.

Temptations always have hatred as their cause. Whoever tempts you, even though he does it under the appearance of friendship, is never your friend, but always your enemy. Trials have their motive in love. Temptations always intend your fall. They have as their purpose to seduce you to sin, to cause you to be unfaithful to your confession, to deny your Lord and savior, to cause you to forsake the ways of God's commandments in order to cause you to seek your happiness in the world, in the lust of the flesh, the lust of the eyes, and the pride of life. But trials intend your salvation. They intend to strengthen the work of grace that God has accomplished in you. Trials are employed to cause the work of grace to shine more brilliantly to the honor of him who wrought it in your heart. Temptations are directed toward your sinful flesh, to your covetousness that lives and works in your heart, in order to awaken it and to move you to satisfy it. But trials are directed toward the work of grace in your heart. Trials oppose the powers of Satan, the world, and our flesh to the work of grace, in order to goad it to the battle, to strengthen it in and through the battle, and to cause it to be victorious and purified, just as one would purify silver by fire.

Therefore, God never tempts.

God cannot be tempted with evil and he tempts no one.

If anyone is tempted and he yields to and falls into sin, he attributes it to his own covetousness that deceived and seduced him. Whatever is conceived by the world and Satan soon gives birth to sin and death.

The text does use the words "fall into divers temptations" in this sense. When understood in this sense, it is not a cause of joy, but a cause of deep sadness and bitter remorse that you do fall, that you do yield to temptations, through which by your own covetousness you are seduced and led astray.

But the meaning is that you may and should esteem it as a great joy when the powerful forces of Satan and of the world surround you on all sides, pursue you, and attack you in order to destroy you, to oppress you, and to cause you to suffer for Christ's name's sake, so that your falling into the world's hands and under its power does not allow you any room to exist in the world.

Divers temptations.

Many are the snares of Satan. Manifold are the tricks of the evil world. Many are the endeavors of the powers of darkness to mislead God's child and to ruin God's work in him. There is the direct influence of the prince of darkness, by which he attempts to move you to rebel against God and to murmur in times of adversity, or in times of prosperity to attempt to move you to pride and to trust in self. There is the seduction of the world, in which it offers you honor and greatness, money and possessions, name and position, if only you will do what the world wills and bow down and kneel before its prince. There are also awful threats, rage and hatred, persecution and oppression, by which it deprives you of everything if you refuse to be unfaithful to him who purchased you with his precious blood. In addition, there is also your own flesh, the sinful passions of the body, without which neither Satan nor the world can have a hold on you, but which cooperate in fellowship with the forces of darkness that encircle you.

Indeed, many temptations.

Oh, no, you did not seek them out.

You did not in sinful recklessness enter the pathway that would lead you into the midst of those powerful temptations.

Rather, you sought to flee from them.

But you fell into temptation.

God himself caused all those temptations to come up against you.

And now you are called to the battle.

The battle of faith!

Account it nothing but a joy!

It is no vain joy without a basis in reality to which God's word awakens us.

When Scripture says that we are to account it a great joy— pure joy—when we fall into many temptations, it is because those temptations are really reasons for gladness.

He who has this life as his goal, who sets his heart upon those things that are seen, and who seeks the salvation of his soul in temporal things understands nothing of this truth and its fundamental spiritual basis. How can adversity and suffering in this present time ever be a reason for joy? After all, suffering in itself can never be an occasion for joy. The child of God does not find happiness in pain and misery in themselves.

Yet he who sees things differently and does not look at the visible things that are temporal, but looks to the invisible things that are eternal may really take delight in oppression, and may account it nothing but joy when he falls into divers temptations. A rich spiritual fruit is found in those temptations. This is indicated in the expression "the trying of your faith." Through temptations your faith is tried. This is indeed not the purpose of the tempter. The contrary is truly his purpose. Satan, the world, and our own sinful flesh do not intend to test our faith through temptations, but to destroy it. Yet the Lord our God, who ultimately is the one who leads us into these many temptations, does in fact achieve his purpose. Also the forces of darkness are subordinate to him. The devil, the world, and our sinful flesh must serve him. God uses those temptations as trials. The faith that is being tried is the Lord's own work. That faith cannot be lost, for God himself preserves it. He casts his own work into the flaming crucible of temptations in order to prove it.

God's purpose with his own work in us is thus attained.

Never any other purpose.

That is a reason for joy, nothing but joy, for when God through temptations proves our faith, that faith becomes pure, just as silver is purified by the fire. The false is separated from the genuine, and the genuine shines forth with a more glorious luster. So it is with the Christian personally. Through the battle he is strengthened, confirmed, and grounded. The longer he is tried, the more he learns to have no confidence in himself and in his sinful strength. He learns to hold ever more tightly and always to the God of his perfect salvation in Christ Jesus. It is the same for the church of Christ. In the heat of temptation, pseudofaith cannot endure and cannot sustain itself. The result is that it becomes evident who fears the Lord and who does not.

Consequently, faith receives a proven character through the means of temptations.

Undoubtedly the text must be read according to the meaning of the original: "Knowing that the proven character of your faith works patience."

That tried faith works patience.

Patience is an additional fruit of temptation, in which the child of God who seeks the things that are above may rejoice greatly.

Patience is not a natural decision, a stoic attitude of indifference toward the suffering of this present time. The child of God does not harden himself against life's pains. He feels the suffering. He feels it very deeply. He feels the pain of life ever more deeply, because he has within him the principle of eternal happiness. He yearns and groans under the dreadful weight of suffering, and he longs with all his strength for the perfect and final deliverance.

Patience is not a certain natural endurance by which one takes an attitude of resignation in the face of the unavoidable.

No, patience is the fruit of grace, specifically produced by proven faith. It is the resilience of faith by which we are enabled, in the midst of all the attacks of Satan, to remain faithful, to stay standing, and to bear suffering with joy for Christ's name's sake.

It causes us to rejoice in the victory in the midst of the battle. It causes us to be more than conquerors through our savior who has loved us, knowing that the enemy and his temptations must serve our salvation. The child of God in his spiritual patience is clearly conscious of the final, complete, and eternal victory in the day of Christ.

Toward that final glory patience looks, esteeming the afflictions of this present time as very light and transitory.

Of that final victory patience is assured.

By means of the final victory, which rejoices the heart, patience receives new strength and courage to fight on in the battle to its very end and willingly to endure suffering. That patience is the strength by which we struggle to the heights of Zion.

Nothing but joy!

———————

Be not afraid then!

Let patience work her perfect work.

Do not limp along on two conflicting ideas. Be not double-hearted.

Do not attempt to serve your savior and your king, and mammon too. Do not fight and resist the enemy on one hand, while on the other hand collaborating with him and giving him access. Do not be halfhearted. No matter what happens, no matter how the enemy rages, no matter what he may take from you, no matter how fierce the persecution, no matter how deep and bitter the suffering may be, no matter how intense the battle, do not give up anything to the enemy. Never hesitate, never make a peace treaty with the enemy of your king.

Persevere to the very end!

Let your patience be complete; let it be a perfect work.

Then, and only then, will you be upright and wholly upright in this world. Only then will you be lights in the midst of darkness, friends of God as opposed to his enemies, faithful in all things, and never unfaithful.

Soon you will be blessed!

Eternally!

20

Glorying in Tribulations

"And not only so, but we glory in tribulations also:
knowing that tribulation worketh patience; And
patience, experience; and experience, hope."
                                        —Romans 5:3, 4

Not only this!

Surely, this as well: We rejoice in the hope of the glory of God!

Without this rejoicing in the hope of the glory of God, it is absolutely impossible to glory in tribulation.

After all, whoever glories in tribulations is not rejoicing in this
tribulation for its own sake, but glories in it with a view to the fruit
that it produces. Tribulation indeed works patience, and patience
works experience, and experience works hope. In tribulation everything revolves around hope. Whoever rejoices in tribulation, to
him hope is precious above all things. He is willing, therefore, to
give up everything if only he can have this hope. In order to possess this hope, and to possess it in ever greater measure—to taste
it, to feel the joy of it welling up in his heart, to rest in its certainty,
and to reach out to its goal with all the desire of his soul—he gives
up his possessions and riches, his name and position, his freedom
and his life. For that hope he is prepared to suffer and to endure
the slander and abuse that Christ endured—to die!

Therefore, he is able to glory in tribulation.

That hope is, after all, the hope of the glory of God.

That glory of God is its object. Soon, very soon, he who rejoices in tribulation will be clothed with glory himself. It will not
merely encircle him and shine all around him; he will not merely

see it all around him. But it will itself be reflected in his own nature and in his own face; it will be mirrored in his thinking and willing, because then he will be made wholly conformable unto the image of the Son of God.

He will be like him.

For he will see him as he is.

He rejoices, therefore, in that hope of the glory of God. He is assured that he will share in it, because it is in principle his portion already in Christ Jesus.

He rejoices in that hope.

To taste the joy of that hope already in this life is for him above all things most precious.

For this too we hope.

But not only for this.

For standing in the grace of peace with God through Christ Jesus our Lord and rejoicing in the glory of God, we also rejoice in tribulation.

The end of the way of tribulation is hope; the end is a greater hope, an always more confident hope, and an always fuller and richer hope.

Because tribulation works patience.

Patience then works experience.

And experience, hope.

———————

A powerful act of faith!

Marvelous revelation of God's rich grace that is always all-sufficient for every circumstance of life. We glory in tribulation also.

Note that "we." The Bible lays that language of faith upon the lips of all of God's people. It is the intent of Scripture that we take this word upon our lips as a personal confession and that we echo this declaration: We rejoice also in tribulation.

Or at least, it is the intent of Scripture that by sincerely attempting to make this statement our personal confession, we turn inward to examine ourselves whether or not it is true of us that we glory in tribulation.

Truly, it is not appropriate for us to take this language of jubilation upon our lips too easily and too thoughtlessly. Indeed, so often we are very far removed from that position of faith in which alone it is possible to glory in tribulation. It is so very easy to speak about glorying in tribulation. Merely talking about it is easy, as long as the suffering of this present time does not touch us, if the tribulation does not affect us, and if the fire of purification does not singe our clothing. When everything is sunshine and prosperity, and happiness and joy characterize our path of life, we can talk far too easily about glorying in tribulation. But let the tribulation become reality for us. Let suffering according to body and soul—by which our place in the world becomes narrow, so that we are shoved aside and pressured—become reality. Let pain consume our bodies; let our souls wither away in sorrow. Let our enemy ridicule us, taunt us, and walk all over us. Let death rob us of what is dearer than life to us. Let adversity after adversity be our lot, so that poverty and misery are daily our companions on life's pathway. Then let us take the Bible's language of rejoicing upon our lips: We glory in tribulation.

Then it becomes real, the reality of life.

It becomes real when the enemy rages and we are called upon to suffer affliction according to the will of Christ, and following him, to carry his cross.

Or when in a general sense the sufferings of this present time are our lot.

Then it becomes serious: We glory in tribulation.

But this language frequently dies on our lips. We quickly collapse in the weakness of faith and hope. We suddenly lose the proper perspective that all things must work together for the good of those who love God, and instead of rejoicing our unbelieving hearts murmur against our bitter lot, against our difficult way, against God's daily chastisements, and against God.

We glory also in tribulation.

No, this does not merely mean that we can glory *despite* tribulation. Such a glorying while *in the midst of* tribulation is appropriate. It is most definitely proper to rejoice in God's love and grace, rejoicing in many blessings that we may receive and enjoy while we are *in the midst of* tribulation, and rejoicing in the ultimate realization of our hope that awaits us, and in so much more than the thankful heart may be aware of while in affliction. Such glorying definitely exceeds the disgruntled murmuring against God that characterizes unthankful unbelief, or the timid complaint that everything is against us. Such glorying amid tribulation is pleasing unto God and creates joy in the heart of God's child.

Yet such glorying is not the same glorying that Scripture intends when it lays on our lips the words: We glory also in tribulation.

The latter is far superior. It is more significant. It is the language of victory. It makes of enemies, friends; of the evil, an eternal good; of the attackers who besiege us, servants; of tribulation itself, a reason for great happiness. Account it a great joy, my brothers, when you fall into all manner of temptations. That is the meaning of glorying in tribulation. It means not merely to glory in the midst of tribulations, but to glory on the basis of and because of tribulation.

Tribulation is the ground of our glorying.

It is the object of our praise.

Whoever glories in tribulation sees something in it, regards it as being of great value, sets a high price upon it, and speaks well concerning it.

So that he is happy in and with the tribulation.

He is more than conqueror.

Marvelous grace!

———————

Rejoicing because of tribulation!

But why? What is there in tribulation that allows us to glory in it? Certainly there is nothing in tribulation itself about which to glory. It is suffering. And suffering does not effect rejoicing, but occasions complaint. It does not exalt one, but brings one low.

Also God's child—yes, especially God's child—is afraid before the reality of suffering. He does not take an indifferent attitude toward it, as does the stoic. Much less does he seek suffering and find a certain sickly pleasure in suffering as such. When pain is his lot, he is afraid; when tribulation threatens, he is anxious and cries out because of its suffocating pressure. In the midst of deep sadness, his soul dolefully laments. He does not lift himself up above the suffering and the tribulation. He descends into despair.

Was not Jesus' own soul filled with agony and deeply saddened to the point of death itself when he wrestled in the garden, and his sweat was as it were great drops of blood?

When God's child glories in tribulation, he does so because of the marvelous fruit that becomes his in the way of tribulation. For tribulation works patience, patience works experience, and experience works hope. It is that ultimate fruit that motivates the Christian. That hope is his possession. He rejoices in that hope of the glory of God. He proceeds in the way of tribulation from hope to hope and goes through the stages of patience and experience.

On account of that fruit he rejoices in tribulation.

It may be compared to a bitter medicine about which people boast, not because of its taste, but because of its healing properties and power. Or we may liken it to a painful operation that people seek and value highly, not for the operation itself, but for its result.

So it is with tribulations.

They work. And through working, tribulations produce fruit —fruit that he who rejoices in the glory of God values so greatly that he suffers willingly to obtain it. For the tribulation is natural, the fruit is spiritual; the tribulation is temporal, the fruit is eternal: patience, experience, and hope.

Tribulation works patience.

It is a precious fruit of grace produced through the means of tribulation. Patience must not be confused with man's natural power to endure suffering that you sometimes encounter in the world of unbelief. On the part of the natural man you may sometimes find an unusual capacity to endure suffering, whether it is because he has a patient nature, or because he has taught himself not to wince even when enduring the most agonizing suffering. Patience is a spiritual fruit of God's grace in Christ. It is not a proud resolve regarding suffering; it is not a natural patience amid suffering. It is the grace to will the will of God even when God's will for us is suffering. It is the resilience of faith through which we contently endure suffering for Christ's name sake. It is the strength of trusting, through which we know that all things work for the good of those who love God and in which we cast our entire way upon God. It is the strength of grace unto perseverance, through which grace we are faithful unto the end. It is realized through tribulation, not because in tribulation itself there is any operative power unto patience, but because it is God's purpose through tribulation to make his children patient and to bring them presently through suffering to glory.

Tribulation works patience, because it must serve as an instrument of God's grace.

Moreover, patience works experience.

Experience describes the state in which one has been spiritually tested. This is the meaning of the original word. Patience produces a state of proven quality. Gold is cast into the fire and is purified in it. Soon it emerges tested from the fire and found to be genuine. It has been purified. It has been cleansed of all foreign substances. It shines now with greater luster. Likewise, through tribulation the child of God is made patient. God's child is found genuine, for instead of collapsing under the weight of tribulation, he has learned patience, and he has learned to will the will of God in suffering and to regard God's will as his highest delight. God's child is cleansed and purified through suffering. It is good for him to have been oppressed, so that he would learn God's holy rule. He is strengthened while in tribulation, for God's hand upheld him even while it struck him. Thus God's work of grace shines even more gloriously in the life of a tried and tested child of God. Greater wisdom and spiritual capacity for the battle have become his portion. The oppressed, patient believer increases in spiritual strength, in courage of faith, in trust, and in the inward certainty that the victory awaits him.

And so experience, the state of tried and tested spirituality, works hope.

Hope is the new life reaching out to heaven, to the final fulfillment of the promise, to the glory of God. Hope is looking forward, looking upward, anticipating. It is not the shrugging of the shoulders to express uncertainty, but it is certainty in relation to the goal of the glory of God and in relation to personal participation in that goal, and it is a longing for its final fulfillment.

Proving, through trial, works hope!

Not as if hope has its source in testing and trying. On the contrary, hope is present in the heart before tribulation is one's lot. No, hope is already glorying when the believer in hope enters tribulation. We rejoice in the hope of the glory of God; that is the beginning. Without that rejoicing, our courage would fail to engage tribulation. But tested and tried faith increases in hope. Certainty of faith becomes even stronger. The longing for heaven becomes stronger. Indifference to the things below increases, and the seeking of the things above becomes more focused.

The proven child of God is bound to the treasures of heaven with even stronger bands.

Sanctified though tribulation, with ever stronger desire he longs to see the Lord.

To be like him.

To participate in the glory of God.

And he rejoices in tribulation.

Knowing!

God's child glories in tribulation, *knowing* that tribulation works patience, and patience works experience, and experience, hope.

He is convinced of that before he enters tribulation.

Therefore, he glories in tribulation. Not after it is past and after he has been tried and tested, not after the fruit of richer hope has been plucked, and he has learned to love God's justice. No, he already glories even before he enters tribulation. He rejoices when tribulation threatens. He rejoices because of the tribulation even while he is in the midst of it. He is triumphant while he complains. He is happy in the midst of sorrow. He laughs through his tears. He glories in the victory while he is still in the battle.

Knowing!

And this he knows because he stands in the grace of peace with God.

Through Christ Jesus, the Lord, who always gives him peace with all things!

21

Zion, A Secure Refuge

"What shall one then answer the messengers of the
nation? That the LORD hath founded Zion, and the
poor of his people shall trust in it."
—Isaiah 14:32

Zion, a secure refuge!

When all around Zion it becomes dark, when threatening
clouds gather on the horizon, announcing a storm; when the
rumble of the thunder of approaching judgment is heard nearby,
and when the wasting judgments break forth, the people become fearful. The children of Zion recognize the approaching
judgment, the devastation drawing ever nearer for the ungodly
world. And Zion, living in the midst of those upon whom the
judgment will be executed, does not see any possibility of es-
caping it.

Terrified, they send out messengers to ask, "What will now
happen to Zion? How will Zion ever escape the threatening danger, the judgment that will crush everything?" What answer will
be given to these messengers? How will anyone comfort and assure the people who live in Zion that all will be well and that when
judgment will have been executed and the storm will have blown
itself out, the city of God will still stand and her inhabitants will
be safe? The answer will be that the Lord has founded Zion. The
city for which he has laid the foundation will stand. The distressed
of his people will find in her a secure citadel even in the midst of
the most dreadful judgments.

The future looked dark.

It seemed impossible that a safe refuge could be found in Zion for the distressed of the people.

Much rather, it appeared unavoidable that Jerusalem would be crushed in the destruction that, according to the prophet, would definitely come.

The prophet had proclaimed judgment upon the Philistines.

The term "Palestina" in verses 29 and 31 means the land of Israel's neighbors and archenemies. It was proper and good that their judgment was coming upon them. They were the children of Mizraim, the second son of Ham. They had always been the bitter enemies of Zion. They allied themselves with the other heathen nations against Israel and sought the destruction of Jerusalem and the people of the Lord. Since the time of Abraham they had lived in a small strip of land on the Mediterranean seacoast. They had not been immediately subdued by Israel. Although they had to bend the knee in subjection to Israel, as in the days of David, Jehoshaphat, and Hezekiah, they had not been exterminated, and consequently they plagued the people of the Lord whenever opportunity presented itself. Certainly it was a cause for joy that the prophet proclaimed the judgment of the Lord concerning these enemies of Zion. According to the prophetic perspective, swarms of hostile forces were coming from the north as the instruments of the Lord for the execution of his verdict upon the enemies of God's cause and kingdom. Indeed, Zion might rejoice.

A troubling question, however, arose when they saw these advancing enemies who would punish the Philistines.

Were not the Philistines Israel's neighbors?

Would the hostile forces from the north, thick as a smoke cloud and marching ever closer, be satisfied with the utter devastation of the land of the Philistines? Would they not desire to march against Zion as well, and would not Jerusalem also be overwhelmed in the very same judgment that would fall upon God's enemies?

When the messengers come, having been sent out by Zion to inquire about this, what answer will be given to them?

Zion is the church of God in all ages. In the old dispensation it was the temple mount where God lived among his people. At the same time it was the royal mountain where God ruled over his people whom he had chosen for his inheritance. Later, Zion is the church of God throughout all ages, even as God in Christ has established his covenant of friendship with them, lives among them, and has fellowship with them, blessing them with all the gifts of salvation, and as her king rules over her in and through Christ her head.

The church lives in the midst of a world that becomes the object of God's judgments because it is hostile to God and his cause—a world that because of its sin lies under the curse and in death, and that walks inevitably toward God's waiting judgment, according to his sure prophetic word.

The devastation of the first world in the flood, the destruction of Sodom, the destruction of apostate Jerusalem, and wars and pestilences are all the beginning of sorrows and types of the coming final judgment. The end comes soon. Then the ungodly world will suffer a final defeat forever, and in the flames of the final, blazing conflagration even the elements shall melt.

Good. But what will become of Zion amid those divine judgments?

What answer will be given to the messengers who inquire about these things?

What will become of God's church in the midst of the universal flood, by which the first world would perish according to the word of Noah? As Abraham, God's friend, asks out of heartfelt concern for the few righteous individuals who live in Sodom, when the cities of ungodliness are about to be burned to the ground, what will really happen? What will happen to God's church, when presently Jerusalem is laid waste?

And what will become of Zion, when the final judgment comes and everything is cleansed by fire?

What? Oh, what answer will men give to the messengers?

Their answer must be that God's church is perfectly safe amid all of God's judgments. The downcast of his people find in Zion a fortress and will live safely there.

In the flood Zion does not drown. She is saved by the water.

The righteous are not killed with Sodom's ungodly. God knows how to rescue righteous Lot, even through the means of fire.

When God's judgment falls upon Jerusalem, which had become like unto Sodom and Gomorrah, the remnant according to the election of grace is spared and continues to live.

Wars and pestilences do not devour the church of the Lord.

So too, in the final judgment Zion will remain standing.

The distressed of the people will live in Zion eternally.

Safe refuge!

———————

Zion is never crushed!

Whoever seeks a refuge in Zion amid storms and dangers and in the midst of wars and destruction will never be put to shame.

Are you deeply concerned?

In fear do you ask for a sure basis that can give you the confidence that Zion will never be crushed?

Then know this: Jehovah God has established the foundation of Zion. Therefore, it is a strong fortress. Its foundation has been laid by a mighty, an eternal, and a wise master builder. The fortress of Zion is as strong and secure and solid as its foundation! Men build strong forts that are no stronger than they are. God's citadel is as strong and as secure as the eternal God himself.

For he is the Lord.

His name is Jehovah.

He is the eternal one. Therefore, all his work is in him. The foundation of Zion is also an eternal act of God. In the counsel of Jehovah God, the foundation of Zion is eternally established and laid from before the foundation of the world. He is the immutable one; he is unchangeable in himself, in his essence, the one who does not subtract nor add, the perfect and eternally complete one, with whom there is no variableness nor shadow of turning. He is the immutable one also in his counsel, whose work is without regret, who never finds a reason in himself or outside of himself to change the content of his thoughts or the decree of his will, who never abandons the work of his hands, and who brings to completion whatever he has begun. Therefore, the founding of Zion is an unchangeable act of God. Consequently, Zion's foundations can never be destroyed. In the Lord alone lies the cause of the fact that Zion endures eternally, and that it is possible with confidence to tell the messengers of the people that there is no emergency, that the distressed of the people will dwell safely in Zion, even when in the midst of raging storms and violent enemies—God's devastating acts and judgments upon the world.

After all, Jehovah is God and no one else.

Zion's God, the rock and fortress of Israel, is their eternal savior.

He is the Almighty, the only sovereign God. Beside him there is none else. No creature has any power except from God alone. Nothing exists or works but by his will. If he then works, who will resist it? Who will ever oppose his arm of strength? If God has founded Zion in eternity with an unchangeable decree of his counsel, who will ever be able to thwart his firm decree? He is the all-wise God, the omniscient God, the only wise God, and he is infinite in his wisdom. Therefore, he has laid Zion's foundation in such a way that it will be able to endure and to remain amid the storms of all ages, the storms of hostile forces, the storms of destruction and death that are God's judgments and curse upon the world. No, there is more. Even the storms are his, appointed according to his wisdom, and ordained to serve for the great glory of Zion. It is all of him alone. No one gave him advice or counsel to instruct him. What plot of the enemy can be laid successfully against that eternal wisdom and actually accomplish Zion's fall?

What answer will be given to the messengers of the people when the enemies march ever nearer, when judgment comes?

Will men comfort them with mere human wisdom, with something born of vain man, with the basic goodness of man's will, and with the certainty of man's trustworthiness? Will men give the messengers of Zion the advice to seek help from Egypt, from the world?

By no means! What salvation can there be by mere man, whose breath is in his nostrils? He is less than vanity and nothingness.

No! But this answer will be given to them: The Lord has founded Zion.

The foundation that God has laid for Zion is Christ Jesus. He is the foundation of the apostles and prophets and the chief cornerstone thereof, on which everything rests and is secure. He has been set from eternity, for the triune God has chosen and foreordained him to be the foundation on which Zion will eternally stand. That foundation is sure, strong, solid, unchangeable, and immovable, for Christ is the eternal Son, God out of God, Immanuel! The Lord, the triune covenant God, has laid that foundation also in time, for he has sent the Son in our flesh for the purpose of being Zion's eternal foundation. God formed him and prepared him to be Zion's foundation when he delivered him over to death as the foundation of his righteousness, when he raised him up, and when he glorified him and caused him to ascend to the highest heavens, setting him at his right hand as the eternal, sure, indestructible foundation of the heavenly Zion.

The Lord has founded Zion.

The foundation on which he has built Zion will never perish.

That foundation stands amid sin and guilt, storms and devastation, death and judgments. The gates of hell will not prevail against Zion, because her foundation is sure.

Zion journeys straight through every storm unto the glory of the eternal kingdom.

Zion, a secure refuge!

Give that answer, then, to Zion's messengers!

Provide them with the comforting message that the Lord has founded Zion.

And you, messengers of the people, hasten to return and notify the distressed people that they need not be afraid for the security of Zion and that in Zion they will dwell safely!

They live in Zion now; they will dwell there unto all eternity.

Distressed of the people.

The meaning is not that some of God's people are distressed, while others are not. That is indeed true in a certain sense, at various times, and from a particular viewpoint. But here it is different. The distressed of the people are all of God's children in the world. God's people as a whole are distressed so long as they have not yet reached heaven's glory. The church is distressed in the world and by the world. She has no place in the world; she is pressured on every side; she is persecuted for the sake of righteousness and for the cause of the Son of God; she endures the suffering of this present time.

God's people are distressed because of sin.

They themselves make their debt of guilt greater every day. They were born in unrighteousness and conceived in sin. Even as they live in Zion, they constantly carry with them the body of this death. The power of sin still operates and rages in them; the sinful operations of the flesh constantly make themselves known. The people of God must confess until the day of their death that they do not do what they would, but what they would not, that they do. Thus they cry out in great distress and in longing for complete deliverance: "O, wretched man that I am! Who shall deliver me from the body of this death?" They are distressed also because of the enemy, the power of darkness, who hates them because they are of the light and walk in the light. In all kinds of ways and by all sorts of means, the world hinders their way, grants them no room, persecutes them and causes them to suffer for Christ's name's sake. And in their dejection and suffering they cry out to the Lord of Sabaoth: "How much longer, O Lord?"

But they have in Zion a refuge.

There, in Zion, which Jehovah God has founded, they have learned to seek a refuge and a fortress. They seek there a fortress against sin and guilt, a refuge against the forces of destruction and death, a fortress against the enemy and the powers of darkness, in order to be delivered and securely protected by the Lord—and by him alone—from all these forces of destruction. They have sought there a refuge against judgment.

When it becomes ever so dark, what then?

When the enemy, as a thick rolling smoke cloud, comes marching from the north toward its enemies as the instrument of God's judgments, to lay waste the land of the Philistines, what answer will be given? And when it appears unavoidable that in that judgment Zion also will be crushed, what then?

When soon the final judgment comes and the elements will melt, what answer will be given to the messengers of the people?

That the Lord has laid the foundation of Zion!

Therefore, even amid storms and judgments, Zion is always a secure refuge for the distressed of the people. It is God's purpose that every one of his distressed people will dwell safely there.

Fear not then, you who are distressed!

Zion is a secure refuge!

22

A Safe Refuge

"Yea, in the shadow of thy wings will I make my
refuge, until these calamities be overpast."

—Psalm 57:1

Excelsior!

Out of the depths of trouble and fear to the heights of praise
and glorying in the God of our salvation.

On the wings of prayer.

This ascent characterizes the contents of many Old Testament
psalms. Many of them are occasioned by trouble and distress and
are pressed from the heart of the poet by fear and anguish of soul
because of the enemy that oppresses him, that surrounds him on
every side, that makes it humanly impossible for him to survive.
Out of those depths he struggles, clinging by faith to him who is
invisible, embracing his immutable promises, and ascending on
the wings of prayer to the glorious heights of victorious confidence
on which he is able to break forth in joyous praise and glory to Jehovah, his refuge and strength.

Thus it is also in this psalm.

The psalmist is in deep affliction.

His soul is among lions, surrounded by the sons of men,
"whose teeth are spears and arrows, and their tongue a sharp
sword." They have prepared a net for his steps; his soul is bowed
down; they have dug a pit before him. Deeply he feels the reproach
of him who would swallow him up. Calamities threaten to overwhelm him.

Although his soul is bowed down and he sees no way out, his

faith is not crushed. By that faith he struggles upward to the mountain peaks of confidence in the Lord his God. He implores God's mercy over him and cries unto the Lord, the God of his salvation, who performs all things for him. He determines to take his refuge in the shadow of God's wings until "these calamities be overpast." He is confident that Jehovah will send forth his mercy and his truth. His heart is fixed; he will sing and give praise unto the Lord among the nations and will declare that his mercy is great unto the heavens and his truth unto the clouds.

Out of the depths to the heights of faith.

Is not this characteristic of the life of each child of God in the world?

Is he not always in the depths?

Does he not always—as long as he is in this world and in the body of this death—cry unto the God of his salvation out of the depths?

Is it not true that on the mighty wings of prayer he ascends unto the heights of joy, peace, and victory over the world— the victory of faith?

These calamities.

The psalmist refers to the calamities of the moment, to certain special and very concrete calamities that were threatening his destruction at the time that he wrote these words.

The superscription in the original informs us that the psalm refers to a time when David was in the cave. Whether this means the cave of Adullam or the cave of Engedi, we know not. It does not matter as far as the meaning of these calamities is concerned. It is evident that the psalmist at this time was bitterly persecuted by Saul and his men and that they threatened his life. Of this he speaks when he complains that his soul is among lions, in the midst of cruel enemies who set a snare for his feet, and who would swallow him up. He declares that he will make his refuge in the shadow of Jehovah's wings until those particular calamities are overpast.

In that particular, concrete sense, we too may well apply these words, as we are mindful of entering upon a new year.

These calamities.

Oh, yes, there is a special meaning in this phrase also for us, as we stand at the entrance of this year of our Lord 1945.

Dark clouds of evil are lowering overhead.

How miserably superficial and wicked appear now the revelry and shouting, the boasting and bragging, the banqueting and drunkenness, whereby the men of this world, whose god is their belly, whose glory is in their shame, and who seek and mind earthly things, hail the new year, as if there were any reason to expect a better world—a world of peace and happiness—in either the immediate or remote future.

It sounds like the drunken prattle of those whose life's slogan is: "Let us eat and drink, for tomorrow we die."

How vain it seems for men to meet one another on this morning, the first day of 1945, and wish for the blessing of a happy new year!

Is not the world full of misery and corruption as never before? Has there ever been a time when all the idle and proud boasts of mere men have been so utterly put to shame as on this very first day of another year? Is not even now the magnificent structure of man's culture and civilization shaking and tottering on its very foundations? Where is now man's wisdom, man's ingenuity, man's goodwill and purpose to build a better world, to create lasting peace on earth among the nations? Was there ever a war so tremendous in scope, so dreadful in its intensity, so bent upon destruction, as the world conflict in the throes of which we find ourselves at the present time?

Must not the words choke in our throats and die upon our lips when we wish one another a happy new year, while at the same time squarely facing reality and the dark foreboding of the future?

Are not our hearts heavy?

Are not our sons torn from our hearths and hearts to shed their blood on the far-flung battlefields of the world? Is happiness possible when we consider their empty places in our homes and at our tables and contemplate the possible suffering and fear and agony they may have to endure at this very moment? Do not our anxious hearts a thousand times pass in anticipation through the agony of the moment when the messenger of evil will bring us the tidings that our loved ones left their lives on the blood-soaked battlefield in a faraway land?

These calamities.

Indeed, on this first day of the year 1945, there is plenty of reason for us to speak of the calamities of the moment in a very special sense.

In the depths we are.

What then? While our soul is bowed down with grief and anxiety, our faith despairs, and our spirits are crushed, shall we remain in the depths?

Shall we assume the devil-may-care attitude of ungodly men, and in drunken revelry close our eyes to stark reality, and speak of a happy new year anyway?

Shall we put our trust in the vain words of men, the mighty and great of this world, who speak of chariots and horses, of the power of man, when they assure us that soon the calamities will be overpast and that the dawn of a better day is already within the range of their vision?

We will do nothing of the kind.

Vain is the help of man, and the expectation of the wicked must surely perish.

No, we will not remain in the depths to be crushed by grief and oppression. We will not drunkenly and foolishly close our eyes to reality and speak of happiness where there is none. We will not put our trust in princes and in the great of this world, in the might and wisdom of men. But we will cling to the mighty God of our salvation, as seeing the invisible, and out of the depths we will cry unto him.

We will trust in his mercy, which is unto the heavens, and in his truth that is unto the clouds.

We will make our refuge under the shadow of his wings, until these calamities be overpast.

But will they ever come to an end?

To be sure, these calamities may be considered as especially dark clouds that will soon be overpast.

Not always will David's soul be among the lions that now threaten him with death and destruction. His stay in the cave, surrounded by Saul and his men who seek his life, will not be forever.

The same is true of our present calamities.

All men somehow look forward to the time when calamities will be overpast, when the glad news will reach us that war is over, that the armistice has been declared, that the peace treaty is signed, that the nations are about to lay down their arms, and that our boys may return home. They long for that time, and they earnestly scan the sky of events to discover whether or not this dark and lowering cloud of evil is almost overpast, and the sunshine of peace and earthly happiness may presently be expected to pierce the darkness and gladden our hearts.

No doubt there is good reason for this expectation.

These calamities will overpass, sooner or later.

But what then?

Is it of any real avail that the present calamities, the troubles and fears and sufferings of the moment, shall come to an end? Is it not true that calamities like the present are very common in the world, that in recent years they have swept down upon us with increasing frequency in spite of the avowed intentions of men to prevent them, and that they have grown in intensity, so that the periods of relative peace and prosperity seem like patches of pale sunshine between ever fiercer and more destructive storms?

In general, are not the present calamities an emphatic manifestation and reminder of the one great, universal calamity of sin and death, and of the wrath of God under which we pine and die?

Is it then of any avail that we make our refuge under the shadow of Jehovah's wings until these calamities are overpast, unless we include in these calamities all our misery of sin and death, and look forward to the time when the great cloud of universal calamity shall have overpast, and the light of the eternal day shall shine upon us from the face of God in Christ?

In the ultimate sense this is the implication of David's prayer and confession.

David is the anointed of the Lord, ordained by Jehovah to sit on the throne of Israel. As the anointed one, he suffers. Because of this the enemies set themselves against him, and take counsel together to destroy him. Though the royal seed runs in the line of Judah, the present occupant of the throne is from the tribe of Benjamin, and he is determined to maintain his position and to kill the anointed of the Lord. Yet according to the promise of the Lord, David cannot perish at the hand of Saul. He will be exalted out of his present calamities to Israel's throne. Hence, until all these calamities will be overpast, he makes his refuge in the shadow of Jehovah's wings, trusting that he will deliver him.

In all this David is but a type.

His sufferings are but the type of the unspeakable sufferings of him who was to come, upon whose head the dark cloud of all the calamities of sin and death, of all the enmity of the powers of darkness that would set themselves against him, and of the fierce wrath of God against the iniquity of his people, would break and burst, and would pour out its untold agony of hell.

On him were the promises.

He was to be exalted to the throne of the kingdom of heaven forever.

In all his sufferings he truly said, "I will make my refuge in the shadow of thy wings, until these calamities be overpast."

And he was not put to shame.

For it was God who justified him. In his resurrection the lowering cloud of his calamities, and of all our calamities, was dispelled forever.

That resurrection is our only hope.

It is the light of the eternal day piercing the darkness of our present death.

The end of all our calamities!

Finding a safe retreat under his wings.

"In the shadow of thy wings will I make my refuge."

As little chicks run to the protection of their mother hen's wings in the time of danger, so I will seek a safe refuge in the care and protection of Jehovah.

This refuge we need.

Although the enemy is overcome, sin is atoned for and blotted out, the world is overcome, and death is swallowed up in the cross and resurrection of the Lord Jesus Christ. Although centrally in him and in his exaltation at the right hand of God, the dark cloud of these calamities—and of all calamities—is overpast, yet in our flesh we are still under the cloud, and the perfect day cannot dawn until the final resurrection and the perfect revelation of God's tabernacle with men in the everlasting kingdom of heaven.

Under that cloud, in the body of this death, we still suffer many things: pain and sorrow, persecution and tribulation, reproach and scorn, destruction and war, sin and death.

We need the comfort of the conscious assurance that we are under the wings of the God of our salvation, under his power and grace, his protection and care, his truth and faithfulness, his unfathomable love, and his everlasting and abundant mercy—always forgiving, always saving, always preserving, always delivering us from death and leading us unto everlasting life and glory.

That retreat is safe.

For he is the almighty Lord, sovereign also over all our calamities, which he uses unto our salvation.

To make our refuge by faith in the shadow of his wings is rest and strong consolation.

Peace that passes understanding!

23

Saving Mercies

"It is of the LORD's mercies that we are not consumed,
because his compassions fail not."
—Lamentations 3:22

The church of God in the midst of the world, existing in the
midst of a thousand powers that are calculated to destroy her, yet
never consumed.

What an amazing spectacle!

It is like the sight Moses beheld, when at the mountain of God
his wonderment was excited by the appearance of the flame in the
midst of the bush, while the bush was not consumed.

Such is the wonder on which the prophet is reflecting, Sitting
on the ruins of the beloved city of God, grief-stricken and overwhelmed with sorrow because of the downfall of the daughters of
Zion, and contemplating this marvelous phenomenon, he cries
out, "It is of the mercies of the Lord that we are not consumed,
because his compassions fail not."

What fearful history the poet is recalling when he utters these
words!

From the very moment the old dispensational people of God
began to appear in the midst of the world, it seemed as if all the
powers of darkness had been let loose upon them to harass them,
to deny them but the smallest place in the world, to blot out their
very existence, and to swallow them up. It had been thus in the
house of bondage, the country that at the first had been a haven
of refuge to them, but soon proved to be the furnace of affliction
in which they were well-nigh consumed. How the cruel scourge of

slavery had lashed their backs and subjected them to bondage, and how the fierce ravings of the hostile world power had persecuted their children unto death! How they had suffered and groaned under the burden of oppression, until it seemed they must be annihilated!

Yet they were not consumed.

How in the terrible desert the forces of hell had been marshaled and set in array against them! Step by step they had been followed by the devil and his host, who were determined upon their destruction. Sometimes the opposing power had come against them in the form of hostile hordes, and sometimes it had employed the wicked factor of carnal Israel, the reprobate in whom God had no pleasure, but who were of Israel, who had been delivered with them out of the house of bondage, who with them passed through the Red Sea and were baptized into Moses, who with them ate of the spiritual bread in the wilderness and drank out of the spiritual rock that followed them. Oh, how they had made Israel to sin! How they had rebelled against the Most High, despising the bread from heaven, provoking the angel of the Lord to anger, expressing their preference for the carnal pleasures and treasures of Egypt, committing idolatry and adultery! How they had invoked the fierce wrath of God upon them, which threatened to consume them—now striking them down by the sword, now laying them prostrate in the desert by fiery serpents, now kindling the fire of God among them, now having them swallowed up into very hell! How their unbelief had proved them incapable of entering into the promised inheritance, and how the anger of the Lord had caused all that generation to pine away in the wilderness!

What a history!

Yet they had not been consumed.

Had it been different during all those years that they had been in possession of the land flowing with milk and honey?

On the contrary, from without they had been the object of hatred by all the surrounding nations, and the powers of darkness had left them scarcely a moment's peace. From within, the ungodly element among them had continued to corrupt their way before the Lord, and had made Israel to sin and to violate the covenant of Jehovah. No nation had been as corrupt as they. The nations around them served their own gods, but Israel committed whoredom with every idol under heaven. Their children they had caused to pass through the fire, their temple they had defiled, their priests had been corrupt, and their prophets had proclaimed lies unto them according to their own hearts' desire. The messengers of Jehovah who showed them the way of salvation they had persecuted and killed. The Lord had revealed his wrath upon them and had caused them to walk in the delight of their sinful hearts until the day of reckoning, so frequently announced by faithful prophets, had finally arrived.

Now Jerusalem was destroyed, the temple was burned, the people of God's choice were scattered into foreign lands, and strange lords had dominion over them.

What a terrible history had been that of the people of God!

Yet, they were not consumed—not even now.

The remnant still remained. The church of God had not been exterminated.

Amazing spectacle!

Burned severely, yet never consumed!

Cast frequently into the furnace of affliction, yet never destroyed!

Always attacked by the hostile powers of darkness, from within and from without, yet never annihilated!

Thus the wonder presented itself to the mind of the lamenting prophet of Israel when he bewailed the calamities that had befallen his people. Is not this wonderful history of the church of the old dispensation typical of the experience of the church of all ages?

It could not be different. It was the Lord's pleasure to save a church unto himself from the midst of a fallen and corrupt race. With that race the chosen people of Jehovah are organically one by nature. With that race they went down into the darkness of sin and death when the first man Adam willfully turned his back on the Most High and heeded the voice of the prince of darkness. With Adam's race they are by nature allied to him who is a murderer from the beginning; with him they are subject to death and condemnation, dead in trespasses and sins, enemies of God, worthy in themselves of God's consuming wrath.

Although with the human race they fall into sin and death, they are not consumed.

The church is called out of the world.

For the Son of God gathers unto himself out of the sinful human race those whom the Father gave him, and who are chosen unto eternal life.

Yet they are in the world.

And the world hates them.

The powers of darkness never leave them a moment's rest. As it was with the people of Israel, so it was with the church of the predeluvian world, the period famous for its attempt to establish a world kingdom around the tower of Babel that would reach unto heaven. No different is it in the new dispensation, for from the very dawn of history the Lord began to realize his word: "And I will put enmity between thee and the woman, and between thy seed and her seed; it shall bruise thy head, and thou shalt bruise his heel." As it was with Israel in Egypt, in the awful desert, and in the promised land, thus it is with the church of all ages. The hostile powers attack the people of God both from within and from without.

The church is not perfect. All is not Israel that is of Israel. The dividing line that divinely discriminates between elect and reprobate cuts through the midst of the camp of the saints.

This carnal element within the sphere of God's covenant leads the church astray and frequently would surrender her to the powers of darkness. Now it is the demand to introduce the pleasures of Egypt into the life of the church; now it is the attempt to subject the church to the spirit of the age; now it is the temptation of a mere form of godliness while the power thereof is denied; now it is all sorts of winds of doctrine, vain philosophies of mere man, that would betray the church of Jesus Christ to the power of opposition. Frequently she is enticed to bow before the idols that are thus erected before her. Often she goes astray, leaving the path of truth and righteousness and wandering in ways of error, of worldly mindedness, of lust and pleasure and the service of mammon. More than once it appeared as if the powers of darkness had triumphed and the church had been swallowed up by the darkness of superstition, unbelief, and carnal lusts and pleasures. Yet she was never consumed.

From without the openly hostile world raved against her.

Now the enemy sang sweet siren songs, and the devil appeared as an angel of light, sweetly enticing, liberally offering all his kingdoms, the power and might, the glory and wealth, the honor and goodwill of the world at its best. Now he madly shook the very foundation stone of the church, denying that Jesus is the Christ, gainsaying his coming in the flesh, mocking the blood-theology of the cross, and casting the veil of doubt and agnosticism over the reality of the resurrection. Again, he fumed and raged against the faithful, opened prisons and dungeons for them, threatened with the bloody sword, erected scaffolds and stakes. And the church was cast into the fiery furnace of fierce persecutions.

Yet in spite of these hostile attacks from within and from without, and notwithstanding her frequent backsliding and many departures from the way of God's covenant, the church was never consumed.

The church still stands—the wonder of all history.

All things pass away.

Nations rise and fall.

But we are not consumed.

Marvelous phenomenon!

What may be the explanation of this historic wonder of the church, always attacked yet never subdued?

Is there in that church some inherent strength that renders her indestructible and that causes all the attempts of the devil, his host, and all the powers of darkness to be futile?

On the contrary, in themselves the people of God are poor and weak and despised and miserable; they are naught. They have no power of their own. Left to themselves, they would soon prove incapable of resisting successfully the mighty hosts of darkness that set themselves in array against the church. Not infrequently, when standing on imaginary rocks of their own power, they were left to prove that their own strength failed to maintain them in the midst of the world.

No, for the explanation of the wonderful phenomenon that the church is hated and attacked from every side but yet survives, you must not look at the church, but only at Israel's God.

For it is of the Lord's mercies and because his compassion never fails that we are not consumed. Jehovah's compassion is his tender love for his people as they are in misery. The Lord is full of mercy toward those who fear him; he burns with lovingkindness over his people, whom he knew from before the foundation of the world. His mercy is abundant over them. In this abundant mercy he will save them out of all their misery, will comfort them with eternal glory and victory in his eternal kingdom, and will presently wipe away all tears from their eyes. It is not his purpose to destroy, but to glorify them. In his overflowing mercy, his heart yearns for them in their misery. Sooner will a mother forget her sucking babe than the Lord will cast away the people of his love whom he has engraven in the palms of his hands.

This compassion never fails, for the name of our compassionate God is Jehovah. He never changes. Hence his mercy never fails.

His compassion is an eternal compassion. It is, as he, independent. It is sovereignly free mercy. The reason for it is not in his people, but solely in himself. His love is no response to their love of him, but his love is the cause, the unfathomable fount of their love. His love is original, absolute, infinite, immutable as his own being, and boundless as his own divine heart. From that eternal and unchangeable love constantly flows his abundant mercy toward his people. His compassion never fails. It fails not, although in themselves his people are worthy of his wrath and condemnation. His compassion is immovably faithful, although their faithlessness renders them a thousandfold unworthy of his mercy.

His abundant and eternal compassion manifests itself in countless acts of mercy, whereby he delivers the people of his choice.

The prophet speaks of these mercies, using the plural.

While doing so, he is thinking of all the mighty deeds of deliverance whereby Israel was saved and preserved in the midst of the furnace of consuming afflictions.

From the one great, eternal, boundless, and endless compassion in God's heart there flow numberless deeds of mercy, blessing and keeping his people and preparing them for eternal glory. These mercies explain the marvelous fact that we are not consumed.

In the very center of all these boundless mercies stands the great mercy of the cross. For God so loved the world that he gave his only begotten Son. It was the greatest deed of mercy, at once the basis and fount of all other mercies that bless God's people and keep them in the midst of the world. Why are the people of God not consumed? Why is there always a remnant? Why is the church indestructible? Why does she always reappear from the furnace of affliction, severely tried but unhurt, with new and greater glory? If she is by nature sinful and condemned in the sight of God, worthy of wrath and death and hell, why does the anger of God not strike her into destruction? It is of the Lord's mercy, revealed when he gave his only begotten Son for her, that she might be redeemed and justified, delivered and sanctified, purified from the pollution of sin and liberated from the power of death, that she might be to the praise of his glory and grace in the beloved.

There is the reason.

The cross of our blessed savior is the greatest of the sure mercies of God.

This most adorable of mercies fully explains the amazing spectacle that the church of God is not consumed.

From that cross flow a thousand mercies, all wondrous and precious, all mighty acts of love.

By these God's people are freed from the shackles of sin, are liberated from the oppression of the house of bondage, are rescued from the slavery of sin and the devil, are renewed, cleansed, nourished with spiritual bread, satisfied with God's blessed fellowship in Christ, kept in the power of God in the midst of the world unto the day of salvation.

They are not consumed.

And never will be!

PART III
Struggle

24

Internal Warfare

"For that which I do I allow not: for what I would,
that do I not; but what I hate, that do I. If then I do
that which I would not, I consent unto the law that
it is good. Now then it is no more I that do it, but
sin that dwelleth in me."

—Romans 7:15–17

Strange experience!

For here God's word is spoken from the viewpoint of the personal experience of the apostle.

In this text there is no scientific or dogmatic explanation of the psychological state or spiritual condition of the child of God. Even less is there an explanation of what man is in general. It is rather a declaration of what the apostle discovered in his own experience as the result of an intense investigation, according to an infallible light and inerrant guidance.

The apostle looks inward.

Under the leading of the Holy Spirit, who in this text gives us God's word and allows the pure light of divine revelation to shine on the actual condition of God's child in the world, the apostle investigates his own heart, his own disposition and mind, his own understanding and will, and his own life regarding good and evil in relation to the law and to sin. He does not express the result of his investigation in words that merely mirror it in a disinterested manner, but he expresses it with a cry from the heart, a cry of deep misery concentrated in one word: "O wretched man!"

This is an emphatic declaration of personal experience without an attempt to explain any further or to provide a dogmatic construction for the results of his investigation!

It is, therefore, so very strange, and yet something with which the Christian so completely identifies.

It is so clearly paradoxical, so sharply antagonistic, and so irreconcilably contradictory. Yet it finds a constant echo in the heart and on the lips of God's children, who do not live according to the superficiality of satisfying themselves with the notion of an external good, but who stand continually before the mirror of the perfect law of liberty.

Does it not seem strange to you that the most contradictory things are attributed to the same person, to the same "I?" Is it not strange that the very same person finds that he is the subject of experiences that apparently are completely irreconcilable contradictions relative to one another? It is really not a double personality that is spoken of here—not two persons who live in opposition in such a way that the one does what the other does not want, that the one loves what the other hates, and that the one refuses to practice what the other wills to do. Admittedly there is mention made of the "old" and the "new" man. The old man is then someone other than the new man. It is the old man who wills to sin, loves it, and does it. That old man is an "I" in himself. It really then does not matter so much what the old man does. Soon he will be totally destroyed anyway, and only the new man will continue to live. However, God's word in this passage does not mean this. The earnest child of God does not come with such self-serving drivel. But in contrast to his sins, he has a sincere delight in the law of God according to the inner man. On the contrary, he disapproves of what he does; he does not do what he wills, and he does what he hates.

Sharply contradictory!

Is it not psychologically impossible, a spiritual monstrosity, that anyone would speak of himself in this manner?

Pay attention to the fact that this doing and not doing, this willing and hating, is attributed to the same person in the very same sense and with a view to the very same purpose.

From a purely natural viewpoint one can indeed do what he really does unwillingly. That is, he does what he hates to do, but does it because he has in view an ultimate good. He proceeds reluctantly, but he chooses that way as the only way to the desired good end. For example, one can reluctantly subject himself to an operation, but does it for his own good. He does then, nonetheless, what he wills.

In the text, however, the situation is different.

It always concerns the same things; it concerns the good and the evil; it concerns God's law and sin.

He wills the good, but he does not do it.

He hates the evil, and he does it.

And what he does, he does not allow.

Still more strongly: what he does, he no longer does.

Marvelous experience!

Strange, and yet so typical!

This language is so very characteristic of every regenerated heart.

Indeed, it is the Christian who is speaking in the text.

The natural man does not express himself with these words. The spiritually superficial Pelagian wants to explain this entire passage in the manner of the natural man.

What person who is dead in sin and iniquity—who has no fear of God before his eyes, who does not seek God, whose throat is an open sepulcher, who has the poison of asps under his lips, who with his tongue has practiced deceit, whose mouth is full of cursing and bitterness, whose feet are swift to shed blood, and whose way is sown with destruction and misery—would will the good? What man, whose thoughts are hostile to God and who will not submit himself to the law of God, would be able to testify of himself that he wills the good and hates the evil, and that he has a delight in God's law according to the inner man?

No, the evil that he commits he wills, he contemplates, and he loves it with all his heart.

The good that he does not do is something he does not desire, he does not contemplate, and he hates, because he hates God.

Only the regenerated heart is able to identify with the language of the apostle.

This is especially clear if we pay attention to the word choice of the apostle in the original. Throughout the Dutch translation we read the little word "do," whereas the apostle uses a different word three different times. We may literally read the text this way: "What I accomplish, that I do not allow; what I will, that I bring not into practice; but what I hate, that do I. If I then do what I will not, in this way I acknowledge that the law is good. I then no more accomplish the same, but sin that lives in me."

Who of God's children does not know the experience expressed by these words? Who of those who by the Spirit have been renewed and are in Christ Jesus, who were drawn out of darkness into God's marvelous light, who were liberated from the law of sin and death, would hesitate even for a moment to say of his most holy deed, "What I accomplished, that I do not approve?" Is it not true of the very best and the holiest of these works that as long as we are in this life, before the work was accomplished, it was so tainted with sin that it became well-nigh unrecognizable, and that he cannot approve it as the good work that he had begun? Yes, it was good initially. When I began, it arose from my regenerated heart and was a work of faith. In private I fell on my knees before the face of my Father in heaven. I desired to seek him, to taste his fellowship, to pour out my heart to him, to confess my sins before him, to find the forgiveness of sins in the blood of the Lamb, to be delivered from all unrighteousness, to open my soul to the sacred influences of the Spirit, to make known to him my needs, to make known to him my way, to cast my cares upon him, to declare his praise, and to glorify his great name. When I arose and looked back on the good that I had desired, when I subjected that finished prayer to an investigation in the light of God's holy sanctuary, I could no longer approve it. What happened to the performance of that prayer? What evil influences corrupted it? What unholy desires mingled among the sobs for forgiveness? Indeed, evil thoughts tainted that prayer for forgiveness. How quickly the proud "I" declared, at the very beginning of the prayer, that I had made myself well-pleasing to God, that I had brought him something. What abominable self-praise wove itself into the praise of God.

O God, what I have performed, I allow not.

Wretched man that I am!

Well may I immediately fall on my knees again to plead for forgiveness regarding the abomination of my very best work that I have just completed.

For whereas I willed the good, I actually did the evil.

The evil that I hated, that I did.

Who does not know it?

Is then this experience really so strange, so paradoxical, so contradictory as it first appears to be?

There resonates in this language, though apparently characterized by contradiction, a deep, fundamental truth.

The fundamental truth is that of the regenerated heart. In the text there are not two separate persons who are speaking. Nor is the Christian speaking on the one hand according to the old man, and on the other according to the new man. Nor does the passage teach two very different fundamental attitudes in relation to good and evil, that is, to the law of the Lord and sin. Only the new man is speaking throughout, from the beginning to the end. That new man has initiated this self-examination. The new man has pronounced the condemning verdict. And the fundamental truth that you hear in this text arises only from the regenerated heart.

I hate the evil!

Oh, it is indeed true: I do the evil. But even though I do it, I nevertheless hate it. I have no peace when I commit the evil. Then

I experience an inward battle. Before God and men, I declare that I hate the evil. And hatred of the evil that I commit is rooted in the regenerated heart.

I will the good!

Oh, it is true that I do not practice it. I do not perform it. When I have done the good, I can no longer recognize it. But even though I have not executed the good deed to completion, I will to do it nonetheless. I am then filled with sorrow by my failure completely to perform it. Then I pursue the good, if I may attain unto it. Then I experience a fearful battle within me. That willing, that sorrowing, that pursuing, and that struggling have their fountain in the life of regeneration that the Spirit has worked in my heart.

I acknowledge that the law is good. I do so with an inward, spiritual acknowledgment of the heart, for I have a delight in the law of God according to the inward man. And my delight in the law of God is rooted in the love of God. In addition, that love of God is the fruit of the life of regeneration, which God himself has begun in me.

No, the Christian is not two different people.

He is one in the fundamental core of his existence and is also one whole from a spiritual viewpoint. When God by the Spirit of Christ regenerated him, a second man did not come into him next to the old man. He did not receive another or a second heart, nor a second mind and will. He was renewed not externally, not in the periphery of his existence, so that he would be delivered merely from some gross sins or from some sinful habits. But he was renewed in his inward being, in his fundamental character, in the deep fountain of the issues of life, in the depths of his heart. His heart was changed. It was united to Christ Jesus to live out of Christ. The old enmity was severed from its root, and the love of God permeated his heart. It was redirected from darkness to the light, from unrighteousness to righteousness, from Satan and sin and the world to the living God.

He is in Christ Jesus.

Having been born of God, he sins no more.

He cannot sin, for he is born of God and his seed remains in him.

The old is gone, for according to the old he hated God and his law and took pleasure in the evil that he did.

Behold, everything has become new!

For he wills the good and hates the evil.

And he has a delight in God's law.

The new man he is.

Fearful struggling!

Painful experience expresses itself here.

For this perfect man, this new man in Christ Jesus, who has been liberated from the law of sin and death, and who on the one hand confesses triumphantly and victoriously that the old has passed away and that everything has become new, on the other hand experiences and confesses with sorrow of heart that everything is still so old.

What I do, that I allow not.

Is that not in the final analysis the language of the defeated instead of the triumphant cry of the victorious in this battle?

What I will, that I do not? What I hate, that do I?

But do I not then suffer defeat repeatedly, time and again?

No, emphatically not!

The fact remains—if we allow the new man to speak once again—that I still will the good. The fact remains—and again the new man who has been created in Christ Jesus speaks—that I hate my own sin. And hating it, I take it with me to stand before the face of God, and there I wash my clothes in the blood of the Lamb through faith. Daily I do this, again and again. This is the faith that is victorious over the world. The fact is—and once again it is the speech of my heart—that I acknowledge that the law is good. That is my victory.

Yes, I do not hesitate to say, "I do not sin any more, according to the deepest essence of my renewed heart."

It is the sin that lives in me that hinders me from performing the good that I will to do. It takes me prisoner to do the evil that I hate. For I am indeed perfect, but only in principle, not absolutely. The heart is truly renewed, yet body and soul have become old in the service of sin. In that service of sin there are in my nature deep ruts, workings of the flesh that have remained. Operations of sin there are in my soul and in my body, in my mind and in my will, in my eyes and in my ears, in my tongue and in my mouth, in my hands and feet. This is the old nature with its lust of the eyes and the lust of the flesh and the pride of life. In addition, my old nature discovers a powerful friend in the world all around me. I am continually open to Satan's temptations. Those operations and powers of temptation take me prisoner, so that the good, which I in Christ Jesus will to do, is so easily led astray into the old ruts of sin and, consequently, I do not accomplish what I will.

But I do not will it to be so.

Let it be said a thousand times: I do not sin any more. I hate it with a perfect hatred.

And I battle, fighting the good fight.

Who will deliver me?

I thank God!

Through Christ Jesus, our Lord!

25

Life through Death

"It is a faithful saying: For if we be dead with him, we
shall also live with him."

—2 Timothy 2:11

This was a declaration of jubilation by God's church.

A hymn that the ancient church took upon her lips when she
assembled to call upon the name of the Lord, a hymn in which
she sang of her hope, expressing her victory in the midst of the
battle.

A song of triumph, whereby, though struggling, she climbed
to the heights of Zion. She took this song of jubilation with her
in the fires of persecution, with her into prison and exile, with her
to the scaffold and the burning stake, singing it forth until smoke
and flames smothered her voice: "If we have died with him, we will
also live with him."

A song that expressed a faith that the world did not understand. A faith that conquered the world when it appeared as if the
world had conquered it.

The apostle, Scripture, and God the Lord himself set a seal of
genuineness on the faith of the church. This is a faithful word, a
declaration that never brings shame, upon which you can rely with
confidence, on the basis of which you may regard everything else
as error.

A word of the living God.

Eternally certain!

Do you wish to live? You must first die!

Amazing paradox; but there is no other way to life, the life, the true, eternal full and blessed life!

God, whose glory is that he calls light out of darkness and makes the dead to live, has willed it this way and devised it this way from before the foundation of the world in his eternal good pleasure, to the praise of his name and for the revelation of his glorious, divine, covenantal life. The natural seed planted in the earthly ground dies in order to live. God's people through death enter into life!

Do you wish to live? Then you must die.

Dying—but not your own death, and not in yourself and from yourself. Dying—not alone, but with him.

In yourself you can only die in order to die even more—to sink away into death eternally.

But with him, you can die in order to live.

For God, who makes the dead to live, who according to his eternal good pleasure has willed to lead his people through death to eternal life, has also opened the way to life directly through death, and he has revealed the power that devoured death in the cross and resurrection of Jesus Christ. If we die with him, we shall also live with him.

Do you want to live? Will, then, to die.

Because whoever wants to preserve his life—this earthly and physical life—will lose it. He will lose everything of this life, for he must die. But regarding eternal life the reality is different: whoever will lose his life for my name's sake, will preserve it.

Do you will to die? Then you will live.

Amazing paradox, indeed!

Nevertheless: a faithful saying!

———————

Dying with him in order to live!

The entire secret of this peculiar mystery lies in "with him," that is, in fellowship with his death and resurrection.

If you died with him, you entered with him into death and passed through it. At Golgotha you died the death that is payment for all your sins. You died the death in which the complete response of love has been given to God's demand of justice regarding the guilty sinner, the death of atonement and reconciliation by the Son of God in our flesh. You died the death by which you have the right to eternal life.

For indeed, you and I have no rightful claim to life until we die to atone. It is not sufficient to die, for hell does that as well, suffering death eternally without ever attaining atonement. But we must die to atone. We have no rightful claim to life until we have endured and suffered in such a manner that we have emptied the cup of death to its bitter dregs, satisfying God's unchangeable, eternal justice for the payment of the guilt of our sin. For the wages of sin is death. Not only does life not lie on this side of death, but it does not lie on any side of death. Besides, there is unto all eternity no opposite side to death unless that death becomes an act of obedience, even as sin is an act of rebellion. There is no opposite side to death unless the dying of the whole death becomes an act of love, completed for God's sake, just as sin is an act of hostility committed against God's will, and unless death is fully endured and is finally removed by an act of obedience in love.

And that you cannot do, I cannot do it, nor can any mere human person.

A mere man cannot die so completely that death is swallowed up and life emerges, for he is a mere man. If God avenges his eternal justice upon him, he sinks down deeper into the abyss, and there is no end to his suffering of death. Mere man cannot die as a willing act of love, for he is an enemy of God, dead in trespasses and sin, and he only daily increases his guilt. In hell is the absolutely passive suffering of death, but never the death of atonement. In hell death is never an act of eternally sacrificing oneself in death through love toward God.

Therefore, the power to die unto life lies alone in Christ's death.

Immanuel's death!

He died the atoning death for all whom the Father had given to him. In so dying, he merited the right to life—the better, eternal, and heavenly life. He could do that because he, the Son, was foreordained to be the head of his people, to stand at the head of the judicial body of all the elect, so that he, according to strict justice, could represent them because they were truly in him. Therefore, God could cause all our unrighteousness to be visited upon him. Therefore, Jesus could be made sin for us, so that our sins were concentrated in him. Jesus could be responsible for our sin because personally he had no guilt before God; his voluntary humility could expect, according to God's own justice, a reward. Jesus was able to do that because he never was touched with the defilement of sin. He was without any spot or blemish. The holy blood and the holy life of the holy child Jesus was offered at Golgotha on God's altar, the blood of the faultless Lamb. Jesus could do that because he was the Son, God out of God, Immanuel, who is eternally in the bosom of the Father, who eternally loved the Father. Jesus, who in his human nature could lay down his life, could shed his blood, could will to die by an act of his own volition in perfect love; that Jesus laid his life as a sacrifice on the altar of God's most holy justice. He could do that because he, Immanuel, God out of God, offered himself through the eternal Spirit. He could taste death as no other was able to taste it. He was able to enter into the eternal depths of death in such a way that he paid unto all eternity the debt of guilt and merited for all the life that is better and eternal.

The voluntary and vicarious death of the Christ of God, who is the Son in our flesh, is the perfect death that results in life.

He died in order to live.

Therefore, God did not put his servant to shame, but gave him glory and honor and eternal life when he raised him up from the dead.

Therefore, in his death there is the right to eternal life for all who believe in his name.

If we have died with him, then we have all died in him when he laid down his life at Golgotha. Then the debt of guilt is paid for us, life has been merited, as certainly as if we ourselves had personally performed that act of voluntarily dying the death of atonement before the face of God in loving obedience.

Then we enter into eternal life through faith in the power of the Lord's suffering and death.

Then through faith we have the right to eternal life.

With him we have died.

In order to live with him.

Dying with him, in order to live with him!

Amazing paradox, but nevertheless a faithful saying that has its immovable basis in the cross and resurrection of Jesus Christ from the dead, and that even today becomes real in the life of believers!

They have, after all, died with him not only legally, but also spiritually. They also have risen from the dead by the grace of his Spirit and through the power of faith.

His death is indeed the death of death!

By nature we lie in the midst of death; we were born with our race and from our race in the power of death. As a people of misery and as willing slaves of the devil, we are bound with the bands of unrighteousness. Every thought of the flesh is death as well, for the flesh is enmity toward God. It does not submit to God's law, for it cannot. Born under the power of death and living in the sphere of death, we produce dead fruits. That is our death, our dreadful misery.

Besides, the power of that death is our guilt before the law. According to God's own justice, we are accursed. We have no right to be delivered from that power of sin and of death. God's own law declares the judgment that whoever commits sin is a slave to sin. Therefore the law is powerless to help us; it cannot censure sin in our flesh and dethrone it.

But what the law could not do, God has done.

He has condemned sin in the flesh; he has taken away every right and all power from it, so that it cannot rule over us; he has liberated us from the law of sin and death. God did this when he sent his own Son in the likeness of sinful flesh, when he had him take the place of his people, standing with all our unrighteousness upon him in the place of judgment. The cross is the satisfaction of God's justice and thereby the condemnation and dethronement of sin, so that it cannot rule over us, and is the destruction of the old man, who brought forth the dead fruits of sin. He has died for sin once.

Died for all whom the Father had given to him.

If one has died for all, then all have died.

We have died with him, in him, and through him. If the power of the cross is applied to our hearts by his Spirit, then the man of sin in us dies as well. It may be true that sin has not died. Indeed, the motions of the flesh may still fight against us and reveal themselves in our flesh. But we have died to sin. Although we formerly lived for sin, now we are dead toward sin. When earlier we sought sin, we now flee from it.

We have died with Christ.

But we have died in order to live.

This is a faithful saying: If we have died with him, we shall also live with him.

He has risen.

The last Adam has become a quickening Spirit.

We have died with him through the power of his cross; we live with him by the power of his resurrection. We live in order no longer to employ our members as instruments of unrighteousness unto unrighteousness, nor any more to produce dead fruit, but in order to live for him who has died for us and risen again.

His death is our death—the death of death, and the death of the old man.

His life—his eternal resurrection life—is our life.

Dying in order to live!

If we die with him!

Dying even now, dying our bodily death, with him.

Dying next to him, in him; dying in the world, to the world, and at the hands of the world—if we will to lose life with all that it includes, for his name's sake.

So too will we live with him.

For in this manner he died as well. In the world he had nothing, and the world found nothing attractive and desirable in him. He was the light of the world and shone forth in the world, but the world loved the darkness rather than the light and hated the light. He spoke always of God, who truly is God; but the world was hostile to God, his will, his name, and his covenant. The world sought after and loved her idols, but not the living God. Therefore, the world harbored a deadly hatred toward him. It always purposed and attempted to extinguish the light, to kill the living one, to smother the witness of the servant of the Lord, and to silence him unto all eternity. For everything about him was about God.

Therefore the world put him to death.

There was no room for him in this world.

Therefore, the world cast him out and hung him on the tree of shame. Through the rejection of Immanuel, the light of the world, this world condemned itself and revealed fully that it hated the light because its works were evil. Thus the savior, with his eye on the cross that was seemingly his condemnation, could say, "Now is the judgment of this world."

He died at the hands of the world.

Since his death, and as a consequence of his death through the hatred of the world, two kinds of death have become reality for the children of our race.

There is a dying with the world, which is a dying unto death.

And there is a dying with him, which is a dying unto life.

There is a dying with the world for the children of the world, who love the world and are loved by the world. They are of the world. They live out of the world. They seek to preserve their life, the life of this world, doing so in enmity toward God. And with this world they are destroyed. Whoever will seek to preserve his life in this world will of necessity lose it.

There is also a dying with him for those who belong to him, are born of him, and live by him. For where they have died with him, there they also live with him. They live a life that is not born of this world, but that is from God. They live a life not from the principle of enmity toward God, but a life in principle of love toward God, a life arising not from the darkness, but arising from the light, a life not from below, but from above. They live the life that is from God, through the principle of which they confess in word and in deed that God is God, the eternal good. Because they are born of God and because the world hates him, the world hates them also, will make no room for them, and will crucify them even as they crucified him. They die with him.

They die, however, in order to live.

For the Lord is truly risen from the dead. Whosoever will lose his life with him and for him will keep it—preserved in eternal glory, in the day wherein their life with him will be revealed!

To die with him in order to live with him!

In eternal victory!

26

Walking in Darkness

"Who is among you that feareth the LORD, that
obeyeth the voice of his servant, that walketh in
darkness, and hath no light? let him trust in the
name of the LORD, and stay upon his God. Behold,
all ye that kindle a fire, that compass yourselves
about with sparks: walk in the light of your fire, and
in the sparks that ye have kindled. This shall ye have
of mine hand; ye shall lie down in sorrow."

—Isaiah 50:10, 11

Terrifying experience!

Walking in darkness!

Thick darkness is all around you. You find yourself in unfamiliar regions, in places unknown to you. You find yourself on a path that you never walked before and that you do not know; the direction the path takes is hidden from you, and its end you cannot see.

The night is dark—so dark that you cannot know what lies right before your feet, so that you are not confident about even one step you take. Besides, you have no flashlight that you can switch on, so that in the darkness of the night you can at least illuminate your immediate surroundings with it. Yet you must go forward. If you could just remain where you are, where you feel the ground under your feet, in order to wait for the dawn, then you would not be so fearful and anxious. Yet there is no possibility of your standing still, of resting there. You must always move forward. No matter how dreadful uncertainty may grip your heart and seize your mind, no matter that with every step you must anticipate that you could stumble and fall down into the ditch, you must move forward, always forward.

Such is the picture that the text presents to our mind's eye. God's word here speaks of walking in darkness.

In this figure is portrayed the life, the pilgrim's journey of the individual Christian and of the church of the Lord in all ages. Especially three elements are found in this description. First, the element not only of uncertainty and unfamiliarity with the way that God's child has been called to walk in the world, but also of complete ignorance regarding the immediate future. He walks in darkness. He does not see the way that lies before him. He does not know what his circumstances will be in the next moment. From the perspective of the things that are seen, he proceeds toward an unknown future. Second, from the same viewpoint there is in this figure the element of ignorance regarding the end. He does not see any way out. The end of the way is hidden from his eyes. He cannot see where he is walking, nor can he see the end of his way. His destination, from the viewpoint of the things that are seen, is not in sight. Third, there is in the figure of walking in darkness the idea of danger, specifically, unknown and unseen dangers that threaten him—dangers of the path itself, dangers of depths, precipice, and abyss, and dangers of stalking enemies who threaten to attack and are intent on killing him.

Indeed, a true and poignant figure.

So it is with the church in the world. So it is throughout the history of the church. From the viewpoint of the things that are seen, she walks a hopeless journey. She does not see the way on which she must walk, and confidence escapes her. She does not see the end that she confesses to be the object of her hope. She is always threatened by enemies who attempt to devour her and who appear to have gained the victory over her. Such were the circumstances in the period of Israel's history in which Isaiah prophesied. After all, how could Zion understand the way she had to walk, when her way ran straight to and through Babylon? How could she understand when God's covenant appeared to be shattered, when the city of God lay in ruins, when the temple was destroyed, and when the people groaned under the oppressive yoke of a mighty power of this world? How could she understand the way to the end that Zion had been promised—an end of complete deliverance and victory? Zion walked in darkness.

This figure is no less true when applied to each child of God in the world.

The world is a vale of tears. This life is nothing more than a continual death. The child of God, a pilgrim in this vale of tears, is surrounded by high mountains over which he is unable to peer. And in the valley rules the darkness of a pitch black night. He is not able to see his hand before his eyes. For a long time already there has been only darkness on account of this earthly and temporal existence to which he has been bound— darkness that he cannot defeat, darkness made worse by the dominion of sin, guilt, and death. Into that darkness he was born. In that darkness the child of God must journey onward. From the moment that he is born until the moment that he sets his foot in the Jordan of death, he must always go forward and onward. For him there is no rest.

Moreover, the great darkness of this vale of tears, into which he was born and in which he must walk and live, reveals itself to him and is experienced by him in various forms and in many different ways.

The child of God walks not merely in darkness, but in many different kinds of darkness, in darkness multiplied.

There is the darkness of the guilt with which he was born, from which he knows not how to free himself, and which only increases with every step he takes. There is the darkness of the depravity of his heart, of his nature, of his mind, will, and desires, against which he can never gain the victory and from which he is unable to struggle free, a darkness that always appears to become ever more impenetrable. There is the darkness of the shadow of death, which from the hour of his birth hovers over his existence, and which includes the suffering and the misery that is inseparably bound to death and its operations. There is the darkness of the danger presented by enemies: the world, sin, and Satan, the forces of darkness that ever threaten him.

And finally, there is the darkness of the valley of the shadow of death, wherein he will soon set foot, and about which he knows really nothing, for he cannot see through and beyond death's darkness.

Walking in darkness—in darkness multiplied.

Surrounded by the night's dense darkness.

Nonetheless, he must walk ever onward.

Terrifying experience!

———————

Marvelous authoritative word!

He who walks in darkness also lives in trust.

Just exactly the opposite of what you would justifiably expect: trusting!

When the child of God finds himself where he is unable to see any possibility of a successful outcome, when his heart is filled with dreadful uncertainty, when anxiety and fear take hold of his mind, when a thousand deep concerns and necessities and extreme sorrows press his heart, then trusting!

Trusting says that the mind of this traveler in the darkness is filled with a calm certainty and a happy expectation. Instead of sitting down in discouragement or hesitating with every step he takes because of terror, he strides forth in courage and willingly moves forward. He walks in confidence through the darkness of sin and guilt, suffering and misery, passing through affliction, deep concerns, and death. He strides confidently through the midst of threatening enemies. And presently, when he must place his feet in the waters of the Jordan of death, he does not hesitate.

Trusting!

Trust is the spiritual power of the believer's heart of faith that reveals itself as a joyful confidence with every step the child of God takes in this darkness. Confidence that the way is good, so that he need not fear to press onward, even though he does not see his way. Confidence that the end is glorious, an eternal redemption, and that the way, no matter how dark and dangerous and wrong it may appear to be, will bring him to eternal glory. Confidence that the enemies, no matter how they storm and rage, and no matter how it may sometimes appear as if they will have the victory over him, are nevertheless unable to harm him. Yes, confidence even that they must serve his experience of complete deliverance, the blessedness of eternal life.

Trusting!

But trusting in what? In whom?

Not in our own self-provided light. Not in the light that a sinful world may provide. According to the figure of the text, we do not trust in the sparks of a self-ignited fire that glow and sputter in the darkness.

That is what the world does and what sinful man does.

In the darkness of their own guilt, the wicked turn to the light of their own goodness and let the sparks of their own works sputter everywhere, in order to walk in the meritorious sparks of those works until their time of death. Over against the darkness of the misery and suffering of this present time, the darkness of death, they illuminate their way with their own philosophy, with the sparks of human wisdom and learning, and with their attempts to make this world better. They permit these humanistic efforts to glow and sputter, in their impenetrable and engulfing darkness, for the redemption of humanity.

Vanity characterizes all their activity.

They walk in the light of the flame of their own fire and in the sparks with which they have surrounded themselves. This vain endeavor is the divine judgment due them from the hand of the Lord. For the wisdom of the world that will not come to the light and therefore will not trust, cannot trust, nor can will to trust in the Lord must be put to shame and exposed as foolish. Thus they walk and act in the pseudolight of their own goodness and wisdom, which is really nothing other than the glow of hell that overspreads their way. In that glow of hell they walk on, just as the moth flits about the flame of the campfire, until they reach eternal destruction. In sorrow shall you lie down.

But trust in the name of Lord. Through that name of the Lord go forward, leaning on your God.

The name of the Lord is the revelation of Jehovah, the God of your complete salvation. Upon the Lord must trust the traveler in darkness. One who walks in darkness must trust in the Lord. He must rely on his sovereign God. Only then can he have confidence in the darkness through which he must walk. He does not see the Lord, and God, the Almighty, is hidden from view. No one has ever seen God. But the child of God knows his name, for the Lord declared his name in the darkness and made it known to his children, so that they would trust in that name and through that name, rest in the sovereign God.

Trusting and resting in God.

Trusting is to be confident of his love of you, the love wherewith he has loved his own from before the foundation of the world. We are to know with certainty that in eternal love he has ordained the end of everlasting glory for us: life out of death, light out of darkness, righteousness out of guilt, holiness out of sin and corruption, and eternal salvation out of the night of sorrows.

We must also be confident that God has determined the way, and that the way can lead nowhere else but to the glory of the kingdom of heaven and eternal victory.

Finally, we must be confident that throughout our journey and in the darkness, the Lord, the sovereign God, leads the way.

That is true trusting in the name of the Lord.

That is true resting in our God.

An encouraging word of authority!

Heavenly comfort!

Let him trust in the name of the Lord. Let him rest in his God.

His voice sounds forth that message into the ears of the weary pilgrims in the midst of the darkness.

How wonderful! How full of comfort in the pitch black night is the voice of one well-known to us, to hear a friend's voice calling out and instilling courage! Do you know that voice? Do you? Do you hear it? Does the sound of his voice penetrate to the depths of your soul as the voice of most splendid majesty, the voice of eternal love, and the voice of peace that works in your heart a peace that transcends all understanding?

Listen! You still do not see him, but the sound of his voice penetrates the darkness to reach your soul. It is the voice of the servant of the Lord, of him who was sent into the world by Jehovah God, and who confronted the darkness, to prepare comfort and redemption for his brethren who walk in darkness. In obedience to the Father, and as the servant of the Lord, he came into the darkness to dispel it. He came into our night to create the eternal day. He came into the darkness to prepare life out of death. He is the redeemer of the brethren. He is Immanuel, God with us. He journeyed through the darkness upward to the eternal light. Descending into death, he swallowed up that enemy and showed himself to be the Son of God by preparing a way to life as the head of his brethren.

He calls you.

He is the servant of the Lord, who speaks the name of the Lord alone. The Lord has given to him the tongue of the learned, and he knows how to speak the word with and to the weary at the right time. The word of the servant of the Lord does not proclaim human wisdom, but speaks of God—always of God, of his name, his virtues, his glory, of his eternal counsel and covenant with his people, and of eternal things. He knows how to proclaim appropriately the things that are not seen, that are exalted far above the darkness of this present life, things that are hidden behind the mountains that surround this vale of tears and enclose us on all sides. Therefore, he knows how to speak a word to the weary. He cries out to you, "My brethren, do not employ your own light. Refrain from your own works, and do not surround yourselves with the vain sparks of your own kindled fire. I am the light of the world. Whosoever follows me will not walk in darkness, but has through faith the light of life in the midst of the darkness of the things that are seen. Come to me with your sins and your debts, with your sufferings and death, with your fears and dreadful anxieties. I have prepared for you forgiveness and redemption. I will give you rest, light, and peace. Come here."

Do you fear the Lord, pilgrim walking in the darkness?

Has the grace of life been poured out into your heart, whereby you have been delivered from your vain walk? Has the fear of the Lord been given to you, so that in principle you go to him?

Then hear the voice of his servant, not only with your natural ear, as the world does, for they despise, slap, and crucify him. But hear him with the ear of faith.

Trust in the Lord in the midst of darkness of every kind.

You will not be put to shame!

The eternal morning will soon dawn!

27

Patient in Tribulation

"Rejoicing in hope; patient in tribulation; continuing
instant in prayer."

—Romans 12:12

In the world you shall have tribulation.

This is the savior's message given to his disciples, and therefore to his church in the world, shortly before he willingly entered
his great tribulation, which was the hour he would pour out the
life of his soul in death.

He himself knew by experience what this tribulation in the
world and by the world included. He was a castaway. Just as it was
at his birth, when there was no room for him in the inn and he
was forced, as it were, to greet the light of day from the vantage
point of extreme obscurity, so it was throughout his lifetime and
especially during the time of his public ministry in ever greater
measure, until he was pressed out of the world when he was nailed
to the accursed tree, by which act man declared that there was no
room in all the world for him.

Tribulation. That is, men choke you, oppress you, and scorn
you until you can find no place even to stand.

The savior experienced that.

The Lord's disciples would experience it.

His church, which wants to confess his name and by his grace
desires to walk in his footsteps, will experience the same persecution. Therefore, the constant refrain of sacred Scripture is that in
the world you will have tribulation.

It is true that all suffering is tribulation for the child of God in the world. Inseparably joined to existence in this world are much suffering and affliction, much pain and misery, much distress and grief, much sin and imperfection. Suffering can never be separated from this present existence. Oh, the piercing pain and misery that is suffered when the body is attacked by a fatal disease, consuming bone and marrow, which relentlessly drags the mortal and corruptible down and away to the grave. Oh, how one's courage and determination is undermined by life's misery and pain, when the ties and bands that God himself established for this present life are cruelly ripped apart by the indifferent hands of death! Who is able, even in some measure, to conceive of all the suffering that is endured by those on sick beds and in cancer wards, not only before our very eyes publicly, but also the suffering in loneliness behind closed doors, in hospitals and in private homes, by day and by night; not only the suffering endured by the unbelieving world that curses God's name, but also the suffering endured by the supplicating child of God who adores him? From this viewpoint, life in the world is for the believer tribulation, even more so than for the child of unbelief who seeks and loves this world. It is a greater tribulation for the believer not only because he knows another life, a life that is from above and that yearns for the complete redemption that also includes the body, but it is also greater because he knows the tribulation that befalls him is due to the power of sin in his members, the body of this death from which he would happily be delivered.

Most assuredly, he sighs and groans as a Christian, for he longs to be clothed upon with the house that is from heaven. The more the new life of Christ Jesus matures in him, the more sensitive he becomes regarding this tribulation in the world. He does not want to sin, but nonetheless, sin frequently holds him captive. He does not want to suffer, but his chastisement is there every morning.

God's church in general and the individual in particular endure a tribulation in which the world is not required to share and in which it cannot participate. It is the tribulation that is not only *in* the world but also *because of* the world. Such is the meaning of the word *tribulation,* when the savior said that his disciples would have tribulation in the world. In this sense, the apostle spoke of "this present suffering" in the epistle to the congregation at Rome. He presents tribulation in the same way in the text, when he warns the congregation to be patient in tribulation. He refers to the tribulation caused when the world rejects God's people, because the world hates him of whom the church is born, and because God has chosen and called to himself a people that causes his light to shine in a world that is of the darkness. The hated church is a people who will preach the virtues of the Most High God in a world filled with enmity against the radiant beauty of his virtues. They are of the party of the living God in this world, and as God's party they are bitter enemies of all the powers of darkness. Therefore, the world makes the place of God's church extremely narrow; it chokes her on every side, and it will not grant her any space to live as long as she remains faithful to the name of her God. That is the tribulation that the church experiences in the world and at the hands of the world.

In all manner of ways the world reveals its hostility; it shows what it is in many different forms. On occasion the world uses words and speech, and it persecutes by means of slanders and sneers, libel and scorn. Thus the church of God is dragged through the mud and her good name is defamed and mocked. The world also shows what it really is through persecution: God's child is banished as unworthy; the doors of the prison are thrown open to receive him; he is refused name and reputation in the world, so that he is unable to buy or sell; or scaffolds and pyres are erected, by which the people of the world deny him his very existence.

The Roman Christians knew this cruelty; they were required to experience this dreadful tribulation for Christ's sake.

Be faithful, show yourselves to be children of light, and the very same hatred in one form or another will publicly manifest itself even today.

In the world you shall have tribulation. Your savior experienced it as well.

So it was also for the disciples when they began their public ministry with the name of their Lord on their lips.

The history of the church of God in every age confirms the truth.

Tribulation in the world.

So it is even today.

But be of good courage!

Be patient in tribulation.

Not in the way the world sometimes shows itself patient in suffering. The unbeliever wants to steel himself against the suffering of this present time and disciplines himself in order to be reconciled to his suffering. He steels himself and hardens himself, and refuses to bend his proud neck and back under the lashing blows of the Almighty.

Just as the Stoics disciplined themselves to be able to bear suffering and to endure the sharpest pains without wincing in the least, so the world, in deep sinful rebellion, often acts as if it does not feel the pain, and hardens itself in order to despise the Almighty's scourging punishments.

The savior did not do that. Having his eye on the suffering soon to befall him, he could crawl in the dust as a worm and no man, sweating as it were great drops of blood out of dread, and complaining that his soul was deeply troubled unto the point of death itself.

Suffering was for him dreadfully serious.

Likewise, God's child is never patient, and he is never reconciled to his suffering. He cannot be, for he desires to be delivered from this present suffering, and he looks forward to the brilliantly joyful morning of eternity. He does not want to be indifferent to his suffering, for he knows that his suffering and all his fearful tribulation are sent to him from the hand of his God, with the calling to endure unto the end, to God's glory.

Nor should patience be confused with stubborn resignation, placing the suffering in the category of the unavoidable, offering no resistance to the hand that strikes us, and foregoing all murmuring against our lot and against God, who determines our lot according to his good pleasure, because we are conscious of our weakness and inability to change our life's circumstances in the slightest. The world can do that as well. Then the child of God does not distinguish himself from the world. In his thoughts and determination he is, then, completely rebellious against the living God, even though according to his outward demeanor he acts patiently. He then sits there with his mouth shut, not saying a word, submissive to the cruel power of some fatalism against which resistance is pointless. If he could turn back the hand that strikes him, he would in a moment gladly alter his lot. But where this is impossible, he resigns himself to the suffering, completely dumb and overwhelmed with grief.

No, patience is a spiritual power of God's grace in Christ our Lord.

It is the spiritual power of resilience by which we are enabled to carry the burden of suffering, to persevere in tribulation—happily—for God's name sake, and to do so in the consciousness that tribulation will end, that the battle is only for a short time, that the suffering of the present time races past, that the glorious victory is certain, that a marvelous glory awaits us, with which the present suffering is not to be compared, and that our temporal, fearful tribulation can be of little weight in the scales of faith. Patience is one of the fruits of the faith that overcomes the world because it cleaves to the invisible God, a faith that is convinced and maintains the truth that tribulation in the world and by the world has been ordained by the God of the covenant. Faith also holds certain and knows that the suffering of this present time must work our good. This faith knows, moreover, that our enemies, with all their hatred, spite, and persecution, can only serve to provide us the victory. Therefore, faith rejoices in tribulation. Faith rejoices that it is more than conqueror through him who loves us.

Faith deeply experiences suffering. The believer is nearly choked to death in the midst of tribulation. Faith weeps in misery. The believer complains when suffering, and he cries out in the agony of tribulation's life-threatening, suffocating pressure.

But faith is not disabled. It does not spiritually succumb, and it does not abandon the battle because of tribulation. No, faith rejoices in suffering.

It can sing through tears.

The believer is of good courage, even though the way is despairingly deep and fearful.

Faith is loyal to the very end.

———

Patient, for God's sake!

Submissive, by the power of the Almighty, with our eye of faith fixed on the glory of victory, a victory that certainly awaits us.

Only in this way is patience spiritually possible in tribulation. Therefore, this warning cannot stand alone, but includes a threefold admonition, the parts of which appear to be independent. Yet there exists among the aspects of this admonition the most intimate relationship. The connection is such that, on the one hand, tribulation is endured on the wings of a joyful hope, while on the other hand, our patience is sustained by means of the indispensable power of prayer.

If you rejoice in hope, be patient in tribulation and continue instant in prayer.

Only in this way is patience possible.

Without rejoicing in hope, the one oppressed by tribulation for Christ's sake is of all men most miserable.

Hope in the subjective sense is the resurrection life of Christ in our hearts reaching out to take hold of the glorious future laid away for us in Christ Jesus. We know that through the savior's resurrection we are reborn unto a living hope. The resurrection life that has been planted in our hearts is from above. It is in essence heavenly and therefore longs for heaven and reaches out toward the things invisible and eternal. Consequently, hope is a certain anticipation of our future—our marvelous estate in the glory of God's perfected covenant and eternal kingdom. Hope does not waver, but rejoices in the certainty of glory. It does not stagger, but stands resolutely founded upon Jesus' resurrection from the dead. Hope is, then, an earnest longing for the glorious future before us. It causes us to die to the world and to long sincerely to live with the Lord. Hope does not find its satisfaction in the things of this world. But desiring complete salvation, it looks longingly unto the inheritance of the saints in the light of eternity.

In the objective sense, hope is the glory itself. It is the object of our expectation and longing. Hope is the glory that will be initially revealed to us and in us when the earthly house of this tabernacle will be dissolved and we will enter into our Father's house of many mansions. It is ultimately the glory that has been prepared in order to be revealed in the last time, in the day of the Lord Jesus Christ, when everything will be finished and we will dwell in God's tabernacle with all the saints to behold the loveliness and beauty of our God.

That is hope.

Rejoicing in that hope, the child of God is happy.

Through that hope he rejoices in the midst of tribulation. The happiness of that hope carries him along on its wings and causes him to be patient in the midst of suffering, while he looks forward to complete deliverance.

The future smiles upon the believer. The gleaming rays of the approaching glory through hope shine down upon his dark path, filling him with joyful anticipation. But in the light of this hope he understands also that tribulation is necessary and must work for his benefit, to enable him to partake of this glory.

Let this hope make you rejoice. Otherwise there is no possibility of being patient in tribulation.

Let this hope make you rejoice. Then tribulation becomes light and quickly speeds past and disappears.

Let this hope make you rejoice. Tribulation then works for you an eternal weight of glory.

Being happy and blessed in this hope, do not forget to persevere in constant prayer.

No, you are not to pray to express all kinds of carnal desires. That would not be pleasing to God and would be of no profit to you. You are not to demand of the Lord that he transform your lot into one of good fortune and that he lighten your load. That would not be according to his counsel, nor would it strengthen you in patience in the midst of oppression. But a prayer that through faith opens the soul to God, expresses the heart to him, wills God to determine one's way, cleaves to him, and submissively gives oneself to him in order to be and remain one with him in his will without murmuring—such is the prayer that is pleasing to God. That is the prayer that can strengthen you. That is the prayer that enables you to rise up with the power of the Almighty that permeates you and fortifies you for the battle.

In that prayer, persevere.

Pray often. Pray constantly. Pray until you receive. Pray, not only when you bend your knees in your inner chamber, but also in the midst of battle and oppression. Live prayerfully, and pray while struggling and suffering.

In this way we are patient in tribulation, with our eye of faith fixed upon glory, and with the hand of faith prayerfully held securely by God in his hand.

You shall run, then, through a troop, and leap over a wall.

Then you will soon receive the crown!

28

A Threefold Requirement

"Then said Jesus unto his disciples, If any man will
come after me, let him deny himself, and take up his
cross, and follow me."

—Matthew 16:24

Then said Jesus!

And when he spoke, who is the word of God come in the flesh
and dwelling among us, who is the truth, who spoke not as the
scribes and Pharisees but taught with authority, from whose
mouth proceeded gracious words, words of eternal life, it always
was the proper moment for the particular word that flowed from
his lips.

Had not the Lord God given unto him the tongue of the
learned, that he should know how to speak a word in season to
him who is weary?

Never a word was spoken by him out of season; the contents,
the manner, and the occasion of his speech were always in perfect
harmony.

Then said Jesus to his disciples.

It was the proper psychological moment for the Lord to speak
exactly this word, for the disciples to hear and to begin, at least, to
receive it. For it is a moment of conflict between the spirit and the
flesh, between the kingdom of heaven and the kingdom of this
world, between the honor of man and the praise of God, between
light and darkness, between Christ and Belial. Therefore, it is the
moment when the light must judge the darkness, rebuke it, overcome it, and put it to shame; a moment when the light, having si-

lenced the voice of darkness, may calmly and majestically proceed on its way and point out the way to those who are called to walk in it. Clearly, the disciples had discerned that he was the Christ, the Son of the living God, and but a moment ago by the mouth of Peter they had confessed it. Little, however, they as yet understood concerning the implications of that confession. The name Christ for them was synonymous with glory and power, ascent to the mighty throne of David, a way of victory and conquest, and discipleship was by them considered from the viewpoint of the question, Who shall be the greatest?

The conflict was inevitable. And just now it had begun.

The words the Lord had spoken concerning himself had clashed with their own illusions about him, for he had pictured the way that lay before him as one of suffering and shame and reproach, even of death. To be sure, it was a way of glory, of ascent, of life; but the glory was to be reached only through the midst of shame, and the ascent must be preceded by a dark descent; the life was the life of resurrection, to be attained only through death.

And little they had been prepared to abandon their illusions and exchange them for this stark reality.

Flesh had rebuked the Spirit. The desire after the things of men had asserted itself over against the striving after the things of God. The darkness had made a fierce attempt to maintain itself over against the light. And the light had struck back mercilessly.

Lord, this shall not be unto thee!

Get thee behind me, Satan!

Then said Jesus unto his disciples.

At that psychological moment—when the disciples stood abashed, stunned by the clash of their illusions with reality, and when it appeared that they as yet little understood the implications of coming after him—Jesus spoke.

They had been rebuked severely. Their carnal notions had been swept away like a cobweb.

Now it was the moment for further instructions.

And now he spoke.

Would I come after Jesus?

Are you, am I, clearly convinced that we would come after Christ himself, the Christ of the Scriptures, and not after an illusion of him, not after a Jesus of our own imagination?

Are we prepared to leave him as he is, to take him at his own word concerning himself, then to follow him? The question is a profoundly serious one and must always induce introspection, self-examination in the light of the threefold requirement the Lord here announces as inevitable: denial of self, assumption of the cross, and following unconditionally.

The will to come after him could be characterized by nothing less.

To come after him, which is a figurative expression, means to be his disciple. To be his disciple implies that one hears his word and receives it, that he hides that word in his heart and allows it to be the controlling and guiding principle in all his conversation and life.

His word!

His entire word!

Not merely the part of it that may appear acceptable to us, so that after all we change his word of truth into our lie, but the whole, awful word of Christ, the word of God.

The word of him who is the truth. The word that mercilessly tears away all the righteousness of man in order to establish the righteousness of God; that closes the kingdom of heaven against all whose righteousness does not exceed the righteousness of the scribes and Pharisees, because it demands a righteousness that is inward, of the heart, and perfect, flawlessly in harmony with the righteousness of God. The word that must ever condemn the world, not only because it declares that it has not this righteousness, but also because it insists that it cannot attain to it, that declares that we are guilty and undone, worthy of death and damnation, that we are corrupt and wholly inclined to all evil, that leaves us no hope in self, no ground of self-righteousness on which to maintain ourselves. The word that reaches down to us only in our hopelessness, to declare unto us a righteousness that is of God, through the death and resurrection of Jesus Christ from the dead, a righteousness that is perfect, that is ours as an eternal gift of grace, that is imputed to us, that is also wrought in us through his Spirit, that justifies us freely and sanctifies us wholly, that makes us new creatures in an old world, light in the midst of darkness, citizens of Jerusalem in the midst of Babylon. The word that demands of those who are thus justified and sanctified that they shall be holy even as the Lord their God is holy in all manner of conversation and that they forsake the world and its lusts, fight the good fight, and be of God's party in all their speech and walk.

To hear and receive and heed that word in the midst of the world that lies in darkness is to come after him.

If any man will come after me.

Who is he that so wills?

No man by nature. The will to come after Jesus is the fruit of his own almighty grace. For the natural man is carnal, loves darkness, hates the light, loves the world, and seeks not the things of the kingdom of God. To come after Jesus. He must call, efficaciously, irresistibly call, "Follow me."

And paradoxical though it may sound, he who will come after Jesus is already after him.

That will, then, to come after Jesus, is it yours, is it mine?

Again we may ask the question, and in the light of the question examine ourselves, our way and our walk: Will we come after Jesus?

For many there be that say, "Lord, Lord," yet never will to come after him.

And even though we do will to come after Jesus as far as the deepest choice of our heart is concerned, there always remains much within us that wills not to follow him.

Besides, it is necessary and salutary to learn in an ever deepening sense what it means to be his follower.

Would you, would I, come after Jesus?

Strange requirements!

Let a man deny himself, let him take up his cross, let him follow me.

How directly contrary to the spirit of the world! How utterly without inducement or encouragement to the natural man is the call to come after the Son of man!

The world needs men who have self-ambition to spur them into activity, ambition to gain oneself a position, to make oneself a name, to heap riches upon riches, to open the gates of pleasure; and it offers these to its children in order to induce them to follow. Christ offers no inducement to the self-ambitious. On the contrary, if any man will come after me, let him deny himself.

The will to come after him is first of all and chiefly characterized by the readiness to deny oneself.

And mark you well, the word is let him deny *himself*! It would have been comparatively easy, had the Lord said let him deny something *to* himself. One may find this illustrated often in the world. Men will deny themselves many things for many reasons, in principle for their own sake. They will deny themselves food and drink, which they otherwise crave and relish, if their health is at stake. They will deny themselves leisure and rest if the object of their own ambition is involved. They will deny themselves the world and the things in the world, the more to gain the world. But the Lord's requirement is absolute: let him deny *himself*. It is the very opposite of maintaining oneself. It is the willingness and readiness to become nothing, not to insist on one's name and honor, on one's right and position, on one's means and possessions, no, not even on one's very life. It is the readiness to lose all things for Christ's sake, to have oneself wholly set aside, pushed out of sight, trampled underfoot. To deny oneself before God is not to insist on one's righteousness before him, but to confess that one is utterly lost in sin and must be clothed with the righteousness of God in Christ. It is the desire to be nothing before him in self, but to be all in him. To deny oneself before men is not to seek the praise of men, but to be always ready to suffer reproach and shame, prison and death, for his name's sake.

If any man will come after me, let him deny himself.

It is utterly impossible to do the one without the other. And he who imagines already to be after Jesus and finds himself wholly unwilling to deny himself labors under a very deceptive illusion.

For he does not come after Jesus to snatch a crown in the world, but a cross.

He is required, not merely to bear a cross, but to take it up.

And how shall one willingly assume the burden of a cross, unless he is willing to deny himself? For the cross he is required to assume is always centrally and in principle Christ's cross. The cross is not an emblem of suffering in general, of the suffering of this present time as it is inseparably connected with existence in the world. The slogan "Every house has its cross" is not true. All true crosses are but slivers of his cross. Christ's cross and the cross we must take up are related. Not, indeed, when you consider his cross as the emblem and means of atonement. Then it stands severely alone. Then he died that we might never die, but have everlasting life. But as the ultimate expression of the hatred of the world against God and his anointed, his cross is ours. They hated him because he was of God and they were of the world, because he was the light and they were of the darkness. And the servant is not greater than his Lord. If they hated him, they will also hate those who will come after him, for he is in them and becomes manifest through him. And his cross is still reflected in the crosses borne by those who would follow him.

Cross-bearing is, therefore, inevitable.

If any man will come after Christ, that will must be characterized by the will to assume the cross.

And bearing the cross of Christ, such a one must follow him.

He must follow, not lead. He must obey, not command. He must listen, not speak.

And when the Lord instructs him about his own cross, as well as about the cross one must bear who would come after him, the follower of Christ must not assert his own notions and insist, "Lord, this shall not be unto thee."

He must follow, silently, submissively, willingly, trusting that all is well; although the path appears to be rugged and steep.

Renouncing his own judgment to the word of the Lord.

Denying his own will to obey his.

Follow where he leads.

If any man will come after me, he must be thus equipped.

No mighty arm or mental acumen, no armor of steel and keen-edged sword, no record of fame and recommendation of men, no righteousness of the law or worthy deeds, does one need to come after Jesus.

No ambition to become great and mighty in the world, no pledge to conquer the world for Christ, to prophesy in his behalf, to cast out devils and do many mighty works, could possibly characterize the will to come after him.

He must deny himself.

He must take up the cross, the cross that is but the reflection of his.

And follow unconditionally with wholehearted surrender.

And then?

Must this be the last word? Shall then the wicked always prosper, be dominant, have the victory, and heap malice and hatred upon those who come after Jesus, and rage and be furious against them, and crucify and kill those who walk in the light? Shall shame and confusion and defeat be their only reward who follow Jesus? Is there no reward, no hope, no outlook of final victory, when the denial of self shall have an end, when the cross shall be removed from the bleeding shoulders to be exchanged for a crown, when patient and unquestioning following of Jesus shall terminate in the recompense of the reward?

Let him deny himself, let him take up his cross, let him follow?

Is it the very last that can be said?

It is, indeed, as far as this present time is concerned. It is, if your anxiously questioning gaze would fain look for escape from the cross in this world. The cross means death. Be therefore faithful even unto death.

Yet, rejoice and be exceeding glad.

For though you may find no reward in and with the world, and men revile you and persecute you and speak all manner of evil against you falsely for his name's sake, great is your reward in heaven.

If it were not so, you would, in coming after Jesus, be of all men most miserable.

But he is risen! He whom you follow endured the contradiction of sinners even unto the bitter end. Him more than any man the world hated and reviled, and upon him they performed all their evil will. Him they denied a place in this world, made an outcast, trampled underfoot, and made the object all their fury, until they had apparently vanquished him. And he denied himself and took up his cross. But his shame was changed to glory, his death into life, his cross into the crown, and he is seated at the right hand of God forever.

His glory is yours!

If you deny yourself, he will confess you and constantly pray that you may also be where he is.

If you bear the cross, he will prepare you a crown!

If you follow, he will lead you to glory!

Glory, heavenly and eternal!

29

Strength through Weakness

"The archers have sorely grieved him, and shot at
him, and hated him: But his bow abode in strength,
and the arms of his hands were made strong by the
hands of the mighty God of Jacob; (from thence is
the shepherd, the stone of Israel:)"
—Genesis 49:23, 24

His bow abode in strength!

Unharmed and victorious stands the church of God in the
midst of fierce conflict.

For, surely, the archers have sorely grieved him, shot at him,
and hated him. But his bow abode in strength.

The metaphor of the text presents a wonderful picture. It is
that of a single, lonely bowman, surrounded by fierce and bitter
enemies, experts in battle, trained to aim their arrows at his very
heart. They are filled with bitter hatred and are sorely provoked at
him. They can be satisfied with nought but his death. They draw
their bows, they shoot. The arrows fly thick. But the arrows of the
enemy do him no harm. They fly past him. And when all the
deadly shafts of the numerous foes have been shot at him, the solitary archer still stands, without as much as a scratch on his face or
hands, still grasping his bow, a lone victor over all his enemies.

How vividly real is the picture!

How true it had been in the life of Joseph personally. How he
had been encompassed by these fierce and bitter archers who
hated him and shot at him! How they had constantly aimed at his
destruction! His brethren had nourished a deadly hatred in their

breasts against him, until they had wickedly plotted to kill him, had cast him into the pit, and had finally sold him a slave to foreigners. Potiphar's wife had conceived in her wicked heart the hatred of wounded, sensuous love, and had persecuted him until he had been cast into the dark dungeon of the king's prison.

How the picture was realized in the history of Israel! Was there ever a nation so bitterly hated, so surrounded by deadly foes, so constantly shot at, so continually harassed from every side? Follow its history—from the time that wicked Pharaoh attempted to choke the nation to death in the river of Egypt; through the terrible wilderness, where every power of the world rose against it for its destruction; through the period of its being established in the land flowing with milk and honey, reigned by judges or kings, to the captivity; through the post-Babylonian period when it became a veritable plaything of the nations, who hated it, cruelly tortured, and scourged it—and say whether there was no reason for Israel's singer to wail, "Many a time have they afflicted me from my youth...the plowers plowed upon my back, they made long their furrows."

Again, how true the picture is with regard to the Lord, the head of the church. Was ever a man more solitary in the midst of cruel enemies? He did no evil, no guile was found in his mouth, he reviled not again when he was reviled, his foes were compelled against their will to admit that there was no guilt in him. Yet, how the enemy howled at him like a pack of wolves! How all the arrows were directed at his life! How he was despised as a contemptible thing, crushed, bruised, cast out as one who had no rightful place in all creation. The lonely archer in the midst of enemies who are bitterly provoked!

And was it different with the church of the new dispensation? Have they not hated the apostles and bitterly persecuted them? Have they not opened prison doors and dungeons, kindled the fires of stakes, whetted the swords of scaffolds, and invented instruments of most terrible torture for the people of God all through the ages?

Strange, amazing, this spectacle of an apparently harmless and powerless archer so bitterly hated, so persistently persecuted, so constantly shot at by enemies who surround him and leave him no standing room in the world.

What did he do? What wicked thing did he commit to provoke the wrath of these foes? Is his appearance deceiving, and is he not as harmless and innocent as one could imagine?

Or, perhaps, does he possess riches the enemies crave?

Do not misjudge this conflict. It is not a battle of flesh and blood, although it would appear to be. The conflict is essentially spiritual, a battle of darkness against the light, of iniquity against righteousness, of the lie against the truth, of the powers of darkness against the children of light. For the lonely archer, so constantly harassed, is one called out of darkness into the marvelous light of God, that he might show forth the praises of his God. He is in the world but not of the world. His God made him a stranger in the earth. His life, received by grace, is not from below, but from above. And standing by grace for the cause of God and his covenant in the midst of a world that lies in darkness, they hate him and aim at his destruction. The enemies may appear to be mere men, but they are representatives of the prince of this world, his host, inspired by his hatred of the Most High and of all that is of him. And the battle is not physical, but spiritual in character. The foes do not aim at the earthly life of the people of God's covenant, but at their spiritual life. The purpose is not to deprive them of their earthly goods, but of their heavenly treasures. And the arrows they shoot are not aimed at their earthly life, but at their heavenly life.

Spiritually they must be subdued, their light must be extinguished, their testimony must be silenced. And all the rest is but means to this end.

Thus it was with Joseph and the hatred of his wicked brethren and the abominable attitude of Potiphar's wife.

Such is the nature of the enemies of Israel all through its history, rooted as was their hatred in enmity against Jehovah.

Centrally it was thus with Christ and his foes. They hated him because he came to witness of the truth and of the light, and they loved darkness rather than light.

And such is the conflict of the church with the world all through the ages in the new dispensation.

But the marvel of it is that this lonely archer, apparently so weak and helpless, while surrounded by such mighty foes, prevails and gains the victory and remains unharmed!

His bow abides in strength!

How glorious a scene!

All the bitter foes of the solitary bowmen are vanquished, and only the bow of the lone man abides in strength.

But whence the power of him who appears so weak, who would seem to be so hopelessly the victim of the wrath of the foe? What is the secret of his power? Where lies the source of his prevailing strength?

Look at the picture once more and consider it closely.

At first sight the archer appeared alone and helpless and without hope of victory. But if you look again, eager to discover why this lone man is not overwhelmed and how it may be explained that his bow abides in strength, you notice that behind him stands the gigantic figure of the mighty God of Jacob, the shepherd of Israel and its rock. And the hands of this mighty Lord are on the arms of Joseph's hands, and by the touch of these hands of Israel's stone, there is into the feeble hands of the lonely archer an influx of power, the power of God himself, against which the enemy vainly battles and cannot prevail.

The power of the mighty God of Jacob is the safety of the people of God, of the church in the midst of the world.

They are kept in that power!

And, oh, how safe they are in that power, mighty though the foe may appear!

How sure they are of victory, though the enemies count their numbers by thousands upon thousands!

For consider the threefold name that is given to him who stands behind that lonely bowman. He is the mighty one of Jacob. That means that he is Jacob's God, the God of his people, who is not ashamed to be called their God in the conflict, seeing he prepared for them victory. And he is the mighty one. No other being next to him, under him, apart from him, in earth or heaven or hell possesses any might in himself. He alone is mighty, for he is strong in himself, the source of all strength, and even the enemies have no power except from him. Besides, he is Israel's shepherd who loves his flock before the foundation of the world, cares for them, leads them, feeds them, and is their protector in the midst of the foes who surround them and shoot at them. He is the good shepherd who gives his life for the sheep. He is also Israel's stone, the rock, who is steadfast and immutable, who never changes in himself and never alters in his attitude to his people. The Lord, faithful and true. Combine the names and you have the picture of Israel's aid in the conflict, the image of the almighty, loving, and ever faithful God. He stands behind the lonely archer, his arms around him, his hands upon the arms of his hands.

He is the secret of Joseph's power, the sole explanation of the amazing phenomenon that this lone man does not succumb in the conflict, is not overwhelmed in the battle, and that his bow abides in strength.

Of himself he has no power. He is weak and helpless.

And the enemy is apparently strong. The arrows fly thick all about him.

Now it is with arrows of vain philosophy and deceitful lies that the enemies shoot; now the shafts of the lusts of the flesh, the treasures and pleasures of the world, of name and fame, of riches and honor, are directed at their heart; now it is the weapons of the enraged world that are aimed at their very life. Incessantly the instruments of destruction are prepared for them.

Never would they be able to stand in this evil day, were they abandoned to their own strength.

Yea, the enemy would find a powerful ally even in their own

heart, by nature sinful and of the world, inclined to fight with the foe rather than combat him.

But the mighty God of Jacob, the shepherd of Israel, its stone, its almighty, ever faithful God, stands behind him and strengthens him, trains his hands for the battle and protects him against all the assaults of the enemy.

And the foes are vanquished; the lone man remains victor on the field of battle.

Marvelous scene!

———————

Strength through weakness!

Such is the profound message conveyed to the church of all ages by this blessing of the dying patriarch upon the head of his beloved son.

Do not change this message—that leaves all the glory to God and makes the conflict a gift of his grace to his people—into the error of dividing the glory of the victory between the lone archer and the mighty God of Jacob.

Do not say, as many love to say, that the battle and its victory are the result of the combined power and effort of God and man, of the mighty one of Jacob and his people. God a little, man a little; the battle for God by man and the power for the fight from him for whom the battle is fought; the willingness from man and the aid from the mighty one of Jacob; man striking a manful blow for God and God not leaving him to bear the brunt alone. No, emphatically no! Such is not the truth of God, and it is not what the metaphor with its charming picture teaches. It is the lie of proud, sinful man.

Look at the picture again, watch those hands on the arms of Joseph's hands, quickening them by their touch. Whose is the strength that causes Joseph's bow to abide in strength? Whence is the power that brings victory to this lonely archer? Whose is the battle and whose the conquest? It is all of the mighty God of Jacob and of him alone.

Do not say, "God and Joseph fight the battle."

Refuse to say, "God and the lonely archer gain the victory and overcome the enemy in the conflict."

Say, "Strength through weakness." The battle is the Lord's, not ours. The grace, that we may be called out of darkness into his marvelous light, that we may be placed in his battlefront in the midst of the world, is of the mighty God of Jacob, not of us. The power to fight and to gain the victory, the strength to vanquish every foe is from Israel's stone, not from us. The final glory, all the glory, is his. Ours is the place of humble thanks, thanks for the battle and for the enemy, thanks for the grace to fight and the power to win, thanks for the victory itself. All of him and none of us, for the arms of the mighty God of Jacob, of the shepherd and stone of Israel, are on our arms and prepare our hands for the conflict and cause our bow to abide in strength.

Strength through weakness.

Emphatically insist on this *through*!

It is not strength merely surrounding weakness, like a high wall, behind which we can well afford to feel safe, which the foe can never scale, and through which his deadly shafts cannot pierce. The power of the mighty God of Jacob is not protecting us without us, but *through* us; it is not a protection that lulls us to sleep, but that prepares us for the battle; the assurance of his faithful care and mighty power does not make his people careless and profane, but rather alert and strong, eager for the battle, able to fight, willing to suffer, courageous in the conflict, patient in tribulation. For, look once more at the picture. The arms of the mighty God of Jacob do not shield the lonely archer against the shafts of the foe, but the hands of Israel's stone are on the arms of his hands; the power of Jacob's mighty one flows through him.

And thus it is in reality.

Not without us but through us God fights his own battle, and we are of his party. And to fight his own battle through his people, he causes the power of his almighty hands, by grace, through faith, to flow through them, thus training them to gain the victory, which he prepared for them.

And thus all is well, all is grace, all the glory is God's.

It is given us of grace to believe in Christ.

It is grace that we may suffer with him.

Grace that we enter into his victory!

Strength through weakness!

30

Holding Fast Our Profession

"Seeing then that we have a great high priest, that is
passed into the heavens, Jesus the Son of God, let us
hold fast our profession."

—Hebrews 4:14

Seeing then ... let us hold fast!

Doctrine and exhortation follow each other in regular sequence in this profound and beautiful part of Holy Scripture.

While the exhortatory passages with which the epistle is interspersed occupy the position of inferences from preceding didactical expositions, at the same time they frequently are transitions to further instruction in the truth of the Christian profession to come.

Thus it is in the section that is introduced by the words that constitute the basis of this meditation.

In the preceding part of the epistle, the believers had received sufficient instruction to know and to acknowledge that they have a great high priest who is passed into the heavens—Jesus the Son of God. This had been the chief theme of all the author had written thus far. They were now in a position to see by faith that their high priest was far exalted above all that the shadows of the old dispensation could ever offer. In this position they were now quite receptive for the exhortation not to turn back from the reality of the new into the shadows of the old dispensation, but to hold fast their profession.

There was indeed need of this earnest exhortation, for under the pressure of temptation and persecution, there was a tendency to look back and once again to cling to the tabernacle and temple made with hands.

The church in the world is always in need of hearing this same exhortation: Let us hold fast our profession!

Within and without, the enemy of that profession ever tempts and presses us to abandon it.

But we have a great high priest who is gone into the heavens, Jesus the Son of God. Of him much has been written in the preceding section, and of his glory and greatness much more is still to be said.

Upon him believers must constantly fix the eyes of their faith.

Seeing him as the great high priest, beholding him with the eye of faith, they will not waver, though all hell rise up against them.

They will surely hear and heed this exhortation: Hold fast your profession.

Your profession!

Wonderful gift of God's grace!

But at the same time, a sacred obligation before the face of him who is the author of it, and the glory of whose grace is the end of it.

Your profession is that which—in the fellowship of the saints —is given you to know of the marvelous works of God, of the glory of his grace in the beloved, of the blessedness of salvation, redemption, the forgiveness of sins, and covenantal fellowship with the triune God. It is that which—through the word and the Spirit of Christ dwelling in the church—is revealed to you concerning the things which eye has not seen, neither ear heard, nor has ever arisen in the heart of man.

It is that glorious truth, that knowledge of the God of your salvation and of his everlasting covenant, as your profession.

It signifies that in fellowship with the church in the world, you embrace that truth by a true and living faith; that spiritually it has become flesh of your flesh, bone of your bone; that it controls and dominates your whole existence, your very life in the midst of the world; that now you become a living witness of him who called you, to speak of his name, his glory, and of the wonder of his marvelous grace; and that this testimony of your mouth is sealed and adorned by a walk worthy of God who called you into his kingdom and glory.

Your profession.

That is Christ, and yourself only in relation to him.

For the sum and substance of the profession that the Spirit, through the word of God, works in the church—and in fellowship with her, in the heart of every believer—is that Jesus is Lord.

Marvelous profession!

He, Jesus of Nazareth, the son of Joseph the carpenter, who was born in the stable of Bethlehem and found his first bed in the manger; who in all his life never rose above the humiliating level of that stable and of that manger; who had no form or comeliness, no beauty that men should desire him; who was despised and rejected of men, a man of sorrows, and acquainted with grief, before whom men hid their faces; who, as far as this world and his position in it was concerned, never had a name, or power, or glory; who was a servant of servants, and whose life ended in the shameful death of the accursed tree; whom even now, and throughout all the ages, all men, exactly as men, despise and reject—that Jesus is Lord!

That is the heart of the Christian profession.

It means that he is the Lord in himself, the very creator of the world, who in himself has all power and authority over heaven and earth and all they contain and that he is the only begotten Son, who is eternally in the bosom of the Father, God of God, light of light. It implies that this Lord of all assumed the form of a servant and in that form voluntarily emptied himself completely, descending into the deep and dark vale of the shadow of death and of the agony of hell, because he had taken upon himself the iniquities of his own, and with them and for them he walked as the servant of Jehovah, in perfect obedience of love, to bring the perfect sacrifice that would forever blot out the guilt of sin. It signifies also that God raised him from the dead, giving him testimony that he is righteous and that he exalted him at his own right hand, far above all principality and power and every name that is named, not only in this world, but also in that which is to come.

That is the Christian profession.

It is the profession in word and the manifestation of this profession in deed that this Jesus is our Lord, that we belong to him with body and soul for time and eternity, that his mind is our light, that his will is our law, and that we delight to keep his commandments with all our heart and mind and soul and strength, personally and in every relationship of life, in the home and on the street, in the church and in the factory, always and everywhere. For Jesus is Lord over all, and another lordship next to him is not to be acknowledged.

He is not *a* Lord, but *the* Lord—Lord universal and absolute!

And your profession means that you are, and insist on being, his servants in word and in deed.

Radical profession!

———————

Hold it fast!

For to persevere in that profession is a matter of life and death.

For "if thou shalt confess with thy mouth the Lord Jesus, and shalt believe in thine heart that God hath raised him from the dead, thou shalt be saved."

Hold fast, therefore, your profession.

To be sure, this means that you are zealous concerning the truth as it is in Jesus revealed in the Holy Scriptures, that as a church and as individual believers, you strive for the purity of the faith once delivered to the saints, and that you persistently refuse to be tossed about by any and every wind of doctrine.

It signifies too that you appropriate this pure revelation of the living Lord by a true and living faith, and that by this faith you cling to it, so that your mind is constantly enlightened by it as by a certain, spiritual knowledge, so that your will is wholly controlled and determined by it, so that you put all your confidence in him who is your Lord, and so that you are dominated by a sincere resolution to do his will and to walk in the midst of the world as before the face of your Lord without wavering.

It implies, finally, that you let your light shine, never hiding it under a bushel, that you confess the name of your Lord as a church in the preaching of his word and as individual believers in all your walk and life, so that always and everywhere, and come what may, you actually love the Lord your God with all your heart, with all your mind, with all your soul, and with all your strength, forsake the world, crucify your old nature, and walk in a new and holy life. It implies that in the midst of the world you reveal yourself as being of the party of the living God, revealed in Jesus Christ our Lord.

Hold fast your profession.

Preserve it, cling to it tenaciously, and by faith confess it and enact it in and before the whole world.

And take it very seriously.

For it is indeed a matter of life and death, not only of real, eternal life and eternal death, but also of life and death in this world.

In the holding fast of your profession, you must be wholly prepared, fully and unconditionally, without wavering or compromise, to accept the word of your Lord: He who will save his life shall lose it, and he who will lose his life for my sake will save it unto life eternal.

Even as the lordship of him whom you profess is the most absolute and intolerant and uncompromising lordship conceivable, so that it brooks no other lordship anywhere, so your profession of that lordship is most radical: it knows of no adaptation and of no compromise.

Say not in your heart that for the sake of your earthly life, job, position, safety, or well-being you may be excused for adapting your confession to circumstances, for compromising with the world. Say not that you must live and have a place in the world and have food, clothing, and shelter and that, therefore, you may hide your light, keep silent about your Lord, and accommodate your way of life to the demands of the world. For the moment you permit such considerations to influence your profession, you are lost. You are attempting to save your life, and you will surely lose it.

It must be either Christ or Belial.

You either profess or deny.

Hold fast, therefore.

For there is another lordship in the world: the lordship of the man of sin, of the son of perdition, of the beast, and of the false prophet. It too is intolerant. It is radically opposed to the lordship of your profession. It too aims at universal control, and it cannot rest until all the inhabitants of the world wonder after the beast and worship it. It will oppose you and seduce you by its false philosophy, even under the cloak of religiousness. It will tempt you to become unfaithful to your profession by offering you the privileges of the kingdom of this world, by threatening you with its furious wrath, by casting you out so that you can neither buy nor sell unless you openly acknowledge its lordship, and by putting the sword of the world power to your throat.

The power of that lordship is even now operating in the world, mightily striving to realize itself and to reveal itself in its ultimate manifestation.

Soon it will rise up out of the turbulent sea of the restless, sin-motivated, wrath-driven, warring nations.

Hold fast, therefore, your profession.

Yield not to the lust of the flesh, to the desire to save your life, to the seducing pleasures of the world. And be not afraid of its fury and implacable hatred.

Through the word of God, in the power of the Spirit, by prayer and supplication, persevere.

The time is at hand.

Hold fast!

Seeing then ...

Looking unto Jesus, the apostle and high priest of our profession.

Without that look of faith, that constant look upon him, you will surely be swallowed up by the waves of temptation and tribulation. But seeing him, you will be safe and steadfast, without fear of wavering.

He is your high priest.

Your Lord whom you profess is your high priest, who sacrificed himself for your sins and your transgressions and obtained for you the forgiveness of sins and perfect righteousness. He is your intercessor with the Father, who is acquainted by deepest experience with all your infirmities, with your sins and weaknesses, with your trials and temptations, with all your suffering and death, and who constantly prays for you with a prayer that is never denied. He is your all, in whom are all the spiritual blessings of salvation, and the one who constantly fills you with them.

And he is great.

He is Jesus, the revelation of the God of our salvation.

He is the very Son of God, infinite in power and glory, the Lord of all in himself. All things are of him and unto him. Even those mighty forces of darkness in the world that rise up against him to deny and oppose his lordship are of his own design. Therefore, all their raving and fury can only serve his purpose.

For he is passed into the heavens.

This Jesus was indeed the servant of servants in the days of his flesh. He was despised and rejected, and nowhere was he permitted to have a place in the world. This Jesus did indeed leave his earthly life as a castaway on the accursed tree, and the world appeared to have the victory over him. But God did not leave his soul in hell and did not permit his holy one to see corruption. He justified him, raised him from the dead, and gave him life and glory. He exalted him in the highest heavens and put him at his own right hand in heavenly places. He made him Lord of all.

Seeing then ... hold fast your profession.

Seeing the Lord whom you profess is so great a Lord, God's anointed Lord, hold fast your profession of him with fear and trembling, lest in any way you deny his glory.

Looking upon him who has the victory and who holds all the powers of darkness in his mighty hand, fear not.

Hold fast your profession, even unto the end!

The victory is yours!

31

Striving for the Faith of the Gospel

"Only let your conversation be as it becometh the
gospel of Christ: that whether I come and see you,
or else be absent, I may hear of your affairs, that ye
stand fast in one spirit, with one mind striving together for the faith of the gospel; And in nothing
terrified by your adversaries: which is to them an
evident token of perdition, but to you of salvation,
and that of God."

—Philippians 1:27, 28

Only!

This one thing must be emphasized now, at once, and always!

The apostle had confidence that he would abide in the flesh
for the sake of the Philippians and that he would continue with
them all, for their furtherance and joy of faith.

He would see them again, that their rejoicing might be the
more abundant in Jesus Christ by his coming to them again.

But this is not the most important matter. The question—
whether or not he would abide in the flesh and come unto them
again, whether they would see him and speak to him face-to-face,
or never meet him again in this world—is of relative significance.
The question was not without meaning for the Philippians. That
the apostle would abide in the flesh was surely more needful for
them. How edifying was his instruction, how powerful his word,
how encouraging his consolation, how strengthening his very presence!

Yet this was not the chief question.

Only, strive for the faith of the gospel!

There is only one requirement for the church of Christ in the world. She has only one calling, to which all other things are secondary and subservient. The saints must so walk that they realize the manifestation of the glory of Christ, that their conversation is worthy of the gospel, and that they strive for the faith of the gospel. This is the main thought of this whole passage. For the faith of the gospel the church must strive. That is her only concern. She need be concerned about nothing else. And to realize this sole and unique calling she must walk as becomes the gospel that she professes, must be united in unity of spirit and of mind, and must not be afraid of those who oppose.

Only—whether I am present or absent—let me hear of your affairs: that you are so united and so strive for the faith of the gospel.

For in fulfilling this calling, the church is not dependent upon a man, not even upon the presence of an apostle, but on Christ only.

Stand, therefore, and realize your calling in the midst of a hostile world.

Without fear!

_____

Striving for the faith of the gospel.

The gospel is the promise, and the promise is Christ, and the faith of the gospel is the truth concerning Christ, as it is believed by the church and confessed by her in the midst of the world that lies in darkness.

Christ as the revelation of the God of our salvation—that is the gospel. Christ, the anointed, who was ordained from before the foundation of the world to be Lord of all, the firstborn of every creature, unto whom, for whom, and through whom all things were made; the first begotten from the dead; the head of the church; Lord in his own right, because he is the only begotten Son of God and Lord of all things by divine ordination, because he fought the battle and overcame, because he suffered and was obedient even unto death—that is the gospel. Christ for us, who assumed human flesh and appeared in the form of a servant, who revealed unto us the Father in word and work, who made atonement for the sins of his own by shedding his lifeblood on the accursed tree, who was raised to glory and exalted at the right hand of God as the Lord of lords and the King of kings—that is the gospel. Christ in us, who received the promise of the Holy Ghost and in the Spirit returned unto us to dwell in us and to make us partakers of his own life and of all the blessings of salvation—that is the gospel. And Christ through us, who is the vine while we are the branches, who bears fruit in us and we through him, so that we may walk in all the good works God prepared for us—that is the gospel.

Christ—the whole Christ—in all his riches, as the revelation of the God of our salvation.

Christ as the sole Lord, ruling by his word and Spirit in and over his own, and ruling over the world by his power.

Christ, unto whom every knee must bow, in heaven, earth, and hell, and whom every tongue must confess to be the Lord, to the glory of God the Father.

Christ, in whom alone I trust for my salvation, excluding and rejecting every other, and in whom I have redemption, even the forgiveness of sins, and eternal life.

Christ, to whom I belong with body and soul, for time and eternity, whom I acknowledge as Lord over my existence and life in this world; over my body and over my soul; over my thoughts and all my desires; over my talents and powers, my wealth and my possessions, my wife and my children; over my position in the world, in the church, in the state, in shop and office; and over all my walk and conversation.

That is the gospel!

The faith *of* the gospel is not the same as our faith *in* the gospel. The expression is not to be understood in the subjective sense. It rather denotes the truth of the gospel as it is appropriated by the faith of the church, expressed and confessed by her in the midst of a hostile world, and maintained by her over against all opposition. Just as we speak of the Reformed churches, so the text speaks of the gospel-faith, meaning its truth as it is known and believed, appropriated and confessed by the church by the grace of the Holy Spirit. Hence to strive for the faith of the gospel is to contend for all the fullness of the truth of Christ, the Son of God, the Lord of all, the redeemer of his people, the heir of all things.

For that faith the church must strive.

Such is her high, her chief, calling.

The faith of the gospel she must preserve in all its purity, for unto her it has been entrusted. The riches of that faith she must display. That faith she is called to proclaim, in her own midst, preaching the gospel of Christ and instructing the generations to come in its glorious mysteries of salvation. The banner of that faith she must unfurl in the midst of the world, among all nations, even unto the ends of the earth. That faith she is called to confess in word and deed, everywhere and in all relationships of life. All of this must assume the form of strife. For the faith of the gospel she must contend, for the world hates and opposes it. It will gainsay it, attempt to corrupt it, and try to silence the voice of the church. False teachers will ever attempt to creep in unawares and to destroy the faith of the gospel by their pernicious lies. Shame and reproach will be heaped upon the defenders of that faith. A place will be denied them in the world. Hence in proclaiming and confessing the faith of the gospel, the church must expect opposition.

Striving for the faith of the gospel!

For that strife she must ever be prepared, putting on the whole armor of God.

Like athletes in the contests of the Grecian games, she must exert all her efforts and concentrate all her powers in order to be victorious in this strife.

She must strive together in unity.

Standing together in the fellowship of the gospel, the saints must not strive with one another, but together stand opposed to the world of darkness, and as one man contend for the faith, proclaiming the Christ of the gospel, confessing that he alone is Lord, and fighting the good fight of faith.

Even unto the end.

———————

Only, walk worthy of the gospel.

Let your conversation be as it becomes the gospel of Christ.

And stand fast in one spirit, with one mind striving together for the faith of the gospel.

In the sphere of things spiritual, yea, there more than anywhere else, all things are inseparably related and connected. How shall the church strive for the faith of the gospel if her members walk unworthy of the gospel? And how shall she unitedly contend for that faith, unless she stands fast in one spirit and is of one mind?

Walk as becomes the gospel.

Ah, how otherwise shall you be in a position to contend for its faith? Would you strive for the faith that you deny at every step you take on life's path? Oh, you may contend for a philosophy of man, for the wisdom of the world, by word of mouth, without even making an attempt to realize that philosophy in your own life. A mere theory it is to you, a matter of intellectual pastime. But the gospel is the promise, and the promise is Christ. The faith of the gospel is not a matter of the head, but of the heart; it is not a philosophy, but the living truth of God; it is not an intellectual theory, but it is a faith.

It demands your heart and all its issues.

To appropriate that faith means that you know it as you know nothing else, with your whole being and existence, that you put all your confidence in it, that you rely on it in life and in death, and that you esteem the riches of which it speaks more glorious that anything and everything the world can offer. The faith of the gospel demands your life. It requires of you that you stand in the covenant of God in Christ, that you love him with all your heart, with all your mind, with all your soul, and with all your strength, and that you forsake the world, crucify your old nature, and walk in a new and holy life.

That is the implication of a walk worthy of the gospel.

It is a walk that does not put the gospel to shame.

It means that you walk as a people who have been brought under the power and the complete domination of the faith of that gospel, who are called out of the world, redeemed and delivered from sin, sanctified unto the God of your salvation.

Walking thus, and thus only, you will be in a position to contend for the faith of the gospel.

Your conversation being worthy of the gospel, you will maintain the unity of the Spirit and of the mind in which you may strive together in unison, as one man, for the faith of the gospel.

For then you walk in the Spirit.

The one spirit of the church is the Spirit of Christ. He dwells in Christ as the head, in the church as his body, and in the individual believers only in fellowship with that body.

To stand fast in one spirit implies that you are all partakers of that one Spirit of Christ, that he dwells in you and works in you all one mind, one will, one purpose, one desire: the mind and will of Christ, the purpose to strive for the faith of the gospel, the desire to be more and more conformed according to the image of Christ who is the sum and substance of that faith.

Stand fast in one spirit—that Spirit!

Walking worthy of the gospel.

Never fear!

In nothing be terrified by your adversaries.

This too is inseparably connected with all that precedes.

If you do not walk worthy of the gospel and stand fast in the oneness of the Spirit of Christ, there is neither sense nor reason in this exhortation to be fearless over against your adversaries. For then your striving for the faith of the gospel is vain and powerless, and the adversaries of the faith will leave you alone. You are a friend of the world and know nothing of the battle of Jehovah, the suffering of Christ and its fellowship, and the joy of being without fear, though a host should rise against you.

But walk as becomes the gospel of Christ, confess him as your Lord, adorn your confession by a walk worthy of the gospel, forsake the world and be a friend of God, stand fast in one spirit, being dominated by and living in the sphere of the Spirit of Christ, and so strive for the faith of the gospel, and your adversaries will arise on every side. They will arise in greater number and with more determined opposition as the coming of the Lord draws nearer and the man of sin is being revealed in all the horror of his iniquity. They will arise against you according as you contend for the faith.

But you will then be in a position to hear this word: In nothing be terrified.

You will not fear, for in this opposition you will see a double, antithetical token, a divine sign, a word of God to you.

To the adversaries, this opposition will be an evident token from God of their sure perdition. They oppose your walk as it becomes the gospel, and they hate you for striving for the faith of the gospel. Their hatred and their opposition are their own condemnation. As sons of perdition they become manifest. To you this same opposition is a token of salvation. The hatred of the devil is to you a sign that his dominion is destroyed, and that you belong to the God of your salvation. The victory is yours. Eternal glory awaits you.

And it is all of God.

He places the adversary on your way to create the double sign.

Your faithfulness is his grace; the opposition of the adversary is his trial.

Be not terrified at all!

Fight the good fight without fear!

The victory is yours!

32

Labor for the Rest

"Let us labour therefore to enter into that rest, lest
any man fall after the same example of unbelief."
—Hebrews 4:11

Labor for rest!

For *that* rest, *the* rest, the final rest!

For, though there were several days of rest in the past, there still remains a rest for the people of God.

In the first paradise stood the first man Adam, an image of him who was to come, called to labor that he might enter into God's rest. Six days and one marked the period of God's perfected creation. The Most High had labored to enter into his rest. The same sequence of six days and one, of labor and rest, was ordained for the creature that was made after his own image. Always a rest loomed before him, the rest of God, the blessedness of his everlasting fellowship.

Yet it was not the final rest for which the first man might labor. Even as he was an image of him who was to come, so the rest, which by his labor he might attain, was but a picture of a better and more blessed rest God had prepared for those who love him.

Adam did not enter into the rest that was set before him.

He failed through unbelief.

Instead of laboring for the rest that loomed before him, he chose rather the rebellion of sin and the slavery of the devil, and thus became a weary toiler, without the prospect of ever entering into rest, a drudge whom sin bore down with loads of grief and sorrow and suffering, a slave of the prince of darkness, with nought to anticipate but darkness and death and everlasting desolation. For the wages of sin is death. And because of the sin of one man, the rest seemed hopelessly lost and was, indeed, irretrievable for sinful man.

But our covenant God continued to work.

He spoke of another day, of a better Sabbath, of a far more blessed rest than Adam ever knew or could have attained, the fruit of a wondrous work that would be a revelation of God's amazing power and unfathomable wisdom.

For he had chosen unto himself a people.

A city and country he had prepared them, a land of everlasting rest, in which he would always be their God and they would forever be his people, where he would continuously spread his tabernacle over them and where they would incessantly dwell in his presence. He, their own God, would labor to lead them into that rest.

He visited his people as they groaned under the yoke of bondage in Egypt. He revealed the glory of his name and his marvelous power when he delivered them out of the cruel hand of Pharaoh, when he safely guided them through the Red Sea, destroying the enemies who still pursued them. He led them as a shepherd through the terrible desert, feeding them from heaven, satisfying their thirst from the flinty rock, filling the hearts of their enemies with fear, inflicting terrible defeat upon all who opposed them. He divided the swelling waters of Jordan before them and opened the gate for them into the promised rest, drove out the nations, and fulfilled his promises made unto the fathers. He established his own house on Mount Zion, and dwelled among them, ruling over them as their king, loving them as a father, blessing them with covenantal blessings from heaven. He had led his people into the rest.

Yet even this rest was not final.

It was only a shadow of the rest that was to come. Jerusalem on earth was not an abiding city, and Canaan was itself a promise of better things to come.

Still God worked. Still he spoke of another day, indicating that the ultimate realization of the Sabbath still loomed in the future. Toward that rest pointed all the ceremonies, and of it spoke all the prophets who declared the will of God. That rest was to be prepared by the labor and toil of God's own Son, who for that purpose assumed the form of a servant. He came, and in him God visited his people once more, as they groaned under the yoke of sin and the law. With a mighty hand and in wondrous love, he labored to remove that burden, to destroy the enemies who held them in bondage. He toiled and struggled until the bloody sweat was pressed from his brow, and his soul was exceedingly sorrowful even unto death. He continued the battle until he entered into the deepest depth and darkness of the prison of death, shedding his own lifeblood and leaving his earthly form on the battlefield, so that he might lead his brethren into the rest. He battled unto victory. He labored until the end. And on the day of his resurrection, he entered with all his brethren into his glorious rest. At the open grave, whence he issued in glory, victor over the bondage of sin and death, he stands and calls, "Come unto me, all ye that labor and are heavy laden, and I will give you rest." It was the "other day" of which God had spoken. On that day of his resurrection, all his brethren rejoice and celebrate that God has prepared them a Sabbath.

Into his perfected work they enter.

And by faith entering into that perfected work, they are liberated from the law of sin and death and enter into the rest of God's covenant.

Yet, even so, there still remains a rest for the people of God.

In principle they have entered into the rest. But the perfection of that rest looms in the future, in the heavenly city God has prepared for them.

When the earthly house of this tabernacle shall be dissolved and they shall have a house with God, not made with hands, eternal in the heavens; when all the battle is over, and the rest-giver shall come again in all the power of his appearance to destroy the last enemy, to glorify all his brethren, to create new heavens and a new earth in which righteousness shall dwell; when all the weary night is past and there shall be no more night; when God shall spread his glorious tabernacle over all forever—the rest will be perfected!

Labor to enter into that rest!

Yea, let us labor.

Oh, to be sure, the realization of that rest is certain and depends not on our labor, but solely on the amazing toil of the rest-giver, who shed his lifeblood for us. Never vainly and proudly imagine that your labor adds at all to his merit and to the infinite value of his toil.

But has it not been given us in the cause of Christ, not only to believe in him, but also to battle and to suffer with him?

Is it not his own good pleasure that for a short time we should be in the world to the praise of his glory?

The way to the final rest for all the children of God must be a way of struggle and labor, of toil even unto death.

It cannot be otherwise.

For as we enter into God's rest by faith and partake of his liberty, we become estranged from the world, cease from its evil works, and are children of light. These things are inseparably connected. No one is able to profess that he has entered into God's rest unless he also is actually translated out of darkness into God's marvelous light and begins to show forth the praises of him who called him. For no one can serve two masters, God and mammon, and no one can consistently seek two cities, the earthly and the heavenly. If we have become partakers of the rest of God in Christ Jesus and have been made citizens of the heavenly city, we have also become strangers in the world and condemn its evil works. For that reason the prince of this world and all his host are opposed to us. They will impede our progress to the heavenly city. They will attempt to seduce us from the way. And they are powerful masters of many means. Now they sow doubt and unbelief by vain philosophy; now they blind the eyes and captivate the heart by the glitter of treasures and the attraction of pleasures; now they intimidate by threats and menaces of sufferings and persecutions.

And a powerful ally they have in our own evil hearts, so easily induced to believe the lie, to seek the pleasures and avoid the sufferings and persecutions of the world.

Let us labor, therefore, to enter into that rest.

Let us diligently endeavor, let us put forth all our effort, let us faithfully struggle, that we may attain to the heavenly city.

How necessary is the admonition!

How needful that we hide it in our hearts and constantly have it before the light of our consciousness: let us therefore labor to enter into that rest!

How well, to make it our daily prayer: "Lord, grant me grace to labor, day-by-day, that I may enter into the rest!"

For, to labor for the rest implies that we have our minds set on it, fixed on the things above with undivided attention and interest. It signifies that we seek the heavenly things exclusively, not the things on the earth. It means that the rest is the supreme, the sole, object of our hope for which we actually count all other things but dross and dung. Our hearts and minds cannot be divided. We cannot love the things above and the things of the world at the same time. We will not labor to enter into the rest while we labor to gather the treasures of the world. Our minds and hearts cannot be fixed on the untold bliss of the everlasting pleasures of heaven while they are craving after the lusts of the flesh and the pride of life. And, oh, who does not know how his sinful mind is inclined to be captivated by the things of the world and to forget the things that are above?

Let us labor, therefore.

Laboring implies that we make all earthly things subservient to the heavenly. No, it does not mean that we neglect our earthly calling and haughtily despise the things of this present time. Shall the pilgrim disdain the tent, be it ever so humble, in which he finds shelter on the way? But the tent remains to him a means to an end, though he faithfully cares for it and carries it with him from day to day. No solid foundations he builds under it, but pitches it by the roadside, ready to roll it up in the morning and to continue the journey. The tent is for him a means to reach the desired goal. And thus the Christian stranger lives in a tent. With it he must labor to enter into the final rest. He must not seek his abiding dwelling place in it, neither must he so adorn it that he would not gladly exchange the tent for the heavenly building. The tent must not become an obstacle for him to enter into his rest. Temporal things must be subservient to eternal, the things below to the things above. Who is not ready to confess that his soul cleaves unto the dust, that the tent frequently becomes a hindrance rather than a means to enter into the final rest?

Let us, therefore, labor.

Negatively, laboring implies that we are always willing to sacrifice all things for the attainment of that final rest. When confronted with the choice between the rest or the world, the Christian sojourner may not hesitate. Name and fame, honor and position, wealth and possession, father and mother, brother and sister, wife and husband, son and daughter, home and earthly happiness, liberty and earthly life, all must be accounted dross and dung in comparison with the glory and blessedness of the final rest. The Christian must be willing to deny himself and bear the cross of Christ, rather than the crown of the world. For the cross of the Lord yields a crown in the final rest, while the crown of the world yields everlasting desolation. And, oh, who does not realize what a struggle it costs even the firmest of Christians constantly to make that choice?

Let us, therefore, labor to enter into that rest.

And do not forget continually to watch in prayer.

Your own power is nought and the enemy is mighty. Battling on in your own strength you would soon succumb. In the battle you are utterly dependent on the very grace by which you were translated a stranger in the world.

Watch and pray, that you may not fall into temptation.
Yea, labor for the rest!

Humbly labor to enter in!

Working out your own salvation with fear and trembling.

And do not proudly and vainly imagine that you are beyond the stage in which such admonitions are needed, lest you fall.

A terrible example of unbelief you have before you in those who could not and did not enter on account of their unbelief.

With the people of God they had been delivered out of the bondage of Egypt, with them they all passed through the Red Sea and were baptized into Moses, with them they were witnesses of his mighty deeds, and with them they ate of the manna and drank out of the rock. But they had no faith, they did not cling to the unseen God, their eyes were not fixed on the land of rest but on the pleasures of Egypt, they could not endure the hardships of the journey, neither had they courage to fight the battles of Jehovah with the giants of the land. The terrible displeasures of God, as fierce as his grace is sweet, cast them down in the wilderness. They did not enter in.

These things were written to be ensamples unto us.

Lest we fall into the same example of unbelief.

Not, indeed, as if God's saints could perish in the desert. By his grace they were called, by his grace they shall persevere until the end, and by his grace they shall surely enter in.

But by that grace they must travel a way of battle and toil.

And on that way of labor and battle the Most High cheers them on and admonishes them, encourages them, warns them from ways of wickedness, and urges them to be faithful unto death, that no one take their crown.

He does so by word and example!

Positively, they have before them the example of a veritable cloud of witnesses who trod the same pilgrim's way as they, who lived in the same faith, who fought the same battle, who bore the same cross, who passed through the same sufferings inflicted on them by the same enemies, who were supported by the same grace, and who gained the victory of the rest in the end. Negatively, they have before them the fearful example of unbelief, warning them from ways of wickedness and disobedience, reminding them of the weakness of the flesh and the waywardness of their sinful hearts.

That cheerfully they might follow the one, and humbly they might fear the other.

Let us labor, therefore, to enter in!

Humbly labor!

33

God for Us

"What shall we then say to these things? If God be
for us, who can be against us? He that spared not his
own Son, but delivered him up for us all, how shall
he not with him also freely give us all things?"
—Romans 8:31, 32

We shall say, "God is for us."

We shall say, "God spared not his own Son, but delivered him
up for us all."

We shall say, "Nothing and no one can possibly be against us
if God be for us, which he surely is."

We shall say, "He will surely also freely give us all things with
our Lord Jesus Christ, his own Son, whom he did not spare."

That is the answer to the question, What shall we say then?

It is the answer of faith, the Christian answer, besides which
there is no answer, for no one of the princes of this world has ever
found an answer, nor ever will find an answer to the question,
What shall we say then? But the Christian has the answer because
God gave it to him. He has the all-comprehensive answer, the answer that satisfies because it settles the matter, because it is triumphant over all things, and because it is a well-founded answer.
Faith gives the answer with a view to these things, on the basis of
these things, the answer that must follow, the only possible answer because these things are true.

What shall we say, then, to these things?

What is the conclusion with respect to the things that are seen
and that are the object of our natural, temporal, earthly experi-

ence, seeing that these things are the premises from which the conclusion must be drawn?

If we are in Christ Jesus; if there is no condemnation for us; if we are already liberated from the law of sin and death by the law of the Spirit of life; if the Spirit of Christ dwells in us; if by the Spirit we are led so that we mortify the deeds of the body; if, therefore, we are children of God, heirs of God and joint heirs with Christ, so that we look forward to an inheritance so great and glorious that even all the sufferings of this present time are not worthy to be compared with it; if even all creation stands with uplifted head, groaning and travailing in pain, looking for the glorious liberty of the children of God; if we have the firstfruits of the Spirit, an earnest of the full harvest, and groan within ourselves waiting for the adoption, to wit, the redemption of our body; if the Spirit groans within us, helping our infirmities, when we know not what to pray for as we ought; if he who searches the hearts always hears the groanings of the Spirit; if God in his eternal and unchangeable foreknowledge ordained us to be made like unto the image of his Son, that he might be the firstborn among many brethren; if he called, justified, and glorified us; if all things must surely work together for good to those who love God—what shall we say then?

What is the conclusion, the all-comprehensive answer, to every possible question you may further ask in the midst of the world?

We shall say that God is for us.

And if God be for us, nothing and no one can be against us.

He will surely give to us all things freely.

God is for us!

There is a triumphant challenge in these words. Positively, these words express that God loves us, that he makes us the objects of his divine favor and lovingkindness, that he aims at our good, that he works in our behalf, and that he purposes our eternal salvation.

With a view to the antithesis and with a view to the world, in the midst of which this confession is made, the words mean that God is on our side. That this triumphant confession is made in the midst of the world, of the things of this present time, and of the powers of opposition, is evident from the next question: Who can be against us?

Many are the forces that array themselves against us. Many are the influences that appear to be against us. Many are our enemies who seem to be able to harm and destroy us. There are all the powers of darkness; there is the mighty devil and his host; there is the world, its hatred, its temptation, its lust of the flesh and lust of the eyes and pride of life, and its power and persecution; there is the power of sin within us and without us, of guilt that makes us the objects of condemnation, and of corruption by which we increase our guilt daily; there is the operation of the wrath of God in our world, the sufferings of this present time and death.

But God is on our side over against all these powers of darkness.

Mark well: God, the living God, he who is really God, is for us, is on our side, and works on our behalf.

The significance and strength of the assurance that someone is for us depends on the power and authority and character of him on whom we rely, who stands and works in our favor, and who is on our side. Hence when we profess that God is for us, all the emphasis must fall on God. He is God in relation to us—our God; he is God in relation to all things; he is God in relation to all the powers of opposition and darkness. He is the absolutely supreme judge of heaven and earth, from whose verdict there is no appeal, and who most surely executes his own judgments. If he is for us, he will surely justify us and clothe us with his own righteousness. He is the creator of all things in the whole universe, who made all things strictly according to his sovereign good pleasure, calling the things that were not as if they were. If he is for us, he surely created all things with a view to and adapted to our eternal salvation. He is the sovereign ruler over all, who sustains and governs all things according to his own purpose, so that there is nothing that betides against his will. Rather, all things operate according to his good pleasure—things great and small, things good and evil, even the powers of darkness, of the devil, of sin and death. If he is for us, he rules all things on our behalf, and surely all things must tend to our eternal salvation.

If God be for us—God, who is the Almighty, so that he is not merely stronger than all our enemies, but so that all power in heaven and on earth, even the power of the forces of darkness, is his; God, who is the all-wise, who arranged all things according to his sovereign purpose to be perfectly adapted to the salvation of his own in Christ Jesus, and who executes that purpose without fail; God, who is the Amen, the Alpha and Omega, the unchangeable, with whom there is no variableness neither shadow of turning, the faithful one—if this God is for us, he was and is and shall be for us forever.

All-sufficient assurance!

Blessed revelation!

How shall I attain to the assurance that God is for his people, and that I may consider myself included in their number?

If I know that God is for me, I know all that is necessary to know in the midst of the present darkness of sin and death. But how can I know?

Do not all things testify against the profession that God is for us? Do they not all with one accord proclaim that he is filled with wrath against us? Is not his wrath revealed from heaven against all the iniquity and ungodliness of men? Is there not the suffering of this present time, the anguish of the entire world, the agony of death? Does not my own conscience condemn me and testify that God is against me? Am I not a sinner? Is not my nature corrupt? Do I not daily increase my guilt?

Yes, but in the midst of this darkness there shines the light of his countenance upon us in the face of Christ Jesus our Lord.

There is—all testimonies to the contrary—his own word that assures us that God is for us. It is the word of the cross: he spared not his own Son, but delivered him up for us all.

Mystery of mysteries!

Amazing, unfathomable love divine!

God delivered up his own Son. He spared him not—him, his own. To be sure, his own in distinction from us, his adopted children. His own, the eternal, the natural Son of God, being of his being, Spirit of his Spirit, essence of his essence, not born but begotten, distinct from the Father, yet like him, begotten of the Father, yet coeternal with him, God of God, blessed forever, his own, all he had, his most precious, his only beloved, on whom was concentrated all his divine love, who was and is and will be eternally the object of all his good pleasure, his own—himself.

Amazing depths of love!

He delivered him up. He spared him not. He, God, the living God, the triune God, delivered him up. The Father delivered him up, the Son delivered himself up, the Spirit delivered him up.

Delivered him up to what? To the divine wrath. Who can fathom it? God, through and in his Son bearing his own wrath in the likeness of sinful flesh? He delivered him up into the likeness of sinful humanity; he delivered him up into the darkness of his humiliation, suffering, and agony, in the garden and on the cross; he delivered him up into the deepest darkness of death and hell, pouring out all the vials of his wrath over his head—over him, his own Son. Even in that darkest hour he was still his own Son, the well-beloved, eternally in the bosom of the Father. Is then the suffering of the Son in the flesh not also the suffering of the Father and of the Spirit? Did not the love that delivered him up to the agony of the cross suffer with the beloved, delivering himself up into the throes of death?

O God of our salvation, here we only ask and tremble.

But looking at that cross, we know that God is for us.

He spared him not.

Notice the suggestion of the alternative. He spared him. Does this not suggest that before the eternal divine mind, there was—as far as we can humanly stammer about these profound and amazing mysteries—the alternative: bring us to glory and let his Son go into hell or spare his Son and let us go to eternal desolation. Standing before that alternative, he did not hesitate, not even when his well-beloved cried to him in the garden, but he delivered him up for us and spared him not.

Does he then not love us?

Delivered him up for us all, in our stead. The wrath that is poured out over his head on the accursed tree is properly the wrath we should bear. We were enemies of God, and he loved us. We were guilty, and he came to die for us, to bear his own wrath in our stead, for us all and on our behalf, that we might be clothed with righteousness before his face and that he might bring us into the glorious liberty of the children of God.

For us all.

To be sure, these "all" are not all men. They are his own. And his own are the elect.

Yet, do not change the words. Do not say that he delivered him up for the elect. Leave the triumphant shout in that personal form: he delivered him up for us all.

For us, who are in Christ Jesus by a true and living faith, so that we believe on his name. For us, who are delivered from the law of sin and death by the law of the Spirit of life, who are led by the Spirit to mortify the deeds of the body, who are the children of God, who have the firstfruits of the Spirit, who are saved in hope—for us who are willing to suffer with Christ, that we may also be glorified together.

For us all he delivered him up, his own Son.

Look, then, at the cross!

Behold God, your God, the God of your salvation, delivering up his own Son!

And say, despite all testimonies to the contrary: God is for us!

What shall we say then?

We will say, "God will give us all things with Christ. If he is for us—so for us that he spared not his own Son—how can it possibly fail that he shall surely give us freely all things with him?"

All things.

The question is superfluous whether all things must be taken in the unlimited sense, so that the word of God here teaches that the children of God will be heirs of all created and glorified things in the new heavens and the new earth, or if it is to be understood in the sense of all things that God purposed to give them. There is no real difference. Surely God will freely and graciously realize unto his people all things that from before the foundation of the world he purposed to bestow upon them; he will fulfill his promise in all its fullness. That promise includes nothing less than all things in the most unlimited sense. The saints—and they only—will inherit all things in heaven and in earth forever.

With him.

How shall he not give all things with him?

He gave his own Son. Will he then not give the rest? He gave the greater. Will he fail to give the smaller? He gave the greater in order that he might give us all things. Will he then be found unwilling to give us what for the very purpose of giving us the same he spared not his own Son? In Christ Jesus our Lord he has given us all things even now. Christ the crucified, who was delivered into deepest death and hell, is raised and exalted at the right hand of God, filled with glory and honor as the heir of all things. With him we are joint heirs, and with him God will surely give us the eternal, incorruptible, undefilable inheritance that never fades away.

Can he fail? Will the powers of opposition, the powers of sin and death, be able to deprive us of the glorious inheritance and prevent us from entering into it?

God is for us!

Who shall be against us?

Powers there are indeed, and enemies many, who appear to be

against us, who array themselves against the saints of God in Christ in this world—powers that would sometimes appear to realize their wicked purpose.

Yet, how can they? God is for us. Not only must they fail to realize their purpose, they must even work for our salvation, for our God is the living God, God even over them.

We are more than conquerors through him who loved us!

34

Who Shall Separate?

"Who shall separate us from the love of Christ? shall
tribulation, or distress, or persecution, or famine, or
nakedness, or peril, or sword? As it is written, For
thy sake we are killed all the day long; we are accounted as sheep for the slaughter. Nay, in all these
things we are more than conquerors through him
that loved us. For I am persuaded, that neither
death, nor life, nor angels, nor principalities, nor
powers, nor things present, nor things to come, Nor
height, nor depth, nor any other creature, shall be
able to separate us from the love of God, which is in
Christ Jesus our Lord."

—Romans 8:35–39

The final question and its answer!

Who shall separate us from the love of Christ?

I am persuaded that no created thing shall be able to separate
us from the love of God that is in Christ Jesus our Lord.

If this is true, then no one and nothing can be against us.

Our would-be accusers are silenced. Eagerly they appear in the
courtroom of the judge of heaven and earth, who surely will do
right. Gladly they bring their indictments against the elect to prove
their damnable state, but shamefacedly they sneak away, for they
have found that it is God who justifies. Who, then, shall lay anything to the charge of God's elect?

Gladly they would sit on the judgment seat in order to bring a
verdict of condemnation against the people of God. But they have
found that the judgment seat was already occupied by him who

was anointed thereunto from before the foundation of the world. Christ, the one who died and was raised again from the dead, who also is the advocate of all whom the Father gave to him, and who makes intercession for them, is sitting on the right hand of God and has become the sole judge in all the universe. Where, then, is the condemner?

Yet, one question remains.

It is evident that Christ loves us, that God loves us in Christ, and that there is no condemnation for us.

But will someone perhaps be able to separate us from the power of that love?

Suppose that an infuriated mob took me before a judge in a worldly court, loudly accusing me of murder of which I am innocent, and insisted upon my condemnation. Suppose that the accusations against me were found to be without ground, so that the accusers dropped off. Suppose that the judge passed a verdict of not guilty and that I am set at liberty. But suppose that the furious, howling mob of my hostile accusers is congregated before the door of the court room, still demanding my death and eager to lay hands on me, themselves to become my executioners. Then the question arises immediately. Will that mob be able to separate me from the power of the judge who acquitted me?

God loves me and justifies me. My accusers are silenced.

Christ loves me and is the sole judge, with all power in heaven and on earth. There is no one to condemn me.

But I must still be in the hostile world.

My enemies are waiting.

The final question must be faced. Shall anyone be able to separate me from the love that justified me?

The question is a challenge, and the answer is more than a denial.

Not only shall no created thing be able to separate us from the love of God in Christ Jesus our Lord, but we are also more than victors.

Even the enemy must work together for our salvation.
I am persuaded!

———————

Separation is impossible!

Separation from what?

From the love of Christ. From the love of God in Christ Jesus our Lord.

These two are one. The love of Christ is the love of God. The love of God was manifested in the love of Christ, who died for us on the accursed tree. Emphatically, the love of Christ and the love of God to us are meant, not our love to God in Christ.

Who shall separate us?

The question, then, is not, Who will be able to extinguish the flame of the love of God in Christ in our hearts, although in the final sense this is impossible because our love of God is but a flame kindled by his love of us. Neither does the question refer to the possibility of the fire of the love of Christ being quenched, although it is true that the love of God in Christ Jesus our Lord is eternal and immutable. Still less is it the meaning of the question, Who will deprive us of the blessed feeling, consciousness, and assurance that God loves us in Christ? This is possible at times, although he never forsakes us and always leads us back into the sweet fellowship of his friendship and favor.

But the question is, Who shall separate us from the power of that love?

Who is able to intervene, so to force himself between the love of God in Christ and us, so that its power can no longer reach us and that we are cut off from its saving help?

The subject of the entire eighth chapter to the Romans, this triumphant song of faith, is the absolute security of believers in Christ with a view to their eternal salvation and incorruptible glory. This salvation is accomplished to its end by the love of God in Christ Jesus. On its saving power all depends. Without it believers are lost. By that love they are justified, and no one is able to bring any charge against the elect of God. Because of that love they are secure in the hour of judgment, and no one can appear as their condemner. Forensically, their salvation is established. But will that same love of God be able to save them to the end? Are there in the world no powers that can separate them from its saving strength?

Just as a shipwrecked sailor who finds a place of temporary safety on a rock in the midst of the tempestuous sea might ask whether the raging billows will not separate him from the rock of his salvation, so the question is whether anything is able to separate us from the power of the love of God.

Just as a beleaguered city feels itself secure and able to sustain a long siege, as long as it is not separated from the source of its food supply, so the Christian is safe as long as he is not cut off from the love of God in Christ Jesus his Lord.

Even as the vanguard of an army is in danger of annihilation if, pressing forward too recklessly into hostile territory, it becomes separated from the main army, so God's people would be overwhelmed by hostile powers of death and destruction if ever they would be found in circumstances where the power of Christ's love could not reach them.

Who shall separate us from the love of Christ?

Who shall cut us off from the main and only source of our salvation?

The question is a challenge.

The answer is, No one!

Audacious challenge!

Many indeed are the powers of darkness that would appear to be able to effect this separation. Quite consciously the challenge is flung in the face of these hostile and mighty powers.

The apostle is thinking of these powers as a person. Although in the enumeration of the evil forces he mentions chiefly conditions, states, and circumstances, yet he puts the challenging question in a personal form: "Who shall separate us from the love of Christ?" And with good reason. Are not the principalities and powers, with Satan as their prince and chief, the agents that cause all these states, conditions, and circumstances to come upon the church for the very purpose of separating her forever from the love of God in Christ Jesus and destroying her?

The apostle is thinking of the sufferings for Christ's sake, as is evident from his quotation from Psalm 44:22: "For thy sake are we killed all the day long; we are accounted as sheep for the slaughter." The same is evident from the terms *persecution* and *sword*. The hostile world power inflicts this suffering and breathes this destruction against the people of God. It causes tribulation and distress, making the place of the people of God in the world narrow socially, economically, politically, so that they can neither buy nor sell unless they bear the mark of the beast, and so that they have no room to breathe. That power would have God's people go in hunger and nakedness, in physical want of every kind. It would leave the church no place of safety, make her position perilous wherever she may turn, and persecute her with the mighty sword.

Do not remark that this picture is overdrawn.

A real picture it is of the position of the church in the world.

To impress us with the reality of this perilous position, the apostle refers to the song of the church in the old dispensation, when after the captivity, it became the victim of the world's furious hatred, so that without exaggeration, and inspired by the Spirit of Christ, it could exclaim, "For thy sake we are killed all the livelong day; the world regards us as sheep for the slaughter; never a moment are we safe against its fury." Such was the position of the church then; such is her position in the world always in principle, for even as the world hated Christ who loves her, so they will hate those who are beloved of him. Such will be the position of the church at the time of the end, when antichrist will pour the last vials of this furious hatred upon the people of Christ. Do we not hear the rumblings of that final thunder even now?

The end of all things is near.

Be therefore sober and watch unto prayer.

And be not unequally yoked together with the unbeliever.

Even so, be of good cheer!

For who shall separate us? Even in the midst of tribulation and distress, when hunger and nakedness must be suffered for Christ's sake, when peril and sword would kill us all the livelong day, who will cut us off from the source of our salvation, the saving power of the love of God in Christ Jesus?

No one and nothing!

No created thing, in heaven, earth, or hell!

No trouble or distress you may meet in life, no darkness of the shadow of death, no hunger or nakedness, no pain or sorrow, no tribulation or anguish, not even death itself will be able to separate us from that wondrous love. No angels, no evil spirits, not even all the host of them with the devil as their chief, no principalities and powers, no mighty Caesars or wicked kings, no Nebuchad-nezzars or Antiochuses or Neros, no Hitlers or Mussolinis or Stalins, with all their sword power, are able to prevent that power of Christ's love from reaching us with its saving arm. Nothing there is in time or space, nothing there is in the present, nothing can ever arise in the future, nothing there is in the heights of heaven and no power there is in the depth of hell that is strong enough to cut us off from the love of God in Christ Jesus our Lord.

Was anything forgotten in this enumeration?

Well, then, let this set your heart finally at rest: "Nor any other creature."

No created thing!

Not the enemies, not the angels or principalities or powers, not tribulation or distress or hunger or nakedness or peril or sword, not any creature in the present or in the future, in the heights or in the depths can have the victory.

We triumph!

Not they, but we conquer.

Already we are conquerors.

Nay, we are more than conquerors.

A worldly victor may glory in his triumph after he has fought the battle. We have the victory while the battle is still raging. We triumph while we fight; we glory in the victory even when apparently we are overwhelmed. The enemy cannot even touch us. The outcome is never uncertain.

More than victors are we.

An earthly battle may be won, but not without more or less severe losses on the part of the victor. We lose nothing in the battle.

Even the enemy must help us, in spite of himself, to attain to the final victory and glory.

More than conquerors!

Blessed assurance!

For I am persuaded!

Thus the apostle glories, victorious on the heights of faith; and thus this part of the word of our God would have us glory in the midst of the sufferings of this present time.

How is this glorying, this blessed assurance, possible? How can we be sure that nothing can separate us from the love of God?

Emphatically, because it is the love of God on which everything depends. Not on our love, neither on the cooperation of his love and ours, but on his love alone. Not as if it does not matter whether or not we love God. But on our love nothing depends, not even that love itself. We love him only because he loved us first. His love is eternal, sovereign, and unchangeable. Nothing can quench that love. In that love he made all things. In that love he governs all things, even the powers of darkness, even tribulation and distress and nakedness and hunger and peril and sword, even death itself. And that love is omnipotent. It never fails.

Who then can separate us from that love of God?

God's love was manifested, for it is the love of God in Christ Jesus our Lord.

Christ loved us. He loved us in a very definite act of love. He loved us on the accursed tree. On that tree he took our sins upon himself, to bear them away forever. On that cross he fought the battle alone, in our behalf, and was victorious.

For he arose.

He overcame the world. He is victor over sin and death.

Look, then, on that love. It is the love of God in Christ Jesus our Lord.

Look on that cross and triumph.

More than conquerors through him who loved us!

Who shall separate us?

35

Fear Not, Little Flock!

> "Fear not, little flock; for it is your Father's good
> pleasure to give you the kingdom."
>
> —Luke 12:32

Fear not!

If you seek the kingdom of God first, chiefly, and constantly, this word is addressed to you, and you may hear it.

If you seek the things that are below, the things of the world, the things that are seen but that are temporal, this word of the Lord Jesus is neither meant for you, nor can you hear it.

The entire context of this address of the savior to his little flock speaks of the things of the kingdom of God and the things that are upon the earth as a contrast. Not as if they were a contrast in themselves, as if there were an irreconcilable conflict between nature and grace. But as an object of our desire, of our seeking and striving, they stand opposed to each other. You cannot set your affection on the things above and on the things below at the same time. Where your treasure is, there will your heart be. If your treasure is in heaven, the issues of your heart shall proceed to and fasten themselves on the things that are heavenly; if your treasure is in the things that are seen, the affections of your heart cannot rise above them.

You cannot serve God and mammon.

It is either/or, never both/and.

Such is the clear-cut instruction in the context. It was occasioned, it seems, by the request of a man who served as a particularly clear illustration of one who seeks the things below, and who even would make use of Jesus' authority to help him in realizing his ambition: "Master, speak to my brother, that he divide the inheritance with me." Perhaps the man had a righteous cause. Part of the inheritance was probably his. But the deep and very serious trouble for him was that because of his part of the inheritance, he could not see the kingdom of God, but would make use of the king of that kingdom to satisfy his earthly and carnal ambition. Having rebuked the man, Jesus drew in the parable of the rich fool the picture of the covetous man who lays up earthly treasures for himself, but who is not rich toward God. Jesus then proceeded to apply it to his disciples by the exhortation not to seek earthly things, not to be anxious about meat and drink and clothing, but rather to seek the kingdom of God.

Fear not!

Only in the measure that we seek the kingdom does this exhortation not to fear have meaning for us.

If our affection is on the things below, and if we seek the things of this world, we are perhaps successful people of the world, but the Lord will say, "Fear, thou fool, for it is God's pleasure to cast you, body and soul, into hell!"

If we seek the kingdom of God, we may apparently have plenty of reason to fear, and we may have no place in the world, but the word of the Lord directly concerns us.

Fear not, little flock!

It is your Father's good pleasure to give you the kingdom.

———

Even though apparently there are abundant reasons to fear, be not afraid!

Fear is itself suffering. It is a feeling of terror caused by the apprehension that a certain evil is impending and will befall us. The evil that is apprehended may be either unconditional and unavoidable, or its realization may be contingent upon a certain course of action on our part. A person may have an incurable disease and may fear the unavoidable suffering and ultimate death connected with it; the evil he fears cannot be escaped. Or a soldier on the battlefield may be overcome with terror of the enemy, and he may flee to avoid the dreaded evil.

Always fear tends to and results in the endeavor to escape or avoid the impending evil as far as possible.

Fear not, little flock!

Fear not, although as you seek the kingdom of God—and because of this—dark clouds of evil lower, and storms of persecution threaten to break over your head.

It is of this fear and of these evils that the Lord is thinking as he addresses his little flock. The reference is to the fear that may fill the hearts of his disciples and of his church in the world because of the evils that threaten and beset those who faithfully seek the kingdom of God in the midst of a world that is opposed to that kingdom.

Let us clearly understand what it means to seek that kingdom. It does not simply mean to strive to enter into the heavenly glory of that kingdom in its future realization, though this is not excluded. But it signifies that even now and in this world, we are spiritual citizens of that kingdom in which God is freely acknowledged and served as king, and which is established through the cross, resurrection, and exaltation of our Lord Jesus Christ. It implies that we have been translated from death into life and from darkness into light, and that the righteousness of that kingdom, both in its juridical and in its ethical senses, is ours. It means that we set our hearts on the things of that kingdom and on its righteousness and that we walk as citizens of that kingdom in the midst of the world of darkness and iniquity, proclaiming the word of the kingdom, confessing the Lord of that kingdom, striving to manifest in our conversation the righteousness of that kingdom, thus condemning the evil works of the kingdom of darkness.

So seeking the kingdom, fear not!

Your heart may indeed be filled with terror because of the evils that threaten you from every side.

For the world lies in darkness, and it hates the light.

Moreover, it strives for the realization of its own kingdom, the kingdom of man, of this world, with its own righteousness—the righteousness not of God but of man, without the Christ of God, without the cross, and without the atoning blood of the Lamb. If you seek the kingdom of God and its righteousness, condemn the unfruitful works of darkness, and stand in the way of the realization of the proud kingdom of mere man, the world will hate you, persecute you, and speak and do all manner of evil against you for Christ's sake.

Many are the evils that the mighty power of darkness that is called world may inflict upon you.

It may threaten to take away your name, position in the world, job, possessions, home, liberty, yea, your very life on earth. The time will come when, if you persist in seeking the kingdom of God, the world will make it impossible for you to buy or to sell; you will be considered and treated as an outcast, unworthy to occupy the very ground you stand on.

Fear not!

Not as if these evils are only imaginary. Not as if the threatening storm will never break over your head, for it will.

But fear not, though these evils come!

Let them not fill you with terror.

Above all, let the fear of them never induce you to change your course of action and to abandon the cause of the kingdom of God.

Be faithful unto death!

Little flock.

With special and intentional emphasis, Jesus here designates his church as the "little flock."

The flock is his church, the company of those whom the Father gave him out of the world. All the emphasis is on that significant qualifier "little."

Always the flock of Christ is little.

It was little enough at the moment when he first spoke these words, addressing the small number of his disciples that followed him at the time. Even in comparison with Israel as a nation, as it existed at that time in the land of Canaan, his disciples constituted but a small group, for Jesus had come unto his own, and his own received him not. And what did Israel amount to in number and power in comparison with the mighty nations round about and with the world power of that time?

Little is the church always.

The word that the Lord speaks is not limited by time and place and circumstances. It never is. Christ still speaks, and always the content of his word is the same. Always the church is addressed as "little," and always he exhorts that little church never to fear, but constantly to seek the kingdom of God and its righteousness.

And when was the church of Christ ever numerically strong?

All through the ages it was (and still is) a little flock. In spite of the grand display that the church makes in the world—the many churches, the magnificent edifices, the mighty efforts of those who prophesy, the casting out of devils, and the doing of many wonderful works—the church today is smaller than ever. How relatively small is even the nominal church in comparison with the mighty world. In that nominal church, how many are the thousands who have forsaken the kingdom, have denied Christ and his cross, have apostatized, and have been swallowed up by the enemy. How many of those who outwardly bear the name of Christ are seeking not the kingdom, but the world and its lusts. How small in the midst of the church is the number of those who outwardly still profess the truth. How (speaking from a worldly viewpoint) ridiculously small are the Protestant Reformed Churches, which uphold the truth of God's sovereign grace. How many even of those who outwardly profess the truth will fall away in the fires of persecution and will prove to be reprobate. Do not many of us already ask fearfully, "What shall we eat, and what shall we drink?" rather than seeking the kingdom of God and its righteousness?

Why is the church so little? Is this littleness emphasized in order that we should be stirred into action and put forth our every effort to make of this little flock a mighty army? Is the church perhaps little because we did not labor and sacrifice and preach the word of God? Shall we send forth missionaries and more missionaries in order to gain souls for Christ and to lay the whole world at his feet?

No, this would be of no avail to make the church great in this world.

The word of Christ is absolute. He addresses the whole church of all ages as "little flock." Besides, the gathering of the church is not our work at all, but his and his alone. We cannot even preach unless he speaks.

The littleness of the flock of Christ has its ultimate and sole cause in the good pleasure of the Father—in his election and sovereign grace. He chose the church to be little, for his strength must be made perfect in weakness, that the glory of his mighty grace in the beloved might shine forth and receive all the praise.

Do you not see why "little" is intentionally used and why the church is emphatically reminded of her littleness?

Do you not discern that this very littleness would seem to be an additional reason for fear? This smallness of number means that the church is insignificant in the world, that she has no position, no influence, no vote, no power, and no means to fight, and that the power of the world constantly threatens to overwhelm her. This littleness of the church may inspire her with the dread of ultimately being overcome, and may induce her to make an attempt to organize and to develop power in the world at the expense of her specific character as a flock of Jesus Christ, with the result that she would no longer seek the righteousness of the kingdom of God.

But fear not, little flock.

Make no attempt to develop a power that is not properly yours.

Let not your littleness be a cause of terror.

As a little flock, fear not!

Rather, consider that you have the victory!

For it is your Father's good pleasure to give you the kingdom.

That consideration should be more than sufficient to drive out all fear.

The kingdom refers to the ultimate and eternal realization of the kingdom of Christ in glory. It is the incorruptible and undefilable inheritance that fades not away, which shall be given to the little flock when their Lord will appear once more from heaven to make all things like unto himself. The glory of that kingdom is so unspeakably great and precious that all the sufferings of this present time are not worthy to be compared with it. It would be far better to suffer all the evils of this present time a thousand times than to forfeit our place in that kingdom.

Its possession is assured you, little flock. Nothing can deprive you of it, for it is your Father's good pleasure to give it to you. Mark well: he will give it to you. You need not fight for it. You can do nothing to realize it. The enemy can do nothing to prevent its coming. He will give it to you.

Such is his good pleasure, his eternal counsel, according to which he works all things and in which also the enemy, sin, evil, death, and all the powers of darkness have their proper place. It is his unchangeable counsel, as he himself delights in it.

He, your Father, who loved you even unto the death of his Son, will give it to you.

He, the Almighty, whom no one can possibly oppose, will give it to you.

The matter is fully determined.

Fear not!

36

Fear Not!

"But now thus saith the LORD that created thee, O
Jacob, and he that formed thee, O Israel, Fear not:
for I have redeemed thee, I have called thee by thy
name; thou art mine. When thou passest through
the waters, I will be with thee; and through the
rivers, they shall not overflow thee: when thou walk-
est through the fire, thou shalt not be burned; neither shall the flame kindle upon thee."
—Isaiah 43:1, 2

Fear not!

Jacob-Israel, be not afraid!

Let the church of the Lord, God's beloved from all eternity, be
of good courage in the midst of this world!

Thus the Lord himself calls out to his people by the mouth of
his prophet Isaiah in this marvelous text. The Scriptures throughout often thus encourage the covenantal people who are engaged
in the battle that rages about them. There is a reason that the
Scriptures repeatedly bring this encouragement in many different
forms.

After all, there are water and fire and storms and flames that
threaten throughout the way Jacob-Israel must travel to the everlasting victory of heavenly glory. There are powers of darkness that
threaten her from every side. On the pathway are suffering and
pain and death. There are devastating forces that time and again
are determined to make the Lord's people endure pain and suffering. If the situation were merely such that God's people could
escape these ravaging and threatening powers, if in this comfort-

ing text it were true that they would merely *see* the fire and the water, but would not be required to walk through them, if the situation were not so dire and dreadful for the flesh, there would not be an impetus behind this oft-repeated refrain of sacred Scripture: "Fear not!"

However, if you really do go *through* the water, *through* the rivers, *through* the fire, what then?

Oh, do not speak too quickly!

Do not too hastily give your good advice as long as you have no or little knowledge by personal experience of what it means to go through the water and the fire.

We do not deny that it is indeed wonderful and definitely appropriate for the child of God to lift his head with courage and to sing with joy:

> *Full of great courage I will be,*
> *Since his hand protects me;*
> *I will not fear ten thousand.*
> *Even though from every side,*
> *Violently assaulted and*
> *Fiercely oppressed I may be!*

However, first give an accurate explanation as to why you sing that song without restraint and with exultant joy.

If the water only reaches as high as the ankles, then to walk through it without any fear is of little or no importance. It does not require the steely courage of faith to go through the fire without hesitation with your head held high, as long as the fire is not a threat even to singe your clothes. But if the water rises as high as your head, if the flames actually lap at your flesh, if the streams threaten to sweep you down toward the depths, then what?

Yes indeed, then what?

There is so much to endure.

There is so much weeping.

If I consider only the sufferings of this present time, only the pain suffered in this life (because it is nothing but a relentless dying and death), only the bloodcurdling screams and painful moans that are pressed forth from the hearts of thousands and millions, occasioned by physical suffering and psychological distress and pain, then I am terrified. Then I would be ashamed of myself not to acknowledge that my soul becomes alarmed and fearful.

Yet there is more.

There is a suffering that is applicable only to Jacob-Israel. The word of the Lord here points specifically to that suffering. Jacob-Israel is the honorable name of the church throughout all the centuries. Not just the name *Israel* is her honorable name, but also the name *Jacob* is the same, through God's grace. Jacob designates the church as those who have wrestled with men on behalf of the covenant of God. For the sake of God's covenant, Jacob grasped his brother by the heel. For the sake of God's covenant he wrestled with his brother in his mother's womb, at his birth, and throughout his life. Nonetheless, the name Israel belongs with the name Jacob. Jacob all by himself wrestled in his own strength and would soon be defeated, for his brother was stronger according to the flesh. Yet when he wrestled with God for the sake of his covenant and had conquered by wrestling, through tears and weeping, and when in the future he would wrestle in the power of God, he would be secure and would have the victory. Jacob-Israel! Struggling along with God and in the strength of God against men, against the world, against the reprobate world, against the powers of darkness—that is Zion's glory and strength! In that struggling, however, she often becomes anxious and fearful. Frequently the powers of this world and of darkness are overwhelmingly strong. Not infrequently it appears as if the church will lose and will suffer defeat, as if God's covenant and cause will be driven down into oblivion. Then it becomes dreadfully dark. Fear rises. Anxiety permeates the heart.

So it was for the church in the old dispensation at the very moment this mighty word of grace was spoken to her.

Israel was in Babylon.

Oh, things did not go so very badly according to the flesh for the citizens of Jerusalem in the land of captivity. Many of them never really felt any affinity in their hearts for the old fatherland and the city of God's dwelling, and they believed for all intents and purposes that they had become citizens of this foreign land. Spiritually they had been swallowed up by carnal Babylon.

However, for the true Jacob-Israel, for the remnant according to the election of grace, for the little hut in the vineyard, the night watchman's shack in the cucumber patch, things were entirely different. Their beloved Jerusalem lay in rubble, the city of God was ravaged, the temple no longer existed, the throne of David had been cast down into the dust, deliverance seemed to be impossible, and the cause of God's covenant appeared to be lost forever.

For God's church in the new dispensation the very same thing often appears to be true.

Oh, when from every side the world's temptations press upon the church, when the strong suction power of our present society appears to be tugging the children of Zion down to ruin, and Babylon appears to be devouring Jerusalem, whose heart is not gripped by fear?

Then we go through water and fire.

But then the Lord's word in this text becomes doubly glorious. Be not afraid!

My people, fear not!

Jacob's Almighty God is he who speaks.

Even when in the midst of swirling waters or raging fires, with your eye of faith upon him, let that truth be sufficient to enable you not to fear. However dark the way may be, however strong the enemies may be, however threatening the dangers may appear to be, you have nothing to be afraid of, and nothing can harm you.

He who here speaks is Jacob's almighty God, the one who created and formed you. He who calls the things that are not as if they were has also called you according to his eternal good pleasure. He called forth life out of death, light out of darkness, when he gave you your existence. He is your creator not only because he gave you your natural existence in common with the whole human race, but also because you are his creation according to your spiritual existence. You are his workmanship in Christ Jesus. He formed you. He caused you to be what you are according to your spiritual nature. He created you for the revelation of his grace, for the revelation of light in the midst of darkness and formed you in such a way that you are disposed to proclaim his virtues.

He did that in the way of redemption and by means of his almighty calling of you.

Fear not, for I have redeemed you.

He redeemed you.

When you lay in spiritual death, guilty and worthy of damnation in yourself, he bore your debt and paid for you the ransom price. He himself satisfied for you in order to redeem you. He did that from all eternity both in his divine thoughts and in time, when at bloodstained Golgotha he gave his Son over to the fearful death of the cross. He did that when he himself bore your sins on the tree, in order to justify you in the Beloved. Do not fear. Would God, who gave us his only begotten Son, who for us delivered him to the death of the cross, and who for Jacob-Israel finished the fight, ever deliver us into the power of destruction? Would he ever permit the cause of his covenant to suffer loss? Will God not rather give us all things in him?

He called you by your name.

Do not misunderstand this. He did not call in the same way we call. If we call someone by his name, then he must have a name. God speaks, and it is there. He commands, and it exists. He calls things that are not as if they were, for he is God. Your name is your being. In this case, your name is your spiritual identity by which he called you—Jacob-Israel. That name you did not possess before God called you. You did not come to him with that name, so that he could call you. Before he called you, your name was Adam's child, sinner, child of condemnation, dead in trespasses, enemy of God, contemplator of carnal things, and destined for death. But he had foreordained a name for you in Christ Jesus, out of sovereign grace, from before the foundation of the world, in his eternal and omnipotent good pleasure. That name is God's child. Behold, what great love the Father has bestowed upon us, that we should be called the children of God. That name is friend of the Most High God, soldier in his cause, of God's party in the world, Jacob-Israel. By that name he called you with a divine, sovereign call, through which you came forth out of darkness as a child of light. He called you by your name.

Fear not, then.

His calling is without repentance.

God, who formed you and created you, who redeemed you and called you by name, does everything according to his eternal good pleasure. Therefore, he never abandons the work of his hands. What he has once begun he will bring to completion. The name by which he called you will be yours unto all eternity. No powers of darkness will ever rob you of that name. When in the midst of floods and fires, there is nothing to fear.

"You," God says, "are mine."

Surely, in this assertion lies a divine right—a right that he has by virtue of the fact that he created and formed you. Not the world, not Satan, not the power of sin and death can claim any right over you. God alone owns you and is your sovereign. You belong to him with everything you have and all that you are. He formed you so that you should proclaim his virtues. And therein lies above all his divine love. Just as a man speaks to his beloved wife whom he has chosen, so too does God speak here to his people, "You are mine."

You are his, because he chose you; you are his because he formed and created you; you are his because he called you out of darkness into his marvelous light and gave you a name of wondrous glory.

His eternally.

For he is the Lord, who never changes, who is eternally immutable in his love.

Therefore, you are his eternally.

You are his, even when you must go through water and fire.

Have good courage, then!

———————

Jacob-Israel, fear not!

For God, who is the Lord, declares to you, "You are mine."

And he gives to you this assurance: "When you go through the waters or through fire, I am with you."

God, who is your creator and he who fashioned you, is the one who created that water and that fire. He ordained your specific way—a way that of necessity cuts straight through the threatening and ravaging elements.

No, it is not by chance that the way is often dark, that the sufferings of this present time lay hold upon you, that the world of unbelievers frightens God's church, and that the battle appears to be hopeless. Even less is it true that the powers of darkness and death can in their own strength set themselves against the Lord and his people. The Lord is God alone, also over the water and the fire.

Besides, God calls out to you, "I will be with you. When you go through the water, I will be with you." He, the Lord, the creator who formed you, who never abandons the work of his hands; he, who redeemed you from the power of sin and death and for that redemption delivered over his only begotten Son; he, who called you by his sovereign grace, so that you would proclaim his virtues and be a revelation of the honor of his name; Jacob's Almighty God, who alone rules over the threatening currents and violent waves, who is God of fire and flame, and who causes them to blaze or be extinguished according to his good pleasure; he, without whose will the water cannot overwhelm you and the hottest fire cannot singe your hair—*that* God will be with you. He is in the water with you. He goes with you through the fire, encircles you, leads you, strengthens you, protects you, and does not forsake you even for a moment. Therefore, the swirling water cannot overwhelm you, the fire cannot consume you, nor the flames kindle upon you. You will prevail! The fire and the water may indeed cause temporal suffering. They may take away and destroy everything that does not belong to your eternal name by which God called you.

But you, Jacob-Israel, according to your spiritual name and eternal existence, will successfully complete your course; and through water and fire you will enter into heavenly glory, which your creator and divine architect foreordained for you before the foundation of the world.

Fear not, then.

Do not anxiously attempt to escape the water and the fire when they threaten. Do not become unfaithful when the forces of darkness terrify you and cause your circumstances to become exceedingly distressful in the world. Let not the heat of the fire drive you out toward the darkness of the world beneath, but let it drive you to Jacob's Almighty God, who is above all. He will be with you, not when you skirt the fire, but when you choose to go through the fire by his grace.

Going through the flames with God or skirting the fire without God.

Fear not, then!

Let your trust be in him alone. Reject every little idol upon which you would rely next to God. Our eye of faith must be fixed upon him alone.

Then he is with you! Then you are with him.

Then you walk onward in perfect peace.

37

The Battle Is the Lord's

"When I have bent Judah for me, filled the bow with
Ephraim, and raised up thy sons, O Zion, against
thy sons, O Greece, and made thee as the sword of a
mighty man. And the LORD shall be seen over them,
and his arrow shall go forth as the lightning: and the
Lord GOD shall blow the trumpet, and shall go with
whirlwinds of the south. The LORD of hosts shall
defend them; and they shall devour, and subdue with
sling stones; and they shall drink, and make a noise
as through wine; and they shall be filled like bowls,
and as the corners of the altar."

—Zechariah 9:13–15

The battle is always the Lord's battle.

Even when the church in the world is the church militant in
that battle, the battle remains the Lord's.

In that battle it is forever so very sure and absolutely conclusive
that the church will obtain a decisive and complete victory.

I will restore double. Such was the promise in verse 12. This
includes that God's people will not only be released from the pit,
where there was no water, that is, that they would be liberated
from the supremacy and oppression of their enemies, while these
enemies would go scot-free; but it also means that, having regained
their strength, they will fight the Lord's battle to the very end.
They will see the complete victory in that battle over their enemies, over the evil world powers, and by vengeance upon their
enemies they will be completely and publicly vindicated. The suffering caused to God's beloved people, the oppression with which

the evil world power tormented them, and the blood that was spilled by the enemies of God's cause throughout the whole world—all of this did not happen in an obscure corner. On the contrary, God's people were made a spectacle before the entire world. Their deliverance may not and cannot be accomplished in secret. Publicly, before the entire world and all of creation, it must become apparent that their cause is the cause of the Son of God, who alone must have the victory.

The fight is the Lord's fight.

But that battle he fights in the world through a people that is of the Lord's party.

He himself prepares them for that battle. He makes them to be the weapons with which he fights.

He himself appoints them their places in the battle array in opposition to the world power.

He himself fights for them and through them in the battle.

He protects them, so that they have nothing to fear.

And he gives to them the victory.

God's weapons are his people.

The text speaks of Judah and Ephraim.

Certainly the text speaks first of the people of Israel, for indeed the prophecy views the battle of the Lord from the perspective of the historical moment of Zechariah's prophetic proclamation—the time after the exile.

In the battle mentioned here, all of God's people are united. It is not only Judah that fights in the Lord's battle, but Ephraim as well. The Lord never acknowledged the secession of the ten tribes as lawful. Was not Israel's secession a rejection of Judah, of the house of David, and of Christ? But here Judah and Ephraim are united again. Already before the exile, elements of the ten tribes were added to Judah and with Judah had returned to the land of their fathers. But even though the battle of the Lord is considered in this text from the viewpoint of that time, yet this word of prophecy, just as all prophecy does, looks directly to the new dispensation and to the end of the ages.

The battle is fought throughout all the ages.

The forms that this battle assumes may indeed change. The battle array may be differently arranged, and different weapons may be employed in that battle. But it always is the same battle of the Lord in all the ages of time.

The text presents God's people as his weapons in this battle—weapons that God employs. Judah is depicted as a bow, strung by the Lord, who fills the bow (sets the arrow upon it) with Ephraim. Such is the literal meaning of the text. Moreover, God appoints his people as the sword of a warrior. His people are, therefore, his weaponry. This may not be understood in such a way that the people are passive in the battle, as dead instruments. On the contrary, when they as arrow, bow, and sword are in the hand of the Lord, they remain conscious, rational, and moral instruments who fight the Lord's battle with all their understanding, with all their will, with their whole heart, and with all their strength. They are very willing in the day of the Lord's power. But it is certainly the meaning of the text to express very emphatically that the battle is and remains the Lord's. Only as fellow-laborers of the Lord—formed by him, called by him, and employed by him in the battle—can we fight.

We are God's weapons.

Literally, the text refers to the time of the Maccabees, when the battle of the Lord (as so often in the old dispensation, when God appointed his church as a nation in the midst of the nations of the world) took on the form of actual warfare against the world power of the Greco-Macedonian kingdom. Then God drew his bow and placed the arrow upon it. Then he prepared his people in a literal sense to be as a sword would be to a mighty man, not only to equip them in a physical sense for the battle, but also by bestowing the power of faith and the courage of faith to fight.

Centrally this word of prophecy has its fulfillment in Christ Jesus. He is God's bow and God's arrow, drawn and equipped by

God, and God's sword, the sword as of a mighty man who is fully prepared for the battle. Christ fought the Lord's battle to the very end—so much so that he has decided the battle all along its front and has won the victory. He was formed for the battle, called and prepared by the living God, the God and Father of the Lord Jesus Christ. God foreordained him for this battle before the foundation of the world and placed him at the head of the Lord's armed forces. He sent him in the fullness of time into the world, in order to confront the enemy alone. He prepared him in the womb of Mary and formed him to be Immanuel, God with us. He opened his ear and his mouth in order to be the witness of the living God, and he made him willing and fit to be the servant of the Lord and to humble himself even unto the death of the cross. He gave him the complete victory when he awakened him from the dead and gave him honor and glory at his right hand.

God's sword as of a mighty man.

This word is always being fulfilled, in the new dispensation as well as in the old, for the church in Christ is God's arrow, bow, and sword, as of a mighty man. He has chosen her, called her, and formed her by his Spirit and word through regeneration, calling, and faith, and by indwelling and sanctifying her to fight the battle of the Lord. In addition, God provides for her, causes her to put on the whole armor of God to fight the good fight of faith to the very end.

The battle is the Lord's.

He sets the army for battle.

So the text reads: "...and raised up thy sons, O Zion, against thy sons, O Greece, and made thee as the sword of a mighty man."

Greece refers to the Greco-Macedonian world power and to the evil world power of the Seleucid era, historical enemies as temporal representations and revelations of the antichristian world power as it is always in the world, and as it will develop and be revealed at the end of the age.

But God determines when and where the battle is fought. The battle is wholly his.

It may appear differently in history. From a worldly point of view it always appears as if the world power is the aggressor. They bring the fight to God's people. They hate and distress, they oppress and persecute, they taunt and kill the church of the living God and grant her no room in the world. They even attack the Christ himself, bind him, abuse and whip him, hang him on the tree of shame, and cast him out of the world.

But reality is very different.

The positive party, the only party, the party that decisively determines everything, is the party of the living God, represented by Christ and his church in the world. To her all things have been promised. She is the inheritor of the world. She attacks the world, denies it every right, and conquers it.

She does not rest until all things are hers.

The battle is the Lord's.

God's exclusively.

The battle remains the Lord's.

Even though the Lord himself fights the battle, he always does so through his church in Christ. In this sense as well it is true that the Lord himself fights the battle, even when it is through his church in Christ. Fighting through his people, the Lord preserves them in the battle by his almighty power. The Lord appears over his people: "And the Lord shall be seen over them, and his arrow shall go forth as the lightning: and the Lord God shall blow the trumpet, and shall go with whirlwinds of the south. The Lord of hosts shall defend them."

Oh, of a truth, if the people actually had put on the whole armor of God and fought the battle with utmost exertion, what would it help if the Lord himself did not fight in his own battle? Not by might, not by power, but by my Spirit! What did Israel amount to in the old dispensation compared to the powers of the world that were all around her, if God himself did not stand at the head of the armed forces and did not fight the battle for her and with her? What would the church of the new dispensation be able to accomplish over against the powers of darkness if God the Lord were not active on her behalf? The church can preach, minister the word, witness, watch, and struggle. But what is the significance of this witness, even if it be perfectly in harmony with the Bible (and therefore God's word), if God himself does not speak his own word and by his Spirit make the preaching an irresistibly powerful word? Who will build God's house, if God is not building? Who will gather God's church, if God is not gathering? Who shall conquer the world, if God himself does not give the victory?

It would all be vain.

Our work never has any significance even in the smallest degree if God himself does not perform his own work in and through it.

But he walks before us, taking the lead into the battle. He appears to his people as he who stands and fights at the point of attack in his own battle, as the God of their salvation, the God of the covenant, of whose party they are in Christ Jesus, the author and finisher of their faith, who suffered, fought, and had the victory, who arose from the dead, and who has sat down on the right hand of God's power as the head over all, standing at the head of the host of the Lord of Lords.

He blows the trumpet, which means that he calls his people to the battle. By his word he calls those whom he has formed to be his militant host, and moves them to put on the whole armor of God and to fight the good fight of faith, so that no one may take their crown. He encourages them by focusing their attention on the sure victory, on the crown of life that they who are faithful even unto death will receive. He calls by his Holy Spirit efficaciously and irresistibly, thus causing his word of calling to penetrate the depths of the heart, drawing to himself, and effecting obedience. Yet his blowing of the trumpet also indicates that he himself stands at the head of his people and through his people fights his own battle.

He causes his arrows to shoot out like lightning.

Fast, sure, and irresistible.

Only through God's own fighting does the church's war in the world become a world-conquering battle. And in the battle he protects his own people.

They are preserved by the power of God, according to the testimony of Scripture. And the power of God by which they are preserved is a sovereign power. All power, might, and rule are God's. The enemy's power is his as well, so that the power of the world cannot move contrary to God's will and without his power.

They are preserved through faith in such a way that the power of God by which they are preserved does not act only externally, but works through them, so that in the battle they cling tightly to the living God, as seeing the invisible God.

They are so completely preserved that the enemy cannot conquer them nor harm them! Oh, surely, he may cause them to suffer in the flesh. But from the viewpoint of the spiritual battle, this can only serve for their strengthening.

The Lord of Hosts has everything under his rule and at his disposal in this battle to serve for the protection of his people.

He goes before his people by calling up storms from the south—the most violent of storms that have ever raged.

These storms represent everything in the world—all creatures as they must cooperate for the good of God's people and his cause and against the enemy.

The mighty Lord of Hosts, the God of the whole earth in Christ, is at the head of his army.

The battle is the Lord's!

———————

The victory, therefore, is the Lord's as well!

And the victory is both certain and complete.

In the day of victory God's people will participate in that victory. Joyful and exalted they will be, because God's justice will be fully revealed.

The text presents the victory as a conquering in a literal war—

a victory obtained by bow, spear and sword: "They shall devour, and subdue with sling stones; and they shall drink, and make a noise as through wine; and they shall be filled like bowls, and as the corners of the altar."

According to some interpreters the text expresses a cruel, Old Testament theology of revenge.

There can be no doubt that the slingstones are the enemy. They are referred to as such because they will be as slingstones thrown far by those who shoot at God's people. And when the text speaks of eating and becoming full as the bowls and as the corners of the altar, this signifies that they will eat the flesh of their enemies and will drink their blood. They will be joyful over the absolute ruin of the enemy.

Although the form and concepts are explained from the prophetic perspective of the old dispensation, the reality expressed remains: God's people find joy in the eternal destruction of their enemies.

The victory is all about God: his cause, his justice, his honor!

His eternal victory!